PROJECT EUROPA: Imagining the (Im)Possible

PROJECT EUROPA:

BY KERRY OLIVER-SMITH

With essays by
Marius Babias and Boris Groys

Samuel P. Harn Museum of Art
University of Florida, Gainesville

Francis Alÿs

Fikret Atay

Kader Attia

Maja Bajevic

Yto Barrada

Tacita Dean

Beate Gütschow

Imagining the (Im)Possible

Jens Haaning

Susan Hefuna

Eva Leitolf

Aernout Mik

Marcel Odenbach

Dan Perjovschi

Marjetica Potrč

Andrea Robbins and Max Becher

Bruno Serralongue

Superflex

Lidwien Van de Ven

PROJECT EUROPA: Imagining the (Im)Possible

Samuel P. Harn Museum of Art
University of Florida, Gainesville

February 7–May 9, 2010

The exhibition, related programs, and catalogue are made possible by the Andy Warhol Foundation for the Visual Arts; the C. Frederick and Aase B. Thompson Foundation; Étant donnés, the French-American Fund for Contemporary Art, a program of the French-American Cultural Exchange; University of Florida Student Government; the John Early Publication Endowment; the Sidney Knight Endowment; and the Harn Program Endowment. Additional support is provided by the following University of Florida entities: School of Art + Art History Harn Eminent Scholar Chair in Art History; Center for the Humanities and the Public Sphere; Center for European Studies; France-Florida Research Institute; International Center; and Paris Research Center. Additional funding provided by Bill and Hazel Hough and the Exhibition Circle of the Harn Museum.

Library of Congress Cataloging-in-Publication Data

Oliver-Smith, Kerry.
   Project Europa : imagining the (im)possible / by Kerry Oliver-Smith ; with essays by Marius Babias and Boris Groys.
      p. cm.
   Issued in connection with an exhibition held Feb. 7–May 9, 2010, Samuel P. Harn Museum of Art, University of Florida, Gainesville.
   Includes bibliographical references and index.
   ISBN 978-0-9762552-9-1 (pbk.)
1. Art, European–20th century–Exhibitions. 2. Art, European–21st century–Exhibitions. 3. Art–Political aspects–Europe–History–20th century–Exhibitions. 4. Art–Political aspects–Europe–History–21st century–Exhibitions. I. Babias, Marius. II. Grois, Boris. III. Samuel P. Harn Museum of Art. IV. Title.
   N6758.045 2010
   709.4'0905107475979–dc22
                    2010011274

Publication design and composition: Shore Design, Brisbane, California

Editing: Gerald Zeigerman

Project Manager: Tami M. Wroath

front cover: Tacita Dean, British, b. 1965
Palast (detail), 2004, six color photogravures
19.63 x 27.5 in. (49.8 x 69.9 cm) each
Courtesy of Baker Botts L.L.P., Dallas, Texas

Published by the Samuel P. Harn Museum of Art
University of Florida
SW 34th Street and Hull Road
Gainesville, Florida 32611-2700
www.harn.ufl.edu

CONTENTS

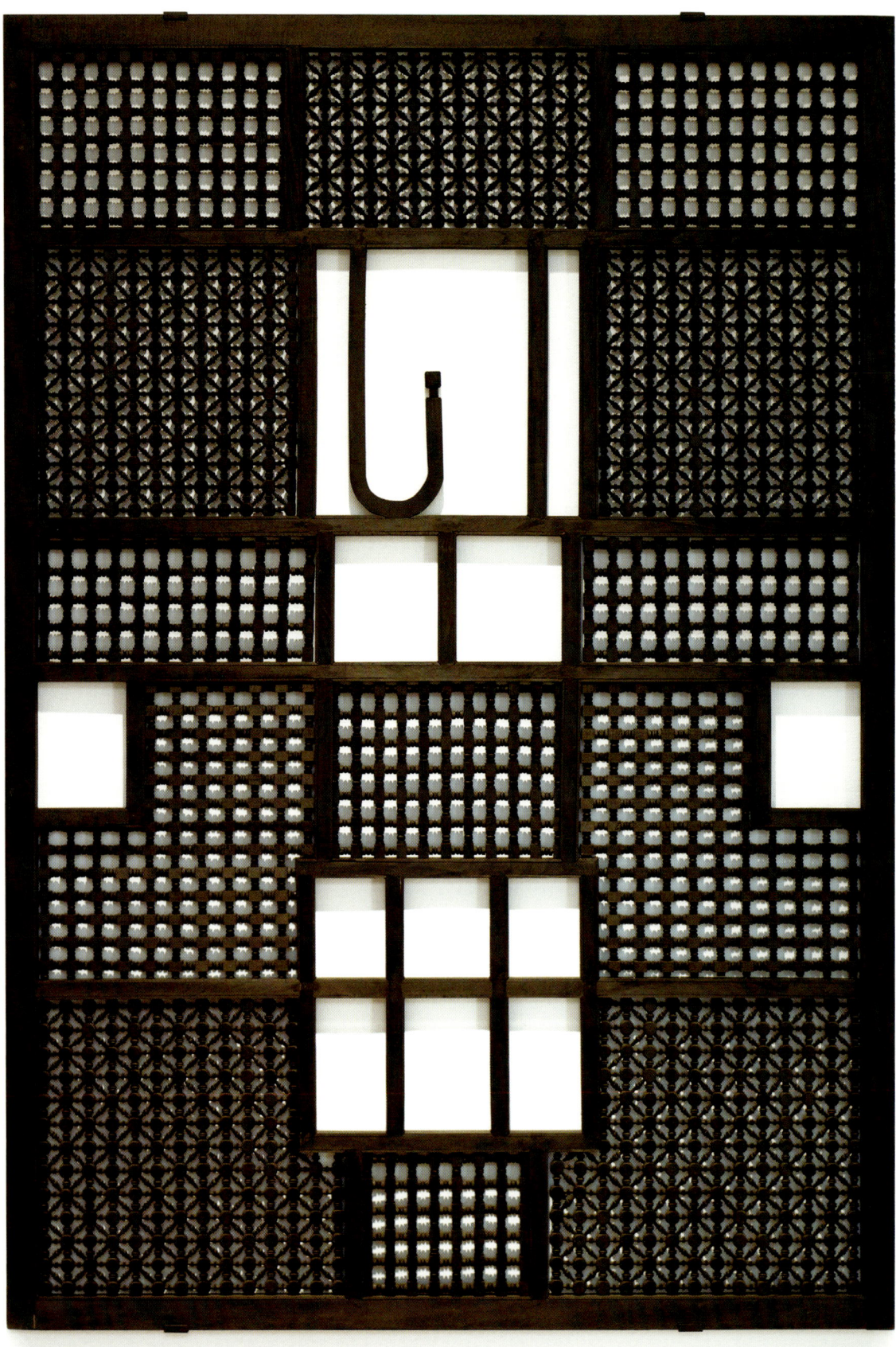

REBECCA M. NAGY

The exhibition *Project Europa: Imagining the (Im)Possible,* supported by this publication, is insightful and thought-provoking. It answers some questions yet raises many others. The featured artists respond to political and social conditions unique to their respective situations, but address issues with universal implications. Living and working in European countries, these artists bring to their work insights and experiences whose relevance extends far beyond Europe's borders. As curator Kerry Oliver-Smith has observed, *Project Europa* provides American audiences an opportunity to reflect on the meaning of democracy both at home and abroad and to grapple with democracy's inherent contradictions and paradoxes. In short, *Project Europa* is an exemplar of the kind of exhibition that a museum at a major research university should offer to its academic and community audiences.

I commend Kerry Oliver-Smith for her excellent work in bringing this ambitious project to fruition, and I extend my thanks to Marius Babias and Boris Groys for their probing essays on democracy and the relationship between art and politics. I share in the curator's gratitude to the artists who made their work available, as well as to the collectors, museums, and galleries that facilitated loans to the exhibition.

Major support for the exhibition and catalogue was provided by the Andy Warhol Foundation for the Visual Arts, for which we are deeply grateful. We also wish to acknowledge additional support from the C. Frederick and Aase B. Thompson Foundation; Étant donnés, the French-American Fund for Contemporary Art, a program of the French-American Cultural Exchange; University of Florida Student Government; the John Early Publication Endowment; the Sidney Knight Endowment; the Harn Program Endowment; and the Exhibition Circle of the Harn Museum. At the University of Florida, Kerry Oliver-Smith's research and programming related to the exhibition were supported by the Center for European Studies and director Amie Kreppel, the France-Florida Research Institute and director Carol Murphy, and the Paris Research Center and director Gayle Zackmann. Programming in conjunction with the exhibition is supported by the University of Florida's School of Art + Art History and director Anna Calluori Holcombe, through the school's Harn Eminent Scholar Chair in Art History Endowment. Additional programming support is provided by the university's International Center and director David Sammons and the university's Center for the Humanities and the Public Sphere and director Bonnie Effros. I extend my gratitude to all of these colleagues for their genuine interest and strong support and for their valuable partnerships with the Harn Museum of Art.

SUSAN HEFUNA

Egyptian/German, b. 1962
ANA
2006
Handmade wood carving, ink
77.5 x 3.54 x 55.12 in. (197 x 9 x 140 cm)
Courtesy of the artist and The Third Line, Dubai
Photography by Randy Batista

ACKNOWLEDGMENTS

KERRY OLIVER-SMITH

Project Europa is a testament to the contributions of many extraordinary people. To begin, I express my gratitude to French philosopher Étienne Balibar, whose provocative and astute critique of democracy in Europe provided a catalyst for the exhibition. Keenly aware of the critical and fragile state of democracy on both sides of the Atlantic, Balibar has produced numerous publications that pose a forceful challenge to the status quo and an urgent call to reinvigorate the practice of equality, liberty, and civility. His writing led me to the realization that an exhibition centered on democracy would be relevant not only to the world of art and politics but to the everyday experience of our own community.

The art itself serves as the galvanizing inspiration for the entire project. My thanks go to the artists, who balance poetry and politics in excellent and diverse work. I am grateful to them and to the galleries, museums, and collectors who generously made work available to us. For their contributions in the research stage of the exhibition, I thank the University of Florida Center for European Studies and director Amie Kreppel; the France-Florida Research Institute and director Carol Murphy; and the Paris Research Center and director Gayle Zackmann. Their generous support enabled me to meet many exceptional artists, curators, and scholars in Europe, each of whom helped shape the exhibition. I give special thanks to Marius Babias, Étienne Balibar, Diedrich Diedrichsen, and Dirk Snauwaert for their critical insights and support.

I am particularly grateful to the entire staff of the Harn Museum, whose energy, dedication, and talent made this project possible. Rebecca Nagy, director of the Harn, was unwavering in her commitment. My thanks also to Phyllis DeLaney, senior director of development, and Kelly Harvey, development coordinator for individual and foundation gifts, for their remarkable efforts and success in securing funding. I would like to thank Brandi Breslin, curatorial secretary, for creating the exhibition's acoustic guide. In addition, she was indispensable in ensuring the smooth progress of the project by drawing on her extensive experience and keen attention to detail. Associate registrar Jessica Aiken deftly handled the loans and care of the works. Thanks also to registrar Laura Nemmers for her oversight. Chief preparator Michael Peyton brought his consummate good humor and expertise to the installation. Tim Joiner's help was invaluable. My appreciation goes to director of education Bonnie Bernau and to the education department, especially the efforts of Rebecca Fitzsimmons and Alyssa Browne Peyton, who organized excellent adult programs that greatly enhance the exhibition. Tami Wroath, director of marketing and public relations, and Courtney Dell, coordinator of marketing and public relations, have brought their considerable talent and attention to detail to the coordination of the catalogue and the promotion of the exhibition. Additional staff members who gave generous help to the project include director of finance and operations Mary Yawn, director of museum technology Dwight Bailey, store manager Kathryn Rush, and the administrative team of Charles King, Donna Duff, and Cecile Sands.

I am beholden to the authors of the catalogue essays, Marius Babias and Boris Groys; their original texts make important contributions to the topic of democracy and the relationship between art and politics. Thanks also to Brian Currid for the skillful translation of the essay written by Babias, and to Gerald Zeigerman for his meticulous editing of the entire publication. Tony Oliver-Smith, Shepherd Steiner, and Maureen Turim generously read drafts of my catalogue texts and provided feedback. I am greatly indebted to Ron Shore for his extraordinary design of the exhibition catalogue. It is with profound gratitude that I acknowledge the invaluable conversations and exchanges with friends and colleagues that furthered the ideas for the exhibition. Warm thanks especially to Alex Alberro, Nora Alter, Max Becher, Roger Beebe, Jill Ciment, Barbara Mennel, Arnold Mesches, Tony Oliver-Smith, Andrea Robbins, Shepherd Steiner, and Maureen Turim. I greatly appreciate School of Art + Art History director Anna Calluori Holcombe, and professors Richard Heipp, Sean Miller, and Jack Stenner for their generous and invaluable support and contributions to the success of the art residencies of Kader Attia and Dan Perjovschi. Special thanks go to Patrick Grigsby and the extraordinary student team that assisted Kader Attia. The faculty and staff of the Center for European Studies provided outstanding support and resources. I am also indebted to my research assistant, Doris Bremm, and to the interns who were instrumental in the realization of the project, including wonderful University of Florida students Louise Michelle Buyo, Lindsay Gordon, Jennifer Fourmont, Kimberly Menninger, Magena Rodriguez, Alexandra Hamilton, and Laura Almeida.

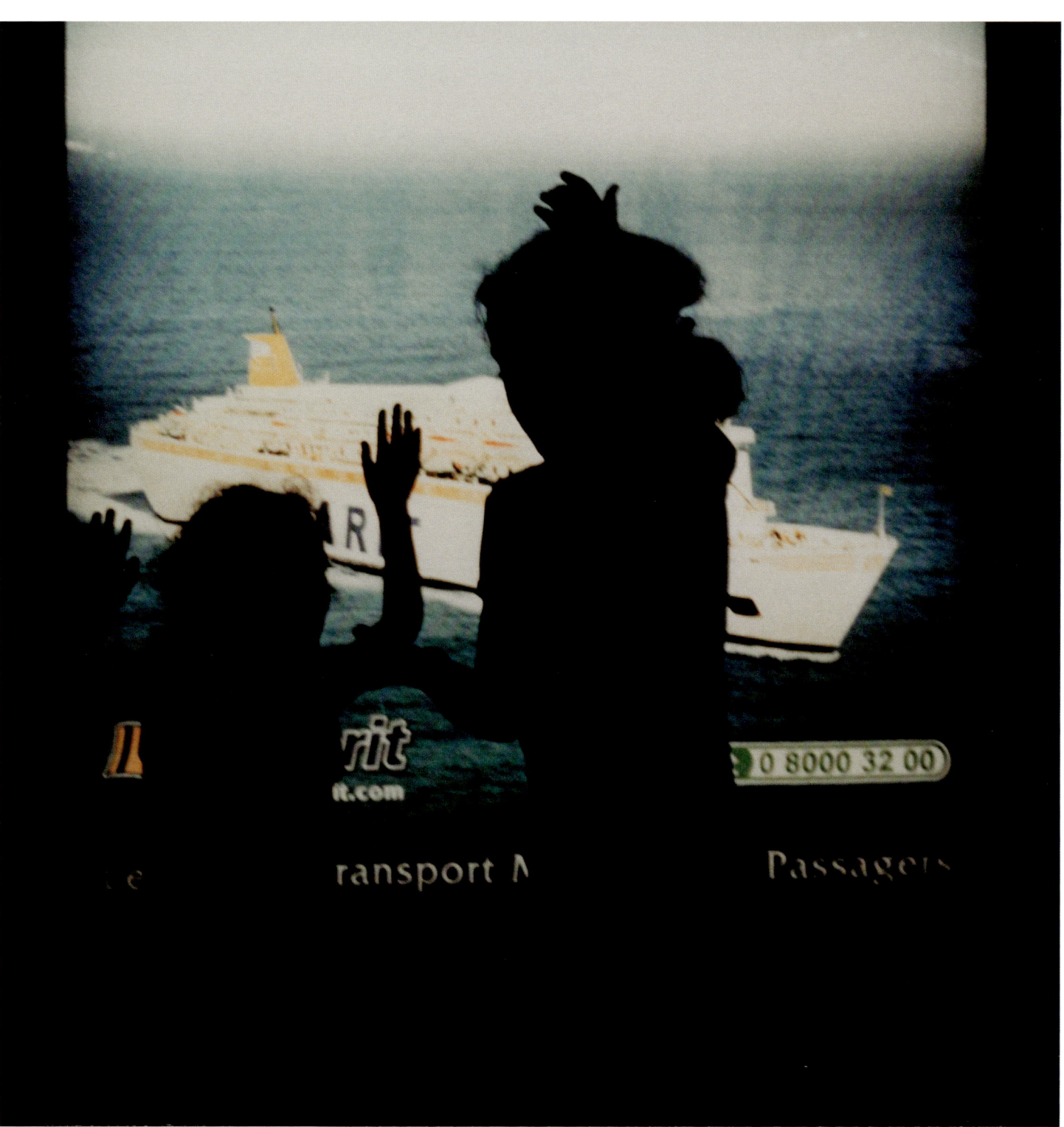

Europe: The Nexus of Possibility

KERRY OLIVER-SMITH

Aporia

Project Europa: Imagining the (Im)Possible is inspired by artists who have critically and imaginatively engaged with the extraordinary transformations of Europe since 1989. The collapse of the Berlin wall, followed by the expansion of the European Union, called the world's attention to the promise of a new Europe. Not just an economic construction, the unification of Europe was conceived as a vital and urgent social project to promote democracy. Twenty years after the fall of the wall, *Project Europa* considers the relationship of art and artists to democracy. What is the role of art in the public sphere? In what ways do artists mediate the vital and critical political issues of their time? What is the emancipatory potential of art? In the exhibition, artists from the British Isles to Turkey challenge the collective imagination of Europe while confronting a paradox: Europe as the site of possibility and impossibility for creating an egalitarian society.

This reflection on Europe is particularly timely and relevant to American audiences. Long coupled as the West, Europe and the United States continue to share an extraordinary and controversial impact worldwide. The acute pressures of globalization, migration, climate change, and terrorism have brought the challenges and mutual destiny of Europe and the United States closer than ever. The two powers struggle with factors that threaten to exacerbate strategic, economic, and cultural divides. In this critical context, it is all the more urgent to question the recent past, examine our global impact, and envision a better future. Looking at Europe provides both the distance and proximity to interrogate our own shifting landscape and to reinvigorate our commitment to a vital democracy.

Europe is a name, a continent, and an abstract idea. Europe was the center of Judeo-Christian tradition and, later, the beacon of the Enlightenment's universal values of equity, tolerance, and reason. Europe is a site of ideological, economic, and cultural convergence, occupying an uneasy but fertile space between socialist and capitalist systems; Christian, Jewish, and Islamic cultures; and the competing influences of Asia, Africa, and America. As an embodiment of the notion of democracy, human rights, peace, and heterogeneity, it has served as a global model. Nevertheless, Europe has also given rise to xenophobia and racism, religious intolerance, and the hardening of immigration policies. After 9/11 and attacks in Spain and England, the fear of terrorism led to heightened security and a climate of distrust and fear. Populist and religious movements replace traditional forms of political and civic society, and consumerism has emerged as a homogenizing form of identity.

YTO BARRADA

French, b. 1971
Advertisement Lightbox, Tangier
A Life Full of Holes: The Strait Project
2003
C-print
23.62 x 23.62 in. (60 x 60 cm)
Courtesy of Galerie Polaris, Paris
Photography by Randy Batista

The barriers to democracy in Europe constitute an aporia. Derived from the Greek word for "impasse," aporia is a paradox or an impossible contradiction. Aporia is also the nexus of possibility.

The barriers to democracy in Europe constitute an aporia. Derived from the Greek word for "impasse," aporia is a paradox or an impossible contradiction. Aporia is also the nexus of possibility. It is a concept central to the ancients and to the ideas of such contemporary philosophers as Jacques Derrida, who theorized the idea in *Aporias* (Derrida 1993), and Étienne Balibar, who extended the concept in his 1999 lecture "At the Borders of Europe" (Balibar 2004, 1–10). Balibar asserts that the heart of aporia lies between necessity and impossibility—the necessity to create a new image of Europe and the impossibility of creating an inclusive political order (Balibar 2004, 9). In his writing, he states provocatively that the "contradictions are more and more acute between a democratic and universalistic claim and self-image, and a neo-imperialist ethnocentric practice…" (Balibar 2006, 5). Based on nationalism and rootedness, past processes of exclusion conflict with policies of inclusion based in transnational politics. Significantly, it is precisely at the crux of contradiction that Balibar sees the opening for new ways of thinking. The confrontation with the impossible provokes a search for the possible, a leap of the imaginary that reveals the potential for a different future (Balibar 2004, 3). Accordingly, Derrida writes that the impossible gives the "movement to desire, action, and decision: it is the very figure of the real" (Derrida, quoted in Reid 2007, 386).

The concept of aporia opens channels of possibility in both politics and art. Pairing art and politics has been construed by some as an impossible contradiction; however, according to Jacques Rancière, they share common ground in the realm of aesthetics. In his book *The Politics of Aesthetics,* he proposes a significant and influential model regarding the politics of aesthetics and the aesthetics of politics that helps illuminate the art in this exhibition. *Aesthetics,* in the broad sense, is about perception and "distribution of the sensible"—that is, what can be said, heard, spoken, and thought. The reigning social order, or "police order," as Rancière calls it, governs the realm of perception with codes of behavior, and the terms of inclusion and exclusion being predetermined by experts. These experts also determine the terms of value and shares within a community. Democracy, however, does not require experts. Power belongs to no one and everyone. Politics, then, involves an opposition or dissensus between the established social order and the excluded who fight for the redistribution of perception and speech. Similarly, art can reverse the hierarchies of representation and reframe the conditions of sensory experience. Art is political when it reconfigures the realm of the visible, challenging boundaries of what is visible and invisible, what is sayable and unsayable, and what can be thought and done. Art also blurs the barrier between those who look and those who act. Rancière writes:

> "Emancipation starts from the principle of equality. It begins when we dismiss the opposition between looking and acting and understand that the distribution of the visible itself is part of the configuration of domination and subjection. It starts when we realize that looking is also an action that confirms or modifies that distribution, and that 'interpreting the world' is already a means of transforming it" (Rancière 2007, 277).

Art expands the landscape of the possible.

The Exhibition   *Project Europa* takes aporia as a point of departure in a consideration of art and democracy in Europe. The exhibition explores the potential of art to locate the possible within the impossible and to reveal new ways of seeing, thinking, and imagining the world. While the exhibition makes no attempt at a geographically comprehensive representation, it includes work by artists from a rich variety of perspectives and cultural positions. Consistently, their work is located at the intersection between art and politics and art and everyday life.

Artists explore the aporias not only within politics but within their own aesthetic practice. In the debate between the separation of art from everyday life or the immersion of art into everyday life, these artists stake a claim at the intersection of both sides. Drawing upon a history of avant-garde strategies and socially engaged art, they do not proselytize or promote ideologies but, instead, strive to disturb fixed meanings and cross the boundaries of what can be thought, seen, and said. Countering the spectacle and singular message of consumer culture and mass media, artists reveal the complexities of the visible and the invisible in everyday reality. They challenge stereotypes and politics of identity and explore the complexity of subjectivity and the relationship of self and other. Furthermore, these artists use a variety of strategies and media from sculpture, painting, performance, photography, and film to integrate the viewer in the creation of the aesthetic experience. Mixing the political with the poetic, these artists look toward new possibilities.

Works in *Project Europa* confront the conflicts and contradictions of Europe's democratic dream and, in the process, open up the promise of democracy. The exhibition concepts are organized by six overlapping areas of contention: *Past/Present, Borders, The City, The Market, War,* and *Future/Tense.* Each part presents specific encounters with the limits of democracy. *Past/Present* begins with the fall of the Berlin wall. Artists examine Europe's democratic ambitions in relation to the absolutism of overarching political and cultural systems of the past, which include nationalism, colonialism, and communism. They consider how aspects of imperialism and xenophobia rooted in the past continue to shape the present. Concentrating on current conditions, artists in *Borders* focus on the geopolitical borders on the edge of Europe. Centering on pivotal divides between the North and the South, the East and the West, they interrogate the condition of the immigrant, migrant, and refugee. Moving from the frontiers of Europe to its interior, *The City* examines barriers within major urban areas, focusing on issues of inclusion and exclusion, communication and altercation, rights of circulation and residence. Artists also consider the role of the law and the media, and trace a disturbing rise in the level of violence. *The Market* looks at globalization, exploring both its liberating and devastating potential. Some artists present a critique while others actively engage in community initiatives and alternative systems of exchange and value. The section titled *War* considers the growing climate of suspicion, police controls, and emergency rule in Europe. Conflicts in the Balkans provide a way for artists to examine the dangers of fundamentalism and to contemplate the incursion of a perpetual state of war. In *Future/Tense,* artists imagine the future of Europe's promise from dystopian and utopian perspectives, leaving the future open to the viewer's imagination. Artists in the exhibition are: Francis Alÿs, Fikret Atay, Kader Attia, Maja Bajevic, Yto Barrada, Tacita Dean, Beate Gütschow, Jens Haaning, Susan Hefuna, Eva Leitolf, Aernout Mik, Marcel Odenbach, Dan Perjovschi, Marjetica Potrč, Andrea Robbins and Max Becher, Bruno Serralongue, Superflex, and Lidwien Van de Ven.

The Catalogue

This book includes three essays and a catalogue of works displayed in the exhibition. The catalogue develops the aforementioned themes while presenting the artists' work. Contributing essayists Boris Groys and Marius Babias consider democracy from the perspective of art and politics, respectively. In his essay "Contemporary Art: Excessive Democracy," Groys deconstructs the radically democratic and emancipatory dimensions of contemporary art. He begins by chronicling changes in current art and politics—one of the most significant changes being our entry into a culture of mass artistic production. Given the new technical and electronic means of image production and distribution, everyone can be an artist. Groys asserts that art is not being created for the masses but by the masses. In addition, he argues that artists work with a potentially infinite variety of images, forms, media, and practices—all of equal value. Thus, the democratic dimensions of art and politics are bound together by equality of forms and practices and infinite possibilities. Artists renew the democratic project by presenting their own alternative art projects while connecting with their audiences, often in collaborative and participatory ways.

The essay by Marius Babias, "The Longing of the East: 'Undemocratic' Democracy and the Dilemma of Political Emancipation in Postcommunism," considers how the tools of political critique may be used to analyze the world. In particular, he is concerned with the condition of democracy in the postcommunist states of Europe, where a "formal democracy" of administrators and experts overrides actual responsibility and representation. He notes how the East longs for the West, confusing capitalism with freedom and emancipation, and how the West longs for the East as a cultural and economic commodity. He traces the erasure of the Communist past and a rise in ideology, nationalism, and racial mythologies. For Babias, political critique is a tool to activate individual agency and to change the way society thinks and acts. Political critique as negative critique opposes the absolute truth claim of rational power; instead, it calls for a politics of emancipation that reclaims its relationship to justice and equality and is committed to universal truths protecting the civil rights of every person. Babias's essay itself stands as a model of political critique.

The essays by Boris Groys and Marius Babias identify strategies that expand the potential of democracy in society. Groys focuses on the possibilities unleashed by mass artistic production, exploring alternative methods through limitless avenues and forms. Babias uses political critique as a way to deconstruct the myths and fictions of society that function as barriers to democratic participation. Both writers consider art and politics in relation to emancipation and equality, providing a stimulating and challenging introduction to the exhibition *Project Europa*.

REFERENCE LIST

Balibar, Étienne. 2006. *Strangers as Enemies. Further Reflection on the Aporias of Transnational Citizenship*. Distinguished Visiting Lecturer address, Institute on Globalization and the Human Condition, McMaster University, March 16, 2006. http://www.ciaonet.org/wps/ighc/0007550/index.html (accessed May 7, 2009).

Balibar, Étienne. 2004. "At the Borders of Europe." In *We, the People of Europe? Reflections on Transnational Citizenship*. Translated by J. Swenson. Princeton, N.J.: Princeton University Press.

Balibar, Étienne. 2003. "Europe, An 'Unimagined' Frontier of Democracy." *Diacritics*: 33.3–4:36–44.

Derrida, Jacques, as quoted in M. Redfield. 2007. "Derrida, Europe, Today." *South Atlantic Quarterly*, 106:2, 373–92.

Derrida, Jacques. 1993. *Aporias*. Translated by Thomas Dutoit. Stanford, California: Stanford University Press.

Rancière, Jacques. 2007. *The Politics of Aesthetics*. Translated by Gabriel Rockhill. N.Y.: Continuum.

Rancière, Jacques. 2007. "The Emancipated Spectator." *Artforum*, March, 271–80.

EVA LEITOLF

German, b. 1966
Hirschgarten, Munich (Hirschgarten, München)
German Images—Looking for Evidence
2007
Color photograph
31.89 in. x 27.17 in. (81 cm x 69 cm)
Courtesy of the artist

The catalogue lists an array of public programs that are an integral and vital component of *Project Europa*. These include a film series, *Crossing Over*, with filmmaker Deimantas Narkevičius and visiting filmmakers Amie Siegel, Helga Fanderl, and Johan Grimonprez. A symposium, *Art and Democracy*, features speakers Alex Alberro, Nora Alter, Claire Bishop, Francois Cusset, T. J. Demos, Tim Griffin, Maria Hlavajova, and Shepherd Steiner. Additional events are a lecture, community meetings, and family and youth programs.

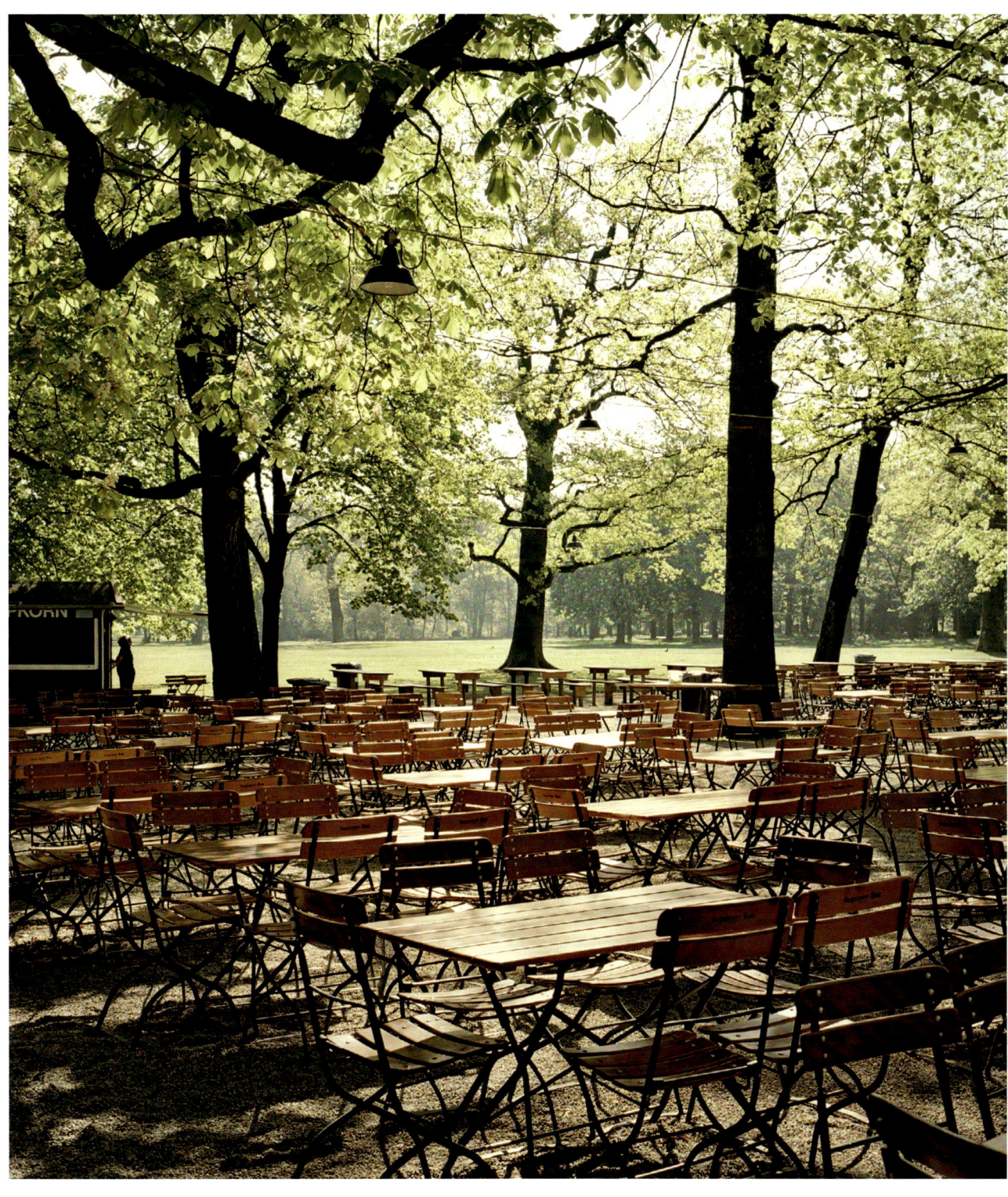

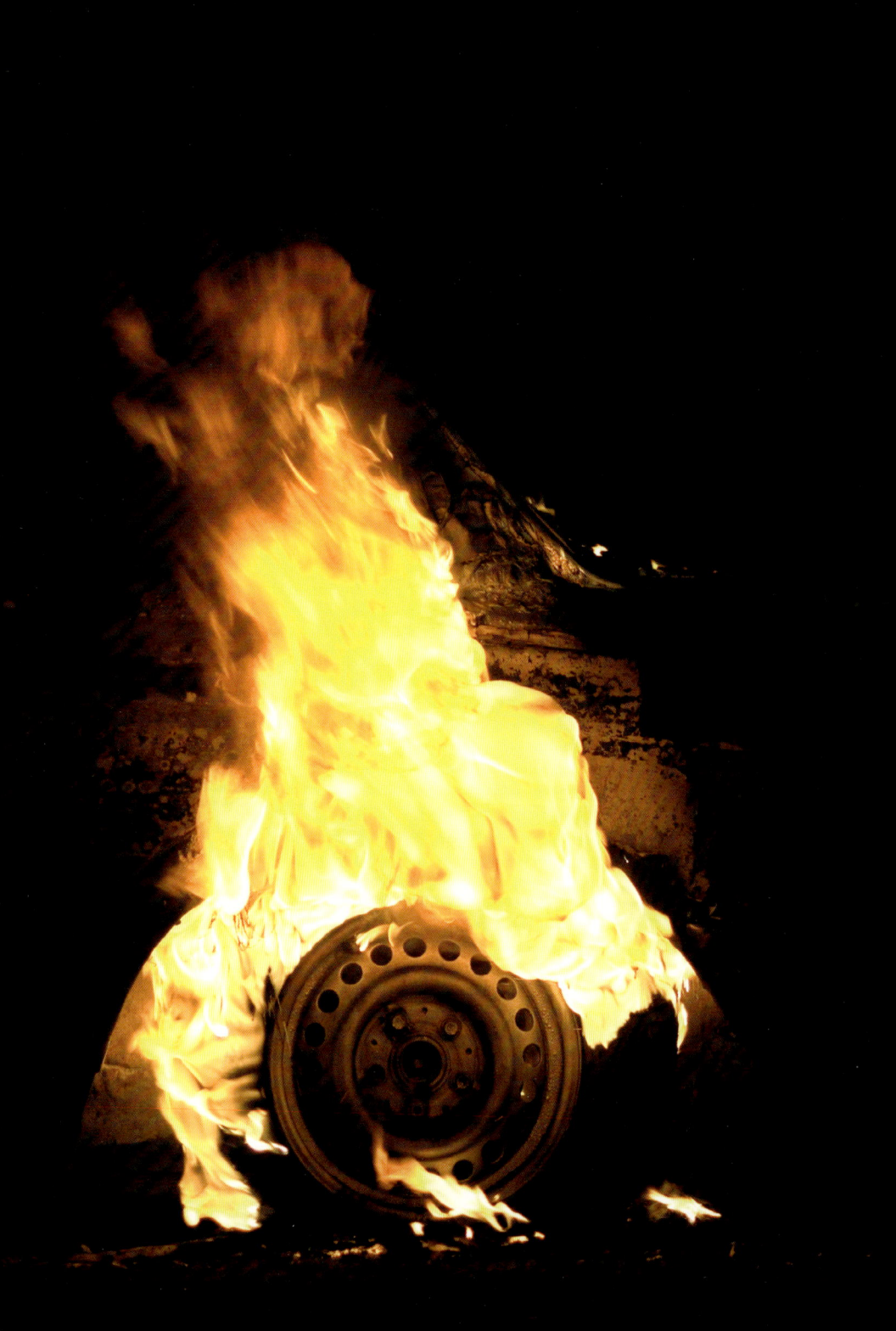

Contemporary Art: Excessive Democracy

BORIS GROYS

Contemporary media-driven Western democracies practice the aestheticization of politics to an extent that historically is almost without precedence. Indeed, in the past, the division of labor between politics and art was clear enough. Politicians made politics, and artists represented politics by narrating, depicting, or criticizing it. But, in our time, the situation has changed drastically: The contemporary politician no longer needs an artist to endow his or her figure and actions with aesthetic representation. Today, every important political figure or event is immediately represented, depicted, narrated, and interpreted by the media. The machine of media coverage does not need individual artistic intervention to be put into motion. Indeed, contemporary mass media has emerged as by far the largest and most powerful machine for producing images—vastly more extensive and effective than the contemporary art system. We are constantly fed images of political events, wars, terror, and catastrophes of all kinds, at a level of image production and distribution with which the artist and his artisan skills cannot compete. Today's political sphere is permanently aestheticizing itself, without any help from, and in a complete disregard of, art and artists. Even in the 1960s, Guy Debord characterized Western democratic societies as societies of spectacle, and this characterization is more valid now than ever before.

The question of how art made by artists must react to this global spectacle and its strategies of aestheticization has remained at the center of art-related discussions for many decades. Historically, we were confronted with different answers to this question, but there is no doubt that the prevailing attitude toward the global spectacle was and still is a critical one: The social and political function of art is seen mostly in critique and deconstruction of the dominating aesthetics of the spectacular. At the end of his essay "Artwork in the Age of Its Mechanical Reproduction," Walter Benjamin famously formulated the opposition between politicization of aesthetics and aestheticization of politics. The latter was, for Benjamin, a way to conceal the real economical and power structure of society—a way that ultimately led to fascism and war, to a totalizing spectacle of aestheticized self-destruction. The politicization of aesthetics was considered by Benjamin as being, on the contrary, a leftist, critical, and salutary practice, because it was supposed to contribute to a revolutionary change in the dominating social and economical order. But, at the same time, Benjamin almost automatically assumed that art and the artist played a decisive, even central role in both cases—be it the politicization of aesthetics or the aestheticization of politics. It is characteristic that he refers to Gabriele D'Annunzio

SUPERFLEX

Jakob Fenger, Bjørnstjerne Reuter Christiansen,
and Rasmus Nielsen
Danish
Burning Car
2008
Blu-ray projection, 11 minutes
Produced by Propeller Group (Ho Chi Minh City)
and coproduced by the Vleeshal, Middelburg,
Netherlands
Dimensions variable
Courtesy of the artists and Nils Staerk,
Copenhagen

and Filippo Tommaso Marinetti when he wants to explain what the aestheticization of politics actually means and how it functions. Accordingly, he expresses the hope that artists can successfully resist the politics of the spectacular by radical politicization of art.

The art of recent decades tried time and again to politicize itself, to transcend the borders of the autonomous art system. In our time, however, almost everybody tends to agree that all the attempts to transcend the art system by practicing the politicization of art never allowed the artist to enter the sphere of "pure politics." This failure is often interpreted as a proof of the incapacity of art to penetrate the political sphere per se. Yet, if the politicization of art is seriously intended and practiced, it mostly succeeds. Art can enter the political sphere and, indeed, art entered it many times in the course of the twentieth century. The problem is not the incapacity of art to become truly political; rather, when art becomes political, it makes the unpleasant discovery that politics already became art, that politics already situated itself in the aesthetic field. The artistic vision of political action transcending the aesthetic field reveals itself as a fiction. If an artist goes beyond the art system, the artist begins to function in the same way that politicians, sport heroes, terrorists, movie stars, and other minor or major celebrities already function. The artist also becomes covered by the media. The transition from the art system to the political field is possible, but this transition operates primarily as a change in positioning of the artist vis-à-vis image production. In other words, the artist becomes the artwork. Now, for many people this means that the critical position has become impossible, because the main condition for such a critical position is seen mostly in the capacity of art to transcend the aesthetic sphere.

One can argue, however, that the real difficulty with criticality has a different cause. Today, the critical position has become so widespread and omnipresent, it can be considered an integral part of the mass culture it intends to criticize. Every act of aestheticization—or of design, of branding—is always simultaneously a critique of the object of this aestheticization; it signals that the object needs an aesthetic supplement to look better than it actually is. Such an aesthetic supplement always functions as a pharmakon, in the sense that Jacques Derrida has used this term: It both cures the object of its application and further contributes to its illness. Design makes a designed object look better—but, at the same time, it raises a suspicion that this object might look especially ugly and repellent if its designed surface were to be accidentally removed. Indeed, the spectacular and the design are primarily machines for production of suspicion. Our contemporary, totally designed world is often described as one of complete seduction, from which unpleasant reality has disappeared. But the world of total design is, rather, one of total suspicion—of latent danger lurking behind the designed surface. Inevitably, we tend to suspect that something terrible is going on behind the aestheticized, designed surface—cynical manipulation, political propaganda, hidden intrigues, invested interests, and, simply, crimes. We are living today not only in the world of design but the era of conspiracy theories. Design and branding demonstrate to us the aestheticized surface of contemporary democracy. But the obvious artificiality of this surface provokes us to react by indulging in conspiracy theories related to the invisible, impenetrable, dark powers assumed to operate behind this artificial surface. The conspiracy theory is the contemporary form of metaphysics (metaphysics being a discourse about the hidden and invisible)—the only form in which traditional metaphysics survived after the "death of God," as some chose to call their sudden lack of belief in a supreme being. Earlier, we had nature and God; today, we have political design and conspiracy theory.

Accordingly, the production of trust became the main aesthetic problem that confronted the contemporary subject under the conditions of media-driven democracy. Now, everybody is scrutinized with suspicion and subjected to aesthetic evaluation—and required to take aesthetic responsibility for his or her appearance in the world, for his or her self-design. Earlier, self-design was a privilege and a burden of the chosen few. Correspondingly, the critical position was also a privilege and burden of the few. In our time, self-design and the critical attitude became the mass cultural practices par excellence.

But the increased aestheticization of the media-political sphere, and subsequent growth of suspicion and criticality, is not the only—and not even the most important—change that differentiates the present art situation from that of the 1960s. Toward the end of the twentieth and the beginning of the twenty-first centuries, art entered a new era—namely, an era of mass artistic production. This era is new because the previous modern age was one of merely mass consumption of art—described by many influential theoreticians as an era of kitsch (Clement Greenberg), of "cultural industry" (Theodore Adorno), or, as mentioned earlier, a society of spectacle. This was the era of culture that was made for the masses—of culture that wanted to seduce masses, to be consumed by the masses. But this allegedly popular culture was produced by the elites, not by the masses themselves. The situation now has changed. There are primarily two developments that lead to this change: one is the emergence of the new technical means of image production and distribution, another is a shift in our understanding of art—the change of the rules used for the identification of what is art and what is not art.

Today, we do not identify an artwork primarily as an object produced through the manual labor of an individual artist; rather, an artwork is seen as an effect of choosing, placing, shifting, transforming, and combining of already existing images and objects. It is precisely what hundreds of millions of people around the world are doing every day in the context of their everyday life. Of course, even after the discourse on the death of the author and the deconstruction of subjectivity and intentionality, we tend to think that all these operations could be interpreted as generating art only if they were to be originally dictated by an artistic project, by an aesthetic intention. We also tend to assume that the masses do not have such an intention but produce aesthetic effects somehow unconsciously—that they become well informed about advanced art production through biennials, documentas, and related media coverage, and, yes, produce their art intentionally. Contemporary means of communication and such networks as Facebook, MySpace, YouTube, Second Life, and Twitter provide global populations with the opportunity to place their photos, videos, and texts in a way that cannot be distinguished from any other postconceptualist artwork. Contemporary design gives to the same populations the possibility of shaping and experiencing their apartments or workplaces as artistic installations, which means that, today, contemporary art has become a mass cultural practice. The question arises, How can a contemporary artist survive this popular success of contemporary art? Or, how can the artist survive in a world in which everybody has become an artist?

Being pressured by this question, one looks back on the age of modernity with deep nostalgia. At a time in which the cynical political and commercial elites propelled pseudoart into the world in an attempt to seduce the masses into political obedience and/or consumerist frenzy, the artist could be proud to produce artworks that had, by their form, signaled resistance to, or, at least, distanced themselves from the dominating mass cultural aesthetics. Avant-garde and modernist art were, time and again, accused of being elitist, but are, in fact, egalitarian and democratic.

Indeed, the classical avant-garde has opened up the infinite horizontal field of all possible pictorial forms, which are lined up alongside one another with equal rights. So-called primitive art, abstract forms, and simple objects from everyday life have all acquired the kind of recognition that used to be granted only to historically privileged artistic masterpieces. This equalizing art practice grew progressively more pronounced in the course of the last century, to the same degree that images of mass culture, entertainment, and kitsch have been accorded equal status inside the traditional high-art context. The artist of the ancien régime was intent on creating a masterpiece—an image that would exist in its own right, that would stand out from all other images as the visualization of a singular truth that, in one way or another, remained concealed by those images. In modernity, on the other hand, artists have tended to present examples of an infinite sequence of images, as Kandinsky did with abstract compositions, Duchamp with ready-mades, and Warhol with icons of mass culture. The source of the explosive impact that these examples exert upon us lies not in their exclusivity but, instead, in their capacity to be mere examples of the potentially infinite variety of images. They not only present themselves but also act as pointers to the inexhaustible mass of images, of which they are delegates of equal standing. This reference to the infinite multitude of excluded images is precisely what lends these individual artistic items their fascination within the finite contexts of political and artistic representation. Hence, it is not to the "vertical" infinity of divine truth that the artist in the modernity makes reference but to the "horizontal" infinity of equally valuable images.

This politics of equal aesthetic rights, this struggle for aesthetic equality among all visual forms and media that modern art has fought to establish, was—and still is, even now—frequently criticized as an expression of cynicism and, paradoxically, elitism. This criticism was directed against modern art, from both the right and the left, as a lack of genuine love for art or a lack of genuine political involvement, of political engagement. Politics of equal rights, on the level of aesthetics, is a necessary precondition. Indeed, contemporary emancipatory politics is a politics of inclusion—directed against the existing exclusions

Art, as such, becomes the socially codified manifestation of fundamental equality between all existing and virtual visual forms and media.

of political and cultural minorities. But this struggle for inclusion is possible only if the forms in which the desires of the excluded minorities manifest themselves are not rejected and suppressed from the beginning by any kind of aesthetic censorship that operates in the name of higher aesthetic values. The modernist ideal of autonomous art encourages not an autonomous hierarchy of taste but abolishing every such hierarchy and then establishing the regime of equal rights for all artworks. Art, as such, becomes the socially codified manifestation of fundamental equality between all existing and virtual visual forms and media. Only against the background of this fundamental aesthetic equality of all artworks can every value judgment, every exclusion or inclusion, be potentially recognized as the result of a heteronomous intrusion into the autonomous sphere of art—as dictated by outside forces. This recognition opens the possibility of resistance against intrusions into art's territory in the name of art's autonomy, or in the name of the equality of all the art forms and media. Of course, when I say "art," I mean art of today, which is the result of a long battle for recognition that took place in the course of modernity.

Democratic art and politics are connected in one fundamental respect: Both are realms in which a struggle for recognition is being waged. As defined by Alexandre Kojève, in his commentary on Hegel, this struggle for recognition surpasses the usual struggle for the distribution of material goods, which in modernity is generally regulated by market forces. At stake here is not merely the requirement that a certain desire will be satisfied but that it will be recognized as socially legitimate. Politics is an arena in which various group interests have, both in the past and the present, fought for recognition, but artists of the classical avant-garde have always contended for the recognition of all individual forms and artistic procedures that were not previously considered legitimate. In other words, the classical avant-garde has struggled to achieve recognition for all signs, forms, and things as the legitimate objects of artistic desire and, hence, representation in art. Both forms of struggle are intrinsically bound up with each other, and both have as their aim a situation in which all people with their various interests, as, indeed, all forms and artistic procedures, will finally be granted equal rights.

The contemporary mass artistic production taking place mostly in and through electronic social networks, such as MySpace and YouTube, inherits this avant-garde project of aesthetic equality. In a way, these artistic practices realize the famous slogan of Joseph Beuys, that everybody should become an artist. Today, we are living not among masses of spectators but among masses of artists. The rejection of the dominating aesthetics now becomes an undemocratic gesture, indeed—and also an impossible gesture. First, to reject the dominating aesthetics of Facebook and YouTube means to reject not art made for the masses but art made by the masses. Second, the aesthetics of this mass-produced art coincides with the most advanced, postconceptualist aesthetics of contemporary art itself. It does not make much sense, then, to start a search for new forms that might be opposed to aspects of contemporary democratic popular culture. It also does not make much sense to look for the strategies of political or ethical engagement, because contemporary Internet culture has enough sites to situate these strategies. Both of these classical modernist strategies seem to be inefficient, so, again, the question arises, Could this mass success of contemporary art possibly be an indication that art as such has come to its historical end?

On the contrary, this success belies a thesis of the end of art formulated much earlier. In the nineteenth century, Hegel asserted, at the beginning of his *Lectures on Aesthetics,* that art was a thing of the past. He argued that modernity is dominated by pure thought that does not need images to be represented but actively resists a possible contamination through images. Accordingly, under modern conditions, art is destined for insignificance; actually, its own insignificance can be its only possible topic. But this Hegelian diagnosis demonstrated itself historically as incorrect. Modern life, in time, became more and more aestheticized, theatricalized, and designed. Today, artistic activity is something that artists share with their public on the most elementary, common level of everyday life. Artists share art with the public as earlier they shared religion or politics. To be an artist ceased to be an exclusive fate; instead, it became representative for the society as a whole on its most intimate, everyday level. Now, the artist once again gets a chance to formulate a universalist claim by revealing the inner structure of contemporary everyday life. And the artist can do it not so much by criticizing the existing art institutions and global spectacle as by proposing alternative art projects and programs that present themselves as being collaborative, participatory, and democratic. A tendency toward collaborative, participatory practice is undeniably one of the main characteristics of contemporary art. Numerous groups of artists throughout the world are asserting collective, even anonymous authorship of their work. Moreover, collaborative practices of this type tend to encourage the public to join in, to activate the social milieu in which such practices unfold. In this way, the artist overcomes the main trauma of modernity: the separation of the artist from his or her audience.

Ultimately, however, there is no fundamental difference between participative and individual art practices. Contemporary art reasserts its democratic vocation primarily when it renews its initial egalitarian promise, when it reclaims the emancipatory vision of an infinite realm of images, media and art practices, endowed with equal rights. By doing so, art operates in the gap between this infinite realm of possibilities and the aesthetics of the global spectacle that necessarily use the limited range of artistic devices to secure their easy and universal recognizability. At the same time, art need not represent only "real" cultural identities or social attitudes that are excluded from this global spectacle. These identities and attitudes can also be imagined, virtual, only possible—and artificially created. After all, in our time nobody can believe in being represented by the *Black Square* of Kazimir Malevich. Today, Internet users create fictional, virtual identities to operate in electronic social networks. As power hierarchies of the past found their extension and legitimization through infinite celestial hierarchies, today's democratic equality finds its legitimization through the horizontal infinity of all possible, virtual forms and media. It is this infinite excess of aesthetic equality that constitutes the true horizon of contemporary political democracy—beyond institutional recognition of any particular interests, demands, and desires.

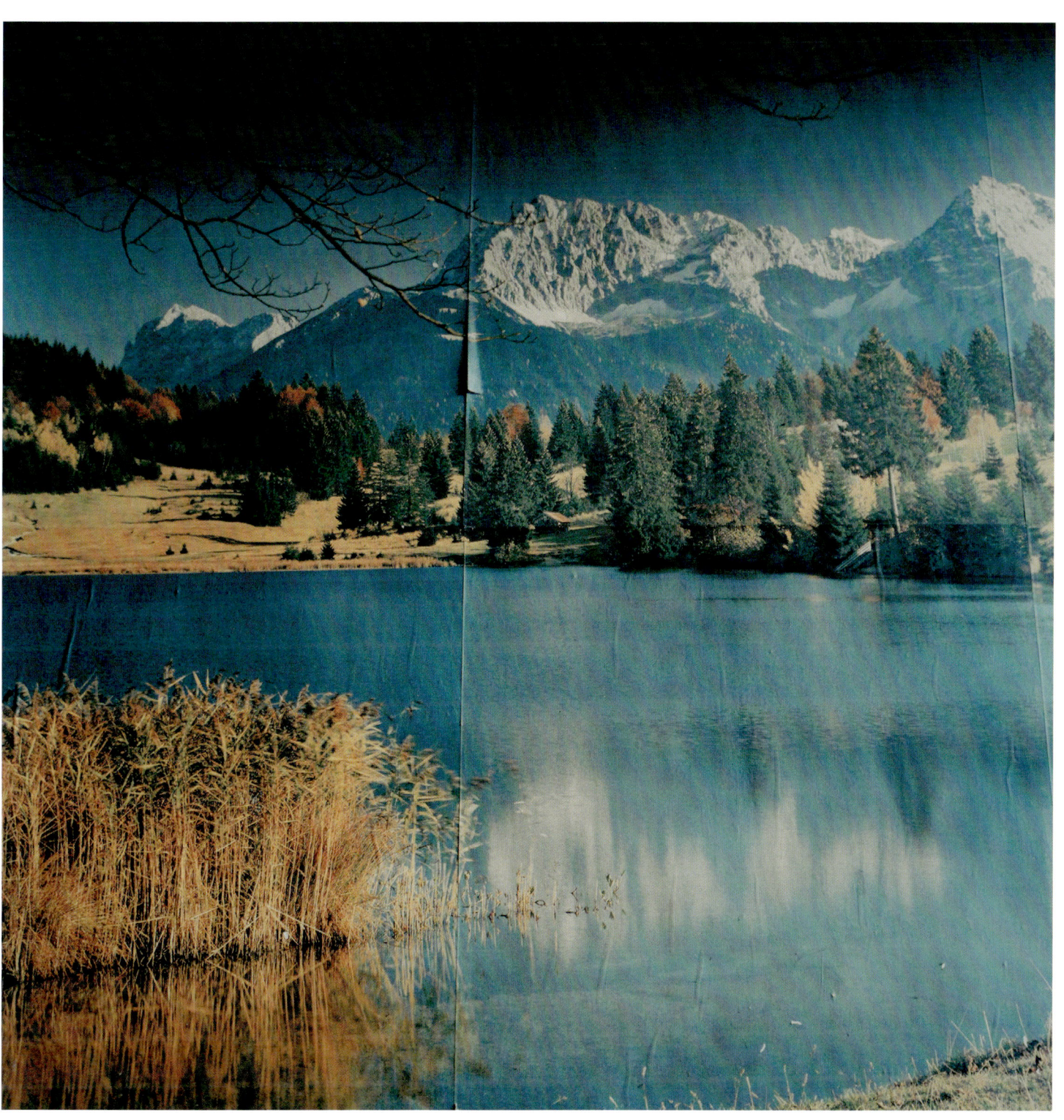

AERNOUT MIK

Dutch, b. 1962
Raw Footage
2006
2-screen video and sound installation (images from
found documentary material: Reuters & ITN, ITN
Source), digital video on DVD
Dimensions variable
Courtesy of carlier | gebauer, Berlin

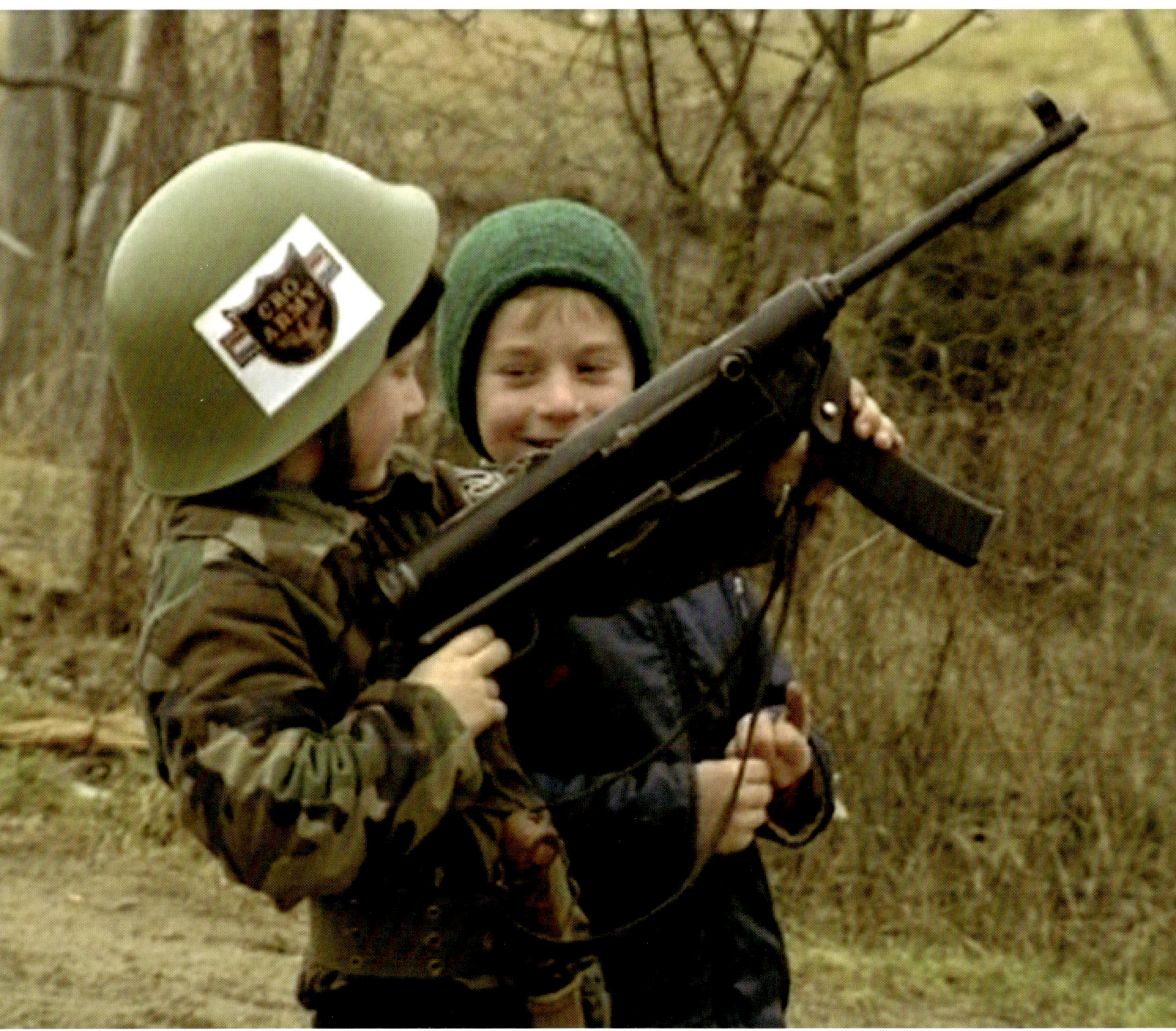

The Longing of the East: "Undemocratic" Democracy and the Dilemma of Political Emancipation in Postcommunism

MARIUS BABIAS

A variety of antagonisms have emerged in politics and culture since state socialism came to an end. Using a concept of political critique, I shall adapt the theoretical tools for analyzing the world in an attempt to make sense of the changing conditions that followed the burnout of Soviet-style state socialism. The term "political critique" may be defined in two ways: the discursive-analytic penetration of the lines of conflict, antagonisms, and contradictions that define postcommunist societies; a category for constituting subjectivity and political emancipation.

These two forms of critique address society as well as individuals active in society, albeit in different ways, but they coincide at one point—in the question of defining action. How can society be changed, how can power relations, ways of thinking, and apparatus be broken up, abstracted, and made useful for defining action? How does a citizen become an active subject, and how can the subject actively define action in agency, instead of being caught as an essentialized substance in society's multiple casting molds?

To arrive at a preliminary answer, take a detour through a more general question: What is democracy? Is it a certain ensemble of institutions and rights, such as parliament and suffrage? Is the presence of classical indicators—the division of powers, human rights, or free elections—what indicates the status of democracy? Or is there a universal all-encompassing notion? Claude Lefort developed a model of democratic universality: He suggests that democracy is more than a collective term for institutions and rights but, instead, a theoretical concept that totalizes several components in a fragmentary whole (similar to the term "manifold" in Gilles Deleuze and Félix Guattari. According to Lefort, the term "democracy" links two social phenomena: conflict and the symbolic institution of the society. The concept of society combines these components by symbolically transforming "conflict" into "society." The legitimization of social conflicts forms the heart of the democratic system, in that the permanent transformation process of conflict is repeated into the regime of the symbolic (institutions, representation, power, elections, etc.). As long as this process of transformation is repeated, there is democracy.

After the collapse of the totalitarian regimes of Eastern Europe, this process of transformation suffered severely, although the majority of the formerly state-communist societies had adopted a democratic-formal form of government. In the Western industrial states, formal democracy had already been subject to constant observation and control by state organs and, in a sense, domesticated, prevented from developing all too freely and radically. But, following the collapse of state socialism, as formal democracy found new territories of domination in Eastern Europe and thus expanded, it lost even more of its utopian content, for the expansion of formal democracy rested upon increasing the power of its own control and administration organizations. The more control and administration grew through the transformation of conflict into society (the keyword here being the EU's expansion to Eastern Europe, with Brussels as its virtual capital, from which thousands of new rules and regulations were issued to the new member states), the stronger became the power of "undemocratic" governmental entities. Since the collapse of state socialism, for instance, there has been, in France "a decline in parliamentary representation, the expansion of the political power of authorities without political responsibility (experts, judges, commissions), the extension of the powers of the president and a charismatic concept of the president as a figure," as noted by Jacques Rancière. This is true across all of Europe. Since the goal of the EU is not to form a Europewide public sphere but solely to guarantee the implementation of a more effective principle of government in the new regions, democracy is now redefined as the protection of neoliberalism, and the expansion of expert authorities within the various nation-states leads to political practice without political responsibility, and, ultimately, to an undemocratic democracy. This undemocratic democracy, which tends to pursue the principle of rationality, is the embodiment of a new kind of exertion of power, characterized by the simultaneity of caring for and controlling citizens.

Critique: The Negation of Power

"Critique" comes from the Greek word *krino*, "to decide." Michel Foucault developed an anthropology of critique that has a surprising affinity to the work of Theodore Adorno. Critique, with methods of operation that Foucault traced back to the Christian Middle Ages, is conceivable "only . . . in relation to something other than itself," and is "an instrument, a means for a future or a truth that it will not know nor happen to be, it oversees a domain it would want to police and is unable to regulate. All this means that it is a function which is subordinated to what philosophy, politics, ethics, law, literature represent as positive" (Foucault 1997, 42). The negative force and/or function of critique is an emancipatory one, Foucault argues, granting subjectivity, and opposing the absolute truth claim of power, tied to ideological premises. Critique, as negation of power, is the "art of voluntary insubordination, that of reflected intractability. Critique would essentially insure the desubjugation of the subject" (Foucault 1997, 47). Foucault, discussing Immanuel Kant's essay "What Is Enlightenment?" (1784), positions the zone of not wanting to be governed in the realm of an autonomy, where the core consists in multiple intersections and enforced mechanisms between knowledge and power. Beyond such moral attributions as "true" and "false," the project of critique lies in examining the triad "power, truth, subject," and answering the question how "a given element of knowledge takes on the effects of power in a given system where it is allocated to a true, probable, uncertain, or false element, such that a procedure of coercion acquires the very form and justification of a rational, calculated, technically efficient element, etc." (Foucault 1997, 59).

The negative force and/or function of critique is an emancipatory one, Foucault argues, granting subjectivity, and opposing the absolute truth claim of power, tied to ideological premises. Critique, as negation of power, is the "art of voluntary insubordination, that of reflected intractability."

This radical micropolitical perspective addresses delicate aspects of the macrorelationship between enlightenment and critique, an explosive and portentous relationship that the Frankfurt school illuminated so fundamentally in a critique of the relationship among rationalization, the hubris of science, and the form of rule. Might it be the case that reason and enlightenment—which, for instance, took a critical stance toward positivistic science and the state in nineteenth-century Germany, but fused, in a delicate point, the notion of rationality—are coresponsible for the power excesses in the name of rationality? This horrible suspicion, which stretches all the way to Auschwitz, is shared by Adorno and Foucault.

Politics of Emancipation

How are these considerations on undemocratic democracy related to the explosive function of critique? How can the notion of political critique become a tool for analyzing the world? How can democracy be liberated from the undemocratic stranglehold of expert culture? How can the subject be charged with resistance, enabled to manage conflict, and activated to choose its own action?

The necessity of a politics of emancipation resting upon universal truths in the age of globalization, where internationalism consists only in the production of capital flows, is becoming ever more evident. The political must reclaim its identitarian relationship to truth, justice, and equality (a relationship damaged and discredited by the totalitarianisms of the twentieth century) without reducing the subject to abstract principles of reproduction, but, on the contrary, engaging the subject in producing the lively, creative, and resistant. Subject production should not serve to generate the substance of a certain people or class, or the teleological finality of existence (in communism, the realization of a dictatorship of the proletariat; in capitalism, the realization of individual freedom); subject production takes place in a radical relation to the here and now. In messianism, the promise of the fulfillment of happiness in the distant future, communism and Christian orthodoxy meet in southeastern Europe in a particularly striking way. This is why Christian orthodoxy could easily fill the spiritual vacuum left behind by communism and usurp power. The radical relation to the here and now consists in creating truths, not principles—free truths that in politics and everyday life should prove to be universal. The radical relation to the here and now is based upon the notion that life is a contingent process of layering and stratifying free truths, and not a holistic principle of applying fixed formulas.

The tactical option of the subject's definition of its own action lies in not considering the political from the perspective of power but from the standpoint of the individual case, the singularity. There is no "subject of history," as Louis Althusser, Jean-Luc Nancy, and Foucault have taught us. This concept was used to legitimize such monstrosities as *Volksgemeinschaft*; rather, the task now is to strengthen a politics of emancipation committed to the generation of free truths that stands up for and represents civil rights movements and such marginalized identitarian groups as gays, lesbians, and other persons experiencing discrimination, and that struggles for ethnic minorities, immigrants, and socially unproductive groups—the sick and the socially fallen and despairing, among others. A climate of fear and the prohibition of critique currently dominates postcommunist society. In a subtle way, intolerance and discrimination are renewing themselves. Fascism and Stalinism, both of which strove in their own way toward the creation of a new kind of person, have delegitimized the project of emancipation for many years to come. After the fall of the Berlin wall, capitalism rose to the surface. Its cover of formal democracy as the apparent sole remaining historical alternative promised to bring postcommunist states affluence and stability, the political, economic, and social asymmetries of this transformation.

At the current time, the struggles of social movements are not sufficiently radical; they do not go far enough to balance out these asymmetries. It is a mistake to carry out political proxy struggles over exchanging places between the powerful and the underprivileged. Such struggles are doomed to failure, because the capitalist organization of society relies upon the presence of both exploiters and exploited. The struggle over the symbolic exchange of places is not only exhausting, it is counterproductive, because—as demonstrated by the example of the Green movement's participation in government coalitions in the 1990s—it ends as a project of modernizing the fissured capitalist order, making the system even more closed and more resilient to resistance and critique. The politics of emancipation has a chance only when the truths and concepts it reveals are universal and potentially address all individuals, when it initiates the process of transforming and empowering citizens to subjects ready to define their actions. Only on this basis can a new form of internationalism and solidarity develop, as shown by Hannah Arendt's example of the figure of the "stateless person."

Money, Freedom, Identity: The Deviant Self of the East

The East's longing for universal ordering principles, for identity and putting the communist past to rest, produced an insoluble paradox: the belief that Europe and the Western civilized world represent everything that the periphery lacks. It is an act of symbolic piracy to desire the supposedly universal of the center rather than accepting the perceived deficit of the periphery as rich and complex, as worthy of recognition. The fundamental problem of Eastern European elites and intellectuals is that they imprecisely equate the project of emancipation, so cynically discredited by the Stalinist form of communism, with capitalism, market economies, and democracy. They cannot or will not see that capitalism aims for the opposite of emancipation and participation—that is, the stratification of new European landscapes according to the primacy of value creation and profit accumulation over cultural diversity, codetermination, and solidarity, the virtues that the theoretical model of communism had promised and so fundamentally spoiled in practice.

The universal ordering principle of the West is freedom—the freedom of markets. Desiring the supposedly universal of the center and to fuse with it, to live as a European in freedom and prosperity, means subjecting oneself to the principle of the freedom of markets, a principle of reproduction and accumulation of capital flows, in which all social relations are, in the end, defined only as financial relations. A politics of emancipation that operates with the notion of political critique can be understood as the opposite of what the elites in the periphery so desire—the internationalism of money and Europeanism. A reformation of identity based on desire and the symbolic exchange of position is equal to a compulsive act of mimesis of capitalist principles, surrendering self-liberation and self-empowerment, the tools of emancipation.

The goal of capitalism and neoliberalism consists of the exploitation of resources, ideas, and subjectivity as well as the expansion of markets. Besides the economic exploitation of the East, it is also about gaining cultural hegemony in the new territories, established with the new political agenda of globalism. On the other hand, the oversaturated cultural markets in the West are longing for cultural manifestations from the East. Culture is successively transformed into a commodity in the current process of reconstitution of a postcommunist Euro identity, in which artists and intellectuals from the East participate, whether they like it or not. The ideology of globalism, centered upon the promise of freedom, fundamentally knows no territorial differences between West and East, North and South. What is meant, however, is market freedom; globalism's concept of freedom no longer entails political emancipation but the production of cultural distinction and the promises of happiness from harvesting of profit (as Marx called it, *Wertab schöpfung*). The more varied that consumer products and flavors become, the more commodified is the production of desire. An effect of this process of transforming the living into a commodity is the harmonization of visual culture around the world. Another effect, however— as defense against Western modernism and its claim to totality, which is felt to be usurpatory—is the formation of regionalisms and national/racial mythologies, whose political impact is worthy of a study of its own. This might show the extent to which the dominant cultural apparatus of antimodernism in postcommunism emerged from communism's national discourse. Especially in the new EU member states in southeastern Europe, we can see how the construction of postcommunist identity as European refers to a deeper-lying apparatus of national discourse, and renews itself under the currently dominant transformative conditions of neoliberalism. The preferred interpretation in the East of communism as a mistake or cul de sac of history does not go far enough. The current process of restructuring postcommunist society, as well as individuals as European, by fading out the communist past (that is, reinterpreted as an accident of national history) and its deep cultural imprint, is not based upon a self-critical engagement with history but, rather, the notion of a continuity of national history, its myths, traditions, and cultural attributions. This notion, amalgamated by the new elites, is the product of the national discourse of communism dressed up in the garb of the now-dominant liberalism.

As long as there is no connection to a fundamental social analysis of transformation—a notion that should be used with the utmost caution, because it implies the false promise of a belated modernization and economic harmonization between East and West—a culture of the critical gaze will only develop tentatively and occasionally, at permanent risk of being transformed into lifestyle and social design. There is the fundamental problem of anchoring such a culture of the critical gaze in the social life of Eastern and southeastern Europe, as well as the problem of lacking institutions and, thereby, insufficient education. The existing cultural institutions, universities, and academies are, to a large part, traditional, which is why the appreciation for critical culture in society is generally very low.

The process of European acculturation can hardly be grasped using the old monocausal or bipolar concepts; success can be had, though, in defining the emerging pan-European relief if we use deterritorialized conceptual definitions. They emphasize that the critical model of a Euro identity must be based upon striving toward delimitation rather than practices of limitation, the old monocausal notions, and constructive principles of nationality, ethnicity, religion, and identity, which in postcommunism paradoxically renew themselves the more the realization of Europe comes to be. They are to be transgressed; new, positive modes of perceiving the Other, the different, and especially the self must replace them. Before this self, which can only be perceived through the Other, as Edward Said noted, is given even a vague definition, we must discard the ballast of cultural attributions and conceptual notions of European identity, some of which are centuries old, by means of disassembly, transformation, and reassembly in discourse analysis. This essay may also be considered an active producer of a model for critiquing the ideology that pretends to have reconciled capitalism with communism—the ideology of Europeanism.

Neoliberalism and undemocratic democracy in Eastern Europe have fused to become a natural state. Money, freedom, identity—these three principles deny the individual's own deviant self. In surrendering this deviant self to these three principles, the psychosocial is completely exchanged, with dramatic consequences for the individual's own psychological economy as well as for the politics of emancipation and representation. The energy center of this notion of political critique grows in proportion to the growth of undemocratic democracy. Schizostructures seem equally oppressive and self-liberating. The revolts are still to come.

Translated by Brian Currid

REFERENCE LIST

Arendt, Hannah. *The Origins of Totalitarianism.* New York: Schocken, 1951.

Babias, Marius, ed. *Das Neue Europa. Kultur des Vermischens und Politik der Repräsentation.* Vienna: Generali Foundation; Cologne: Walther König, 2005.

Butler, Judith. "Against Ethical Violence." In *Giving an Account of Oneself.* Amsterdam: Uitgeverij Van Gorcum, 2003.

Deleuze, Gilles, and Félix Guattari. *What Is Philosophy?* New York: Columbia University Press, 1994.

Derrida, Jacques. *Specters of Marx.* London: Routledge, 1994.

Foucault, Michel. "What Is Critique?" In *The Politics of Truth,* edited by Sylvère Lotringer, translated by Lisa Hochroth. New York: Semiotext(e), 1997.

Groys, Boris, Anne von der Heiden, and Peter Weibel, eds. *Zurück aus der Zukunft. Osteuropäische Kulturen im Zeitalter des Postkommunismus.* Frankfurt/Main: Suhrkamp, 2005.

Klingan, Katrin, and Ines Kappert, eds. *Sprung in die Stadt. Chisinau, Sofia, Pristina, Sarajevo, Warschau, Zagreb, Ljubljana. Kulturelle Positionen, politische Verhältnisse—Sieben Szenen aus Europa.* Cologne: DuMont, 2006.

Kurz, Robert. *Weltordnungskrieg. Das Ende der Souveränität und die Wandlungen des Imperialismus im Zeitalter der Globalisierung.* Bad Honnef: Horlemann, 2003.

Laclau. Ernesto, and Chantal Mouffe. *Hegemony and Radical Democracy: Towards a Radical Democratic Politics.* London: Verso, 1985.

Lefort, Claude. "The Question of Democracy." In *Democracy and Political Theory.* Oxford: Polity Press; Minneapolis: University of Minnesota Press, 1988.

Rancière, Jacques. "Demokratie und Postdemokratie." *Politik der Wahrheit,* edited by Rado Riha. Vienna: Turia+Kant, 1997.

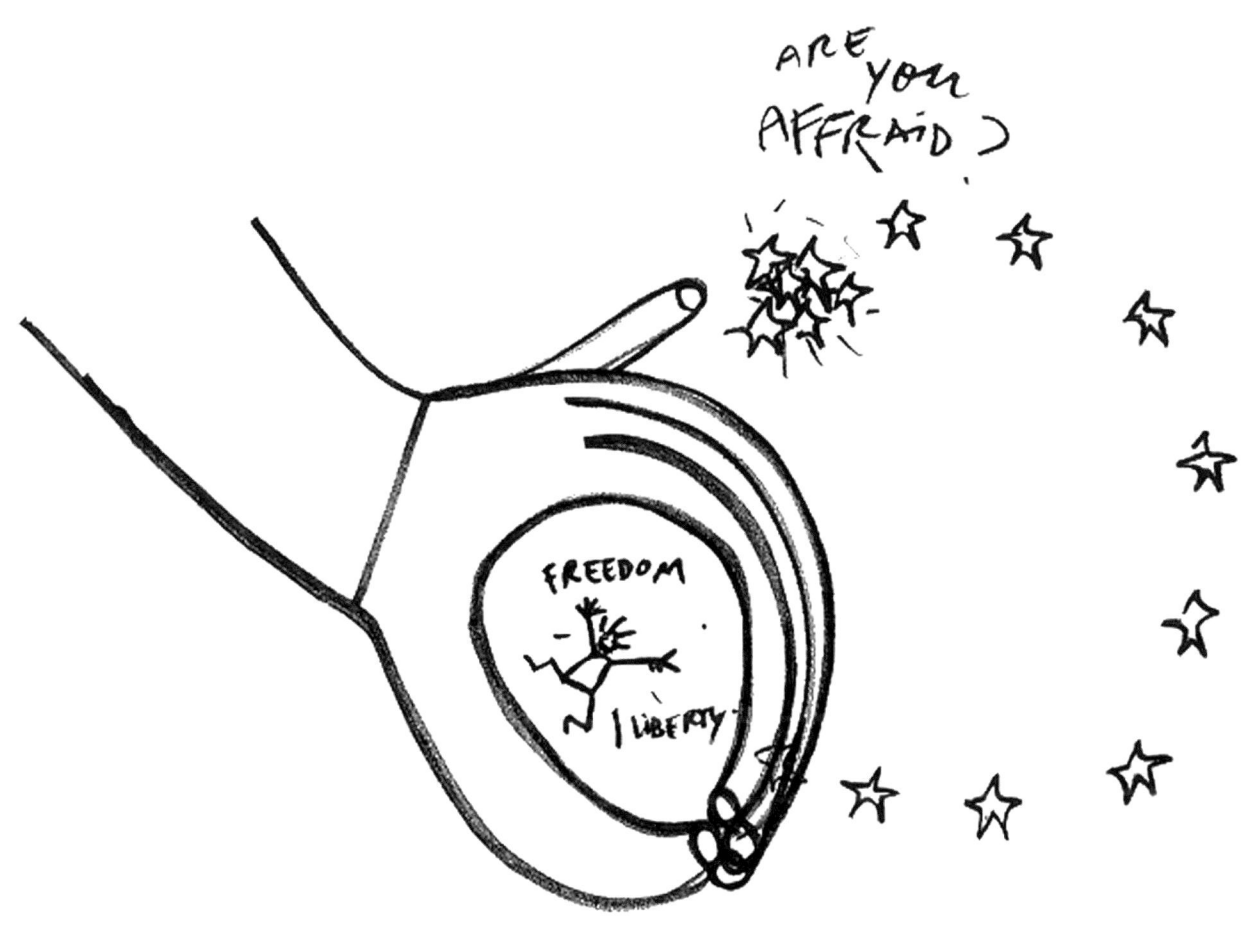

DAN PERJOVSCHI

Romanian, b. 1961
The Round Drawing (detail)
2010
Wall drawing, mixed media
16-ft. wall and rotunda walls
Courtesy of the artist and Lombard-Freid Gallery,
New York
Photography by Randy Batista

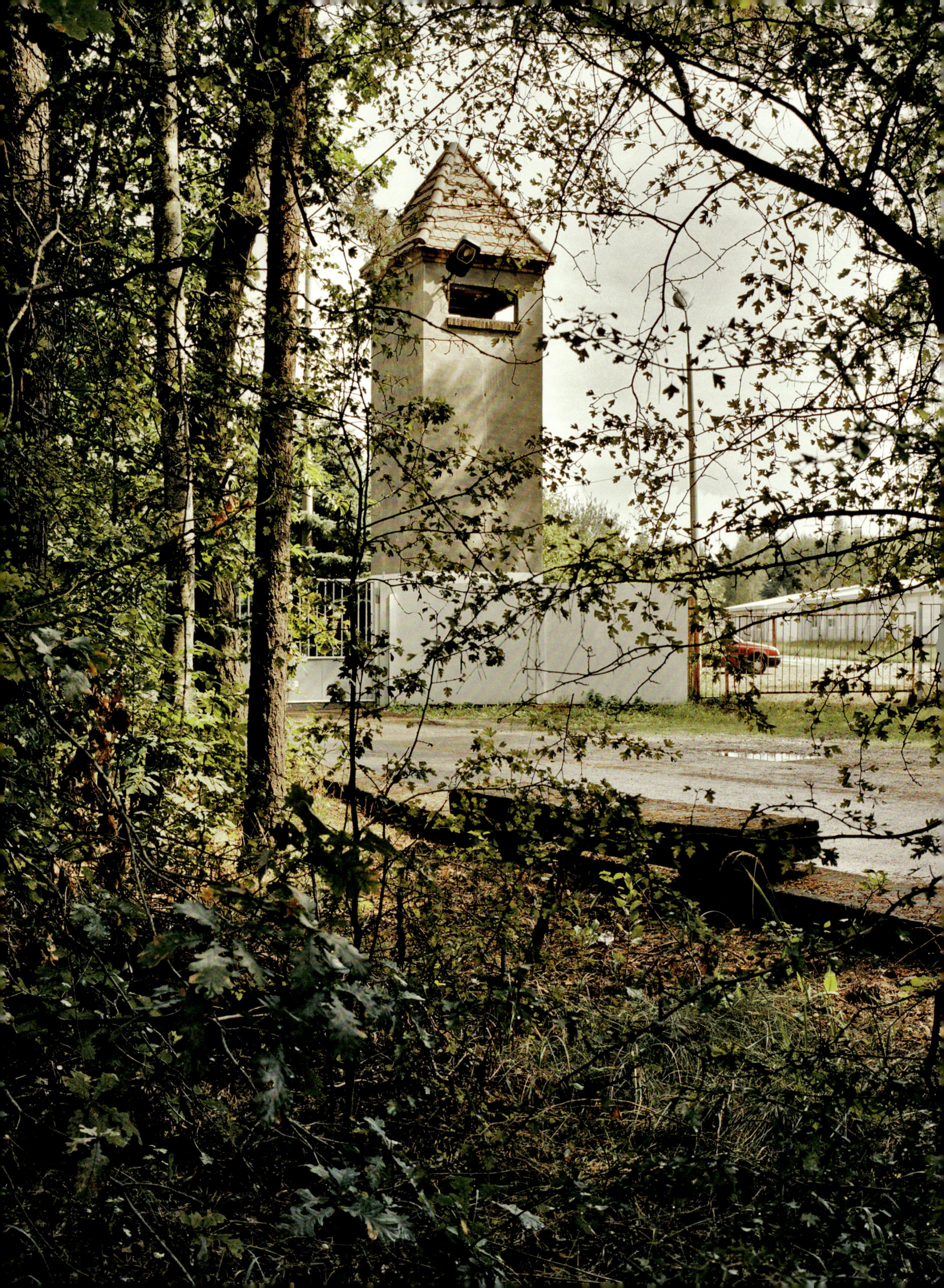

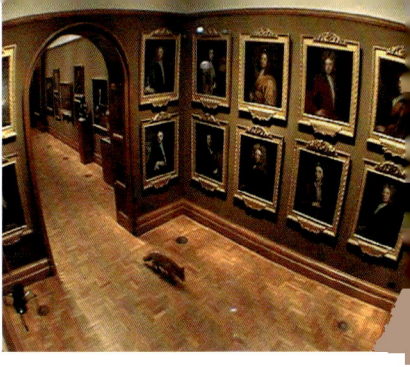

PROJECT EUROPA: The Artists

KERRY OLIVER-SMITH

The fall of the Berlin wall proved a pivotal transformation for Germany, Europe, and the entire world. Precipitating the collapse of the Soviet empire, the event was celebrated as the end of totalitarianism and the triumph of liberal democracy. Berlin stood as an icon of a new era, and the once-beleaguered city began the process of massive reconstruction. In the central space where the wall once stood, a large corporate center was raised. Some historic buildings were marked for demolition while others were restored or rebuilt. Controversial decisions were made regarding what was and what was not sanctioned to represent the history and future of a new Germany.

Artists Marcel Odenbach and Tacita Dean live and work in Berlin, and were present during the days and months that immediately followed the fall of the Berlin wall. Their works in the exhibition unsettle the utopian views of German reunification by questioning the present through the lens of the past. German artist Marcel Odenbach focuses on the literal demise of the Berlin wall in his film *Niemand ist mehr dort, wo er hinwollte* (*No one is where they intended to go*). Recording a sweeping rise of national sentiment, Odenbach captures the jubilation and euphoric spirit of mass gatherings, marches, and candlelight vigils. Through collage, he brings together found footage, newly filmed work, music, and sound. Creating an eerie effect, he superimposes images of Nazi and East German political processions onto the images of the new Berlin marches. By equating the celebrations, he disrupts the collective image of a new Germany and warns about the resurgence of a dangerous nationalism. For Odenbach, Germany has yet to acknowledge and take responsibility for the past; because of this, the country risks a return of populism, racism, cultural essentialism, and religious intolerance.

Odenbach uses a screen split by a narrow vertical image suggesting the shape of the Berlin wall itself. The vertical column creates a gap where sections of continuous images disappear. Their disappearance suggests a momentary amnesia, a passing through a gap in consciousness, as if the Communist regime was a small interruption in a seamless narrative of national identity. One scene within the vertical space is taken from Hitchcock's film *Suspicion*. The film plays on a home television monitor, merging the familiar with the unfamiliar and suggesting the reach of history and media to thousands of private homes. Odenbach foregrounds what is not seen, what is denied, and what cannot be represented. The fragility and instability of the historical moment is embodied in the precarious perching of the television monitor on a set of glasses.

PAST/PRESENT

Tacita Dean concentrates on the windows of perception, on issues of seeing and not seeing, and on histories denied and embraced. In six photogravures that make up her work *Palast*, she also looks at Berlin as a city locating its history and searching for a stake and identity in a new world order. Dean centers her project on the Palast der Republic (Palace of the Republic), the former East German communist parliament building. Condemned, the Palast was set to be demolished and replaced by the building that formerly stood on the site, the Prussian-era Stadtschloss (Palace). The building, described as a piece of wedding-cake finery, is emblematic of Germany's history of empire and lost glory.

The Palast became a symbol of a failed utopia. When built, the Palast der Republic was a beacon of modernist promise and progress. Tacita Dean filmed and photographed the building when it was stripped to its steel skeleton yet still embellished with hundreds of mirrored glass windows. These windows reflected the sun, but also provided a screen for those inside. The opaque windows suggested a former reign of secrecy and a hierarchy of power separating those who observed from those who were observed. The copper-tinted glass also reflected the buildings nearby, casting images in a golden haze of perpetual sunset. Dean captured the fragments of architecture, equestrian statuary, and church spikes and spires that represented different views of the city. In an uncanny way, the vision of the past was projected into the future. Like a mirage, the work creates a temporal and spatial disconnect. History is reimagined and the present appears as an ephemeral and passing dream. As a contemplation of ruins, the images evoke a romantic nostalgia and memory that, far from being passive, can be actively restorative, reflective, and critical (Dillon 2006, 79).

Belgian-Mexican artist Francis Alÿs and German-Egyptian artist Susan Hefuna each live and work in two cultures. Their respective works of art reflect Europe as a site of transnational identity and citizenship. The artists are acutely aware of borders, both open and closed. They are especially interested in devices of perception that establish and affirm social hierarchies. They challenge the distribution of the visual—what is seen and not seen, and who has the power to decide.

The Nightwatch, by Francis Alÿs, concerns the transgression of borders and the power and politics of looking. A former architect, Alÿs was commissioned to create a multidimensional project in response to the city of London. Researching and walking through London, Alÿs encountered an unusual number of surveillance cameras, especially in the financial district, which has the highest concentration of closed circuit televisions in the world. In the neighborhood, he also discovered the National Portrait Gallery, which uses a system of deterrence that openly exposes the monitors and surveillance cameras in the galleries.

Alÿs's art project for the National Portrait Gallery consisted of releasing a fox into the galleries at night. Prior to staging the event, Alÿs spread a rumor about an errant fox in the region. He then set a fox free in the Tudor and Georgian galleries, where he tracked the animal's wanderings with the museum's surveillance cameras. Figures from eighteenth- and nineteenth-century paintings look on as the fox scurries from one gallery to the next. Observed by ghosts of history and the eyes of the state, the fox transgresses a universe of hierarchy and privilege. The fox appears unfazed. Historically, foxes were banished outside the city wall, where they were perceived as unwanted scavengers destined to be hunted down. Foxes have recently returned to the city as unwelcome guests.

Utilizing wit, irony, and allegory, Alÿs creates an incisive metaphor for the contemporary migrant. His critique extends to the history of nationalism, the politics of inclusion and exclusion, and the climate of xenophobia and fear. His primary critique targets the unprecedented omnipresence of surveillance, internalized as a norm of societal policing. Alÿs reconfigures the relationship of seeing and being seen not only with his film but also with his installation. *The Nightwatch* is screened on a television placed in front of a couch. Seated viewers literally become a part of the installation, equalizing and bridging the gap between the observer and the observed.

Susan Hefuna's work *SEE* is a call for visual scrutiny. It constitutes a mandate not only for the eyes but the realm of cultural perception. The word "SEE" is literally embedded within an Egyptian mashrabiya, the intricate latticed window characteristic of traditional North African and Middle Eastern architecture. Created with the help of highly skilled artisans, the window creates a permeable wall between the inside and outside; it also allows for the free flow of light and air. It protects the inhabitant, usually female, from the gaze of strangers, allowing her to see without being seen. The image of a woman behind a mashrabiya evokes the exoticism and Orientalism of the past. Hefuna's work subverts the traditional gender stereotype and reverses the male gaze by asserting her own role as an artist and observer. She reinvents the mashrabiya as a symbol of mutual exchange, one that maintains both individual integrity and open communication. Her work *ANA*, which means "I" in Arabic, affirms the importance of a multidimensional, fluid, and unfixed individual who cannot be categorized by cultural definitions.

Susan Hefuna was raised in Egypt and Germany by Christian and Muslim parents. Foreign yet familiar in each location, she belongs to neither. Her work combines two cultures without one subsuming the other. Multiple meanings can be derived from her work; there is no one truth. English appears on an Arab screen, and her aesthetics emerge from the conventions of both Europe and Africa (Martha 2007). Although the mashrabiya are objects of everyday life in Egypt, they are also related to the abstract grids of modernism in England and Germany. In addition, her work is layered with references to such various cultures and disciplines as architecture, science, and the visual arts. Her piece *Knowledge is Sweeter than Honey* resonates with sacred texts of Christian, Jewish, and Muslim religions. Defying essentialism, nationalism, or the need to erect walls, Hefuna sees possibilities of open exchange among individuals, cultures, and continents.

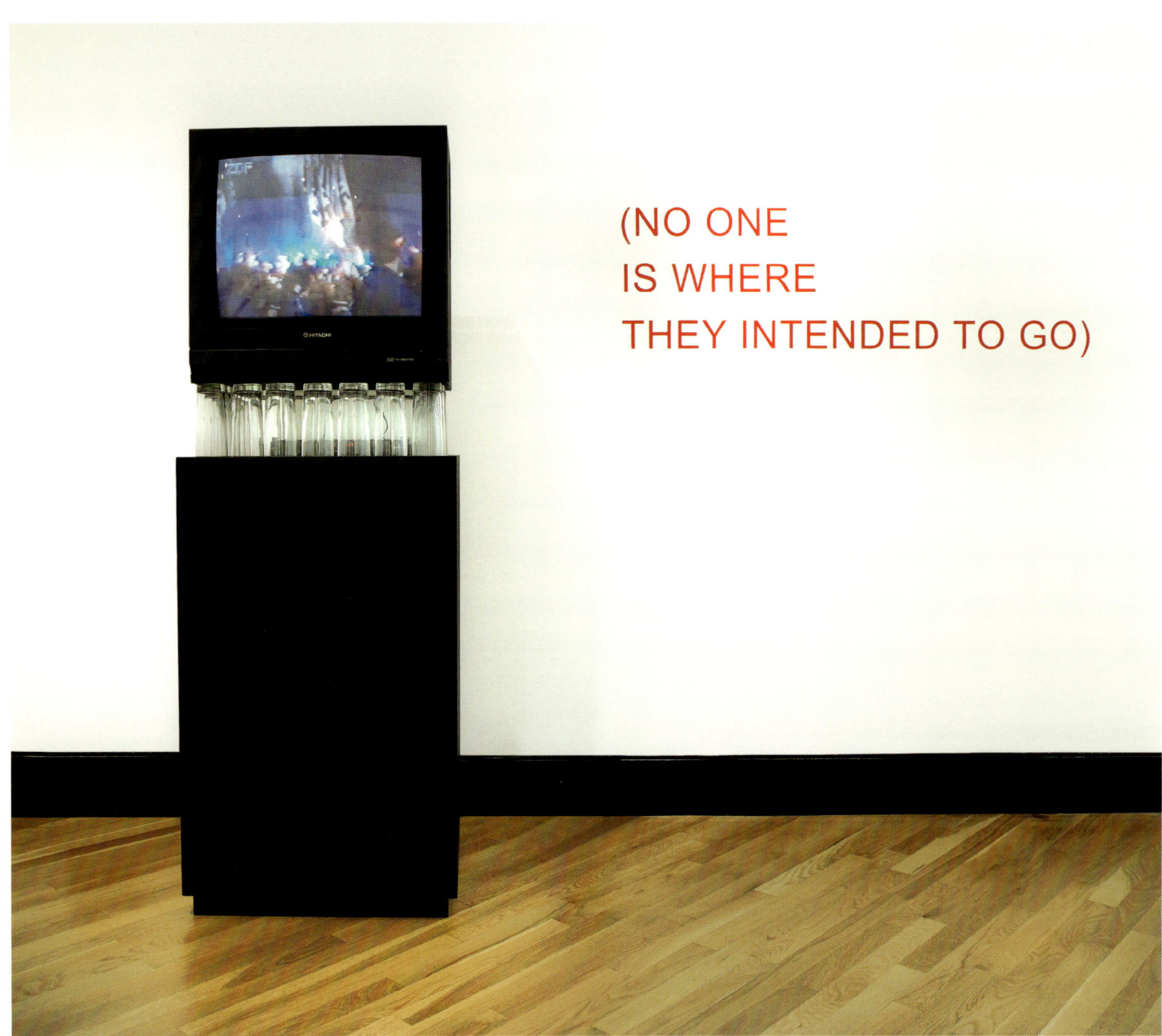

(NO ONE
IS WHERE
THEY INTENDED TO GO)

[pages 36–37]

MARCEL ODENBACH

German, b. 1953
*Niemand ist mehr dort, wo er hinwolfe (No one is where
they intended to go)*
1989–90
Video installation, DVD player, monitor, glasses,
pedestal
Dimensions variable
Courtesy of the artist and Anton Kern Gallery, New York
Installation photography by Randy Batista

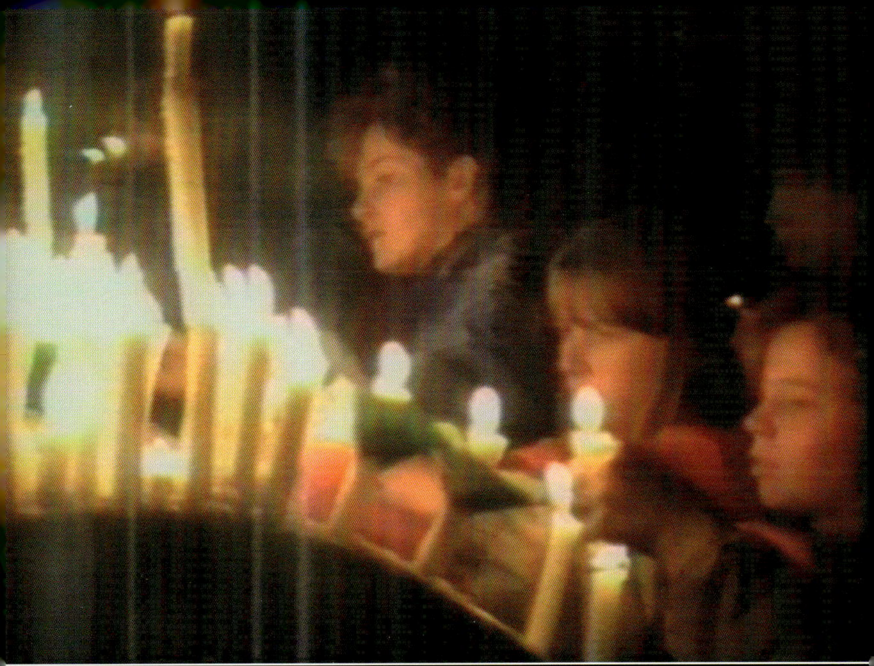

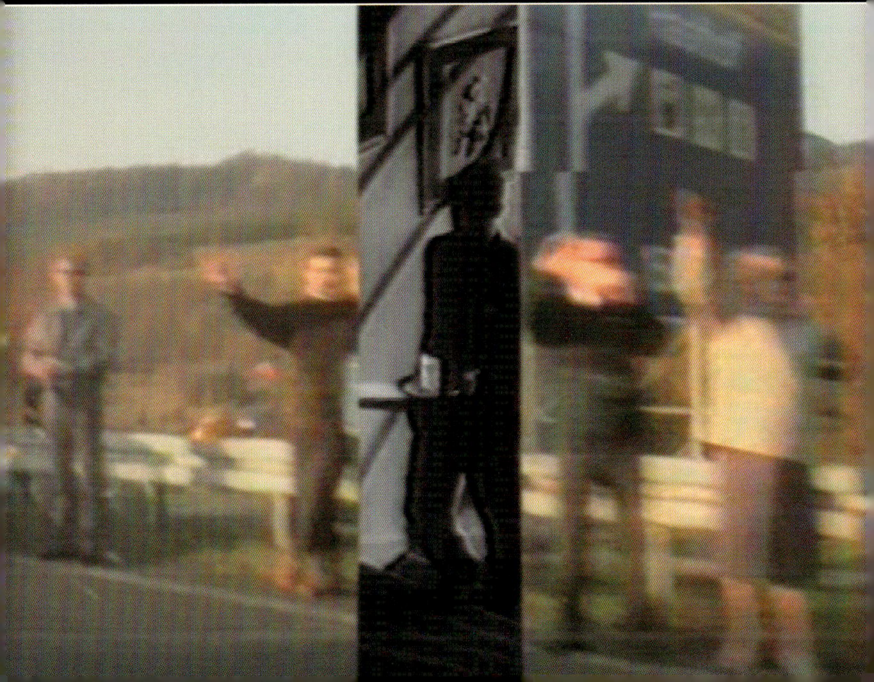

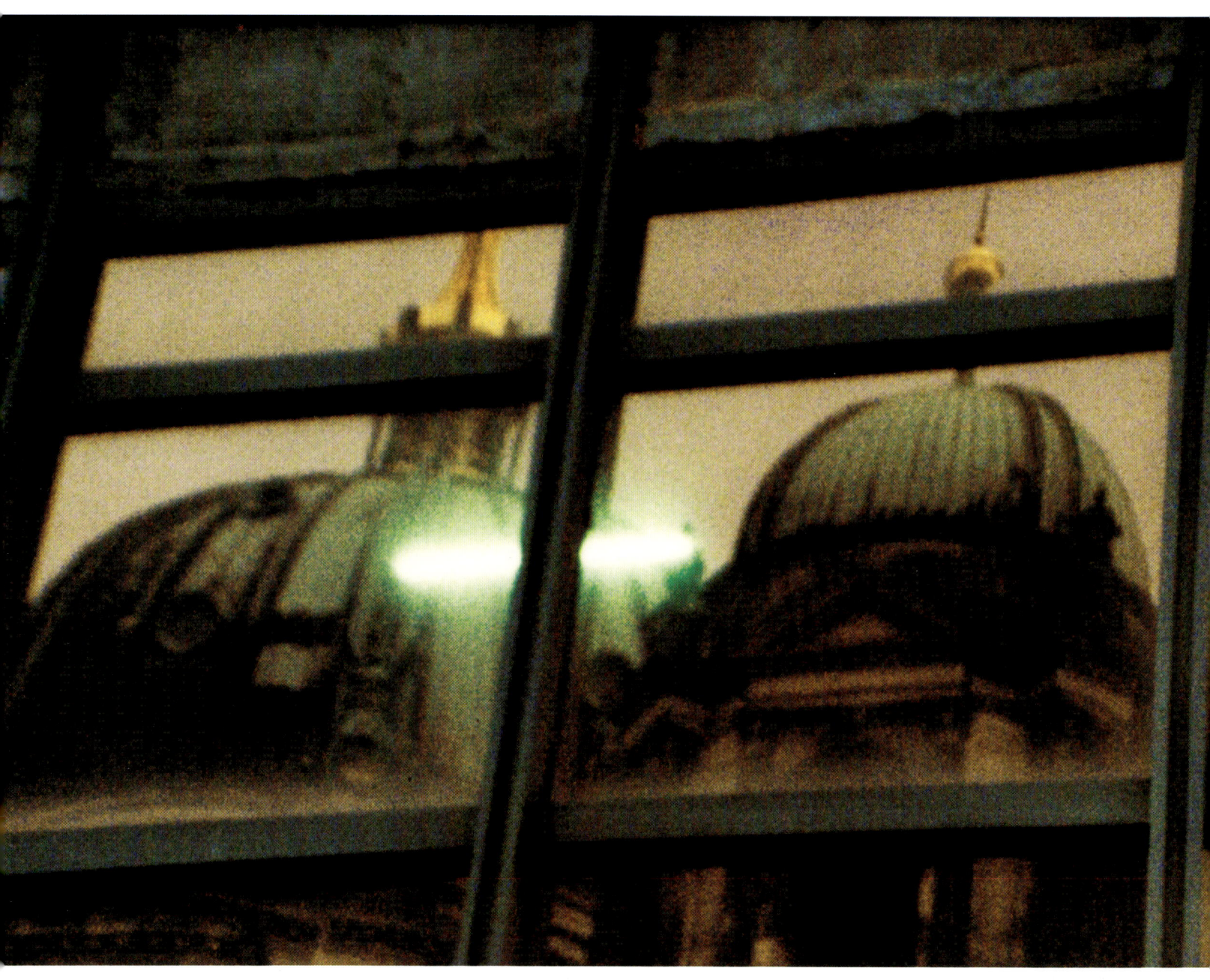

[pages 38–41]

TACITA DEAN

British, b. 1965
Palast
2004
Six color photogravures
19.63 x 27.5 in. (49.8 x 69.9 cm) each
Courtesy of Baker Botts L.L.P., Dallas, Texas

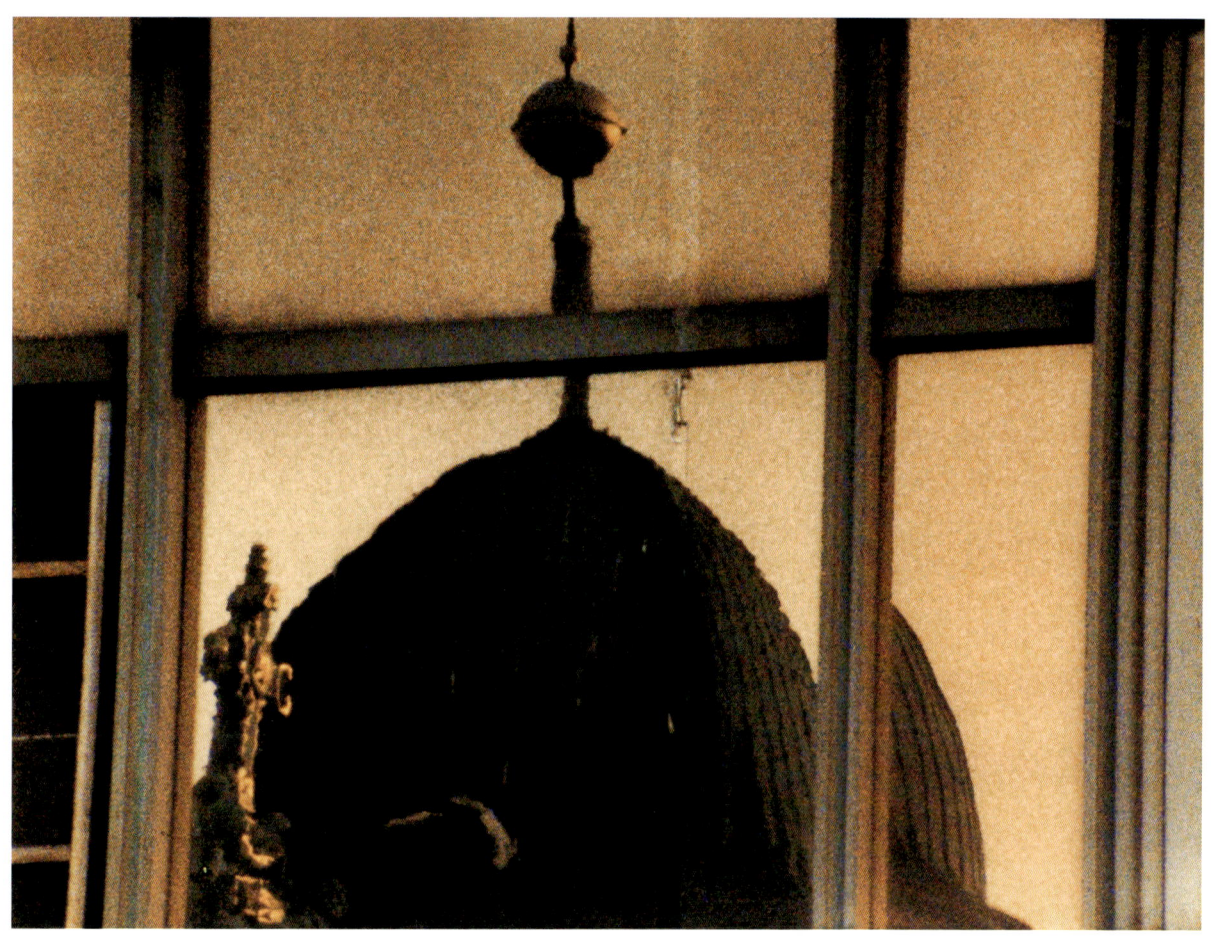

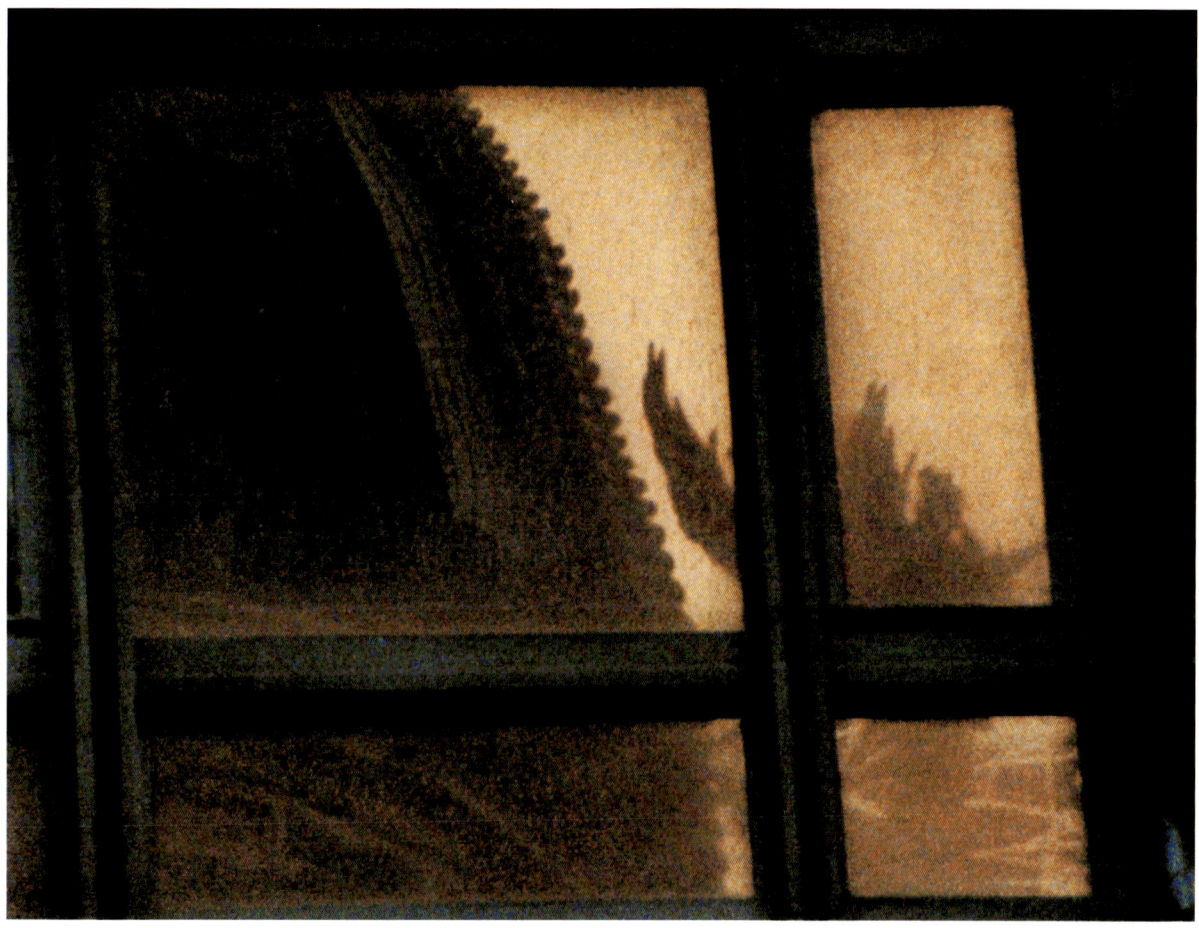

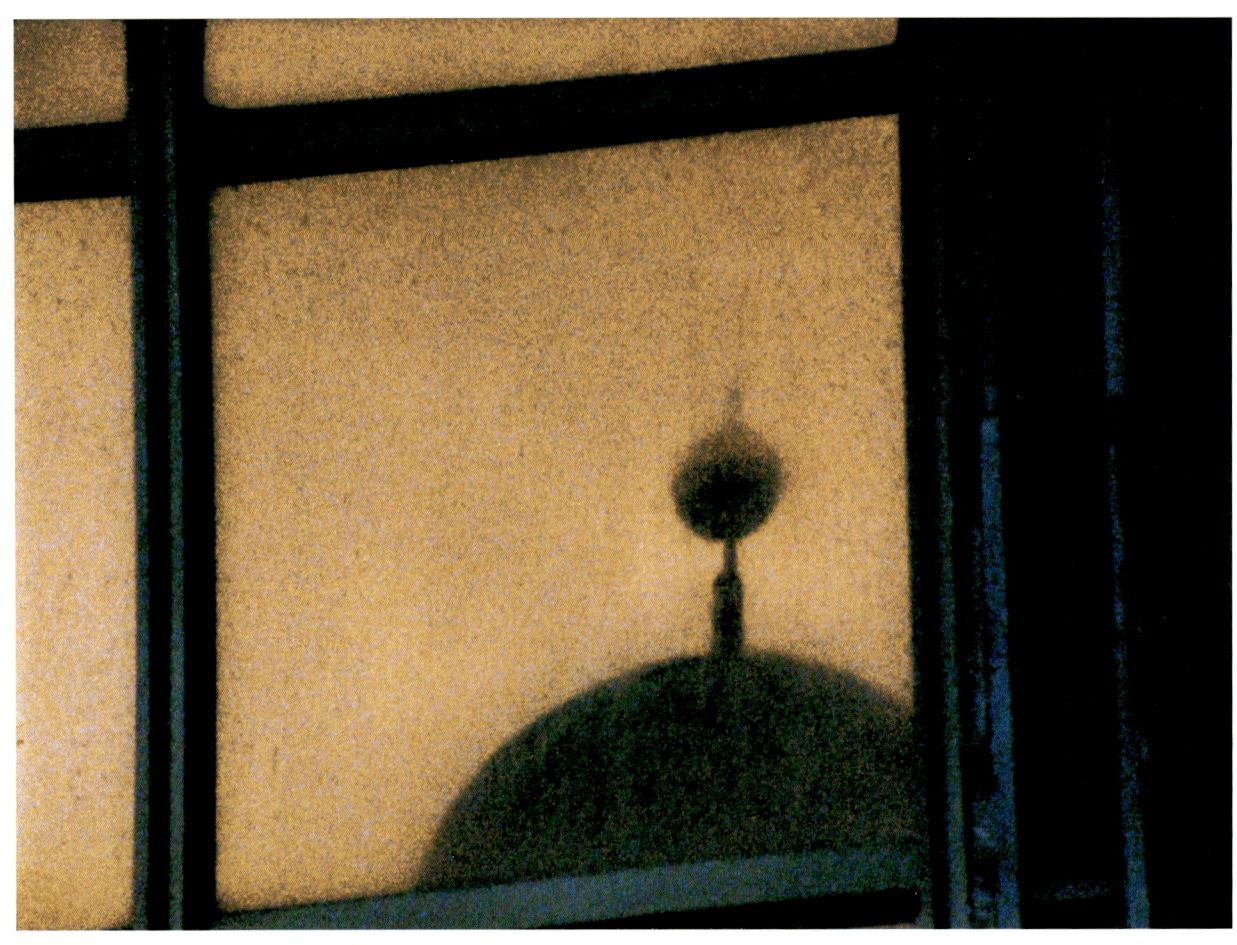

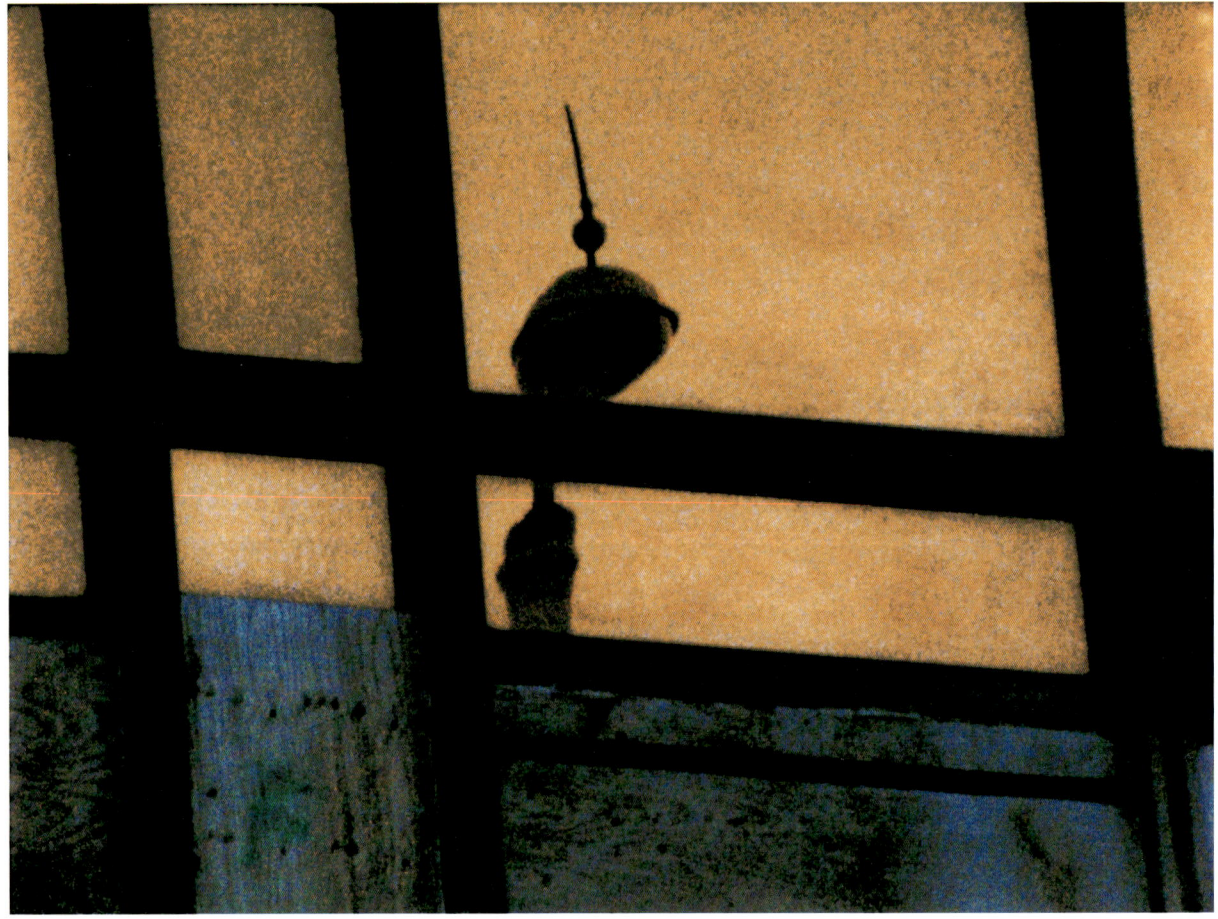

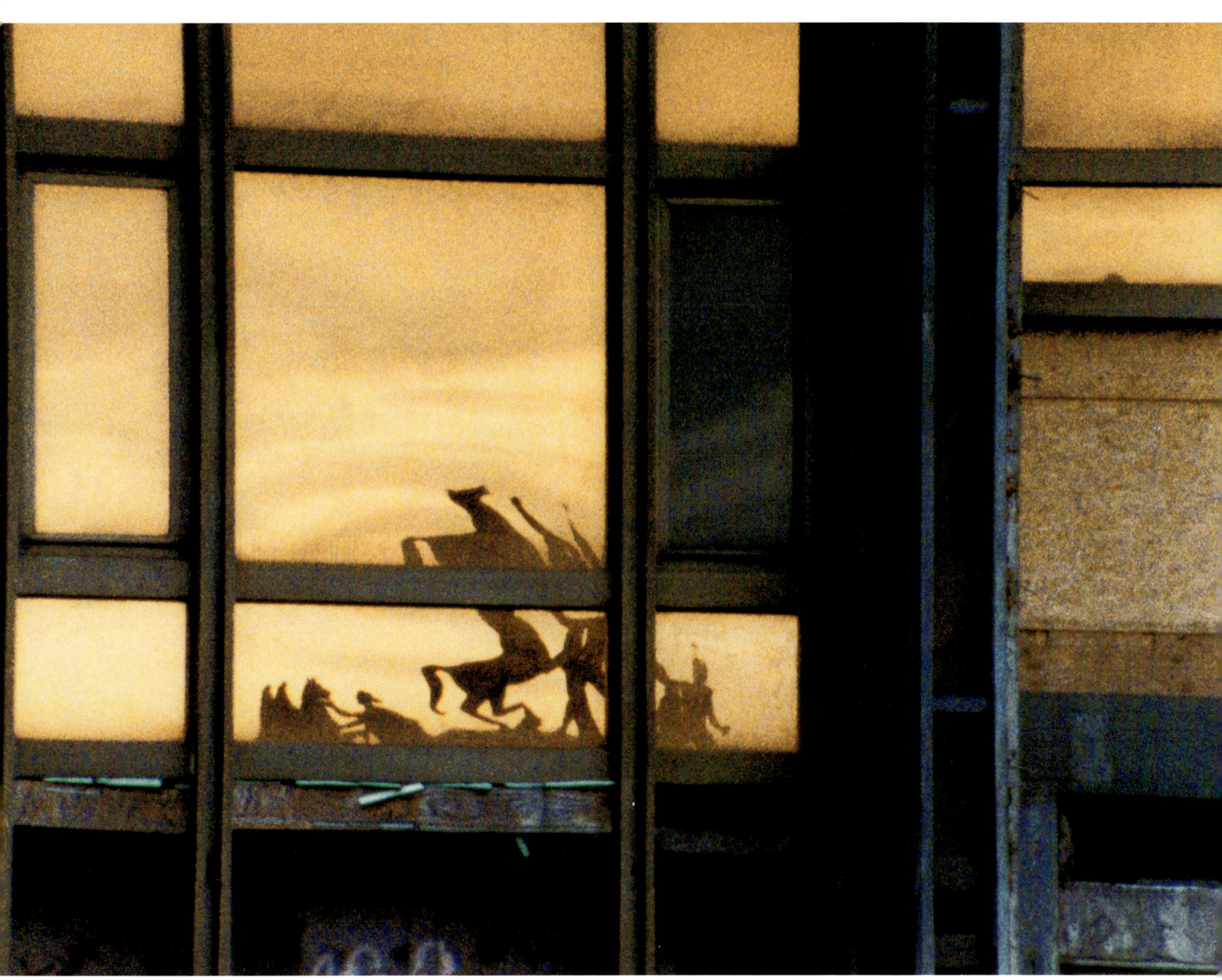

FRANCIS ALŸS

Belgian, b. 1959
The Nightwatch
2004
Video documentation of an action, National Portrait
Gallery, London
Color, no sound, 17 minutes 30 seconds
Dimensions variable
Courtesy of the artist and Galerie Peter Kilchmann,
Zurich

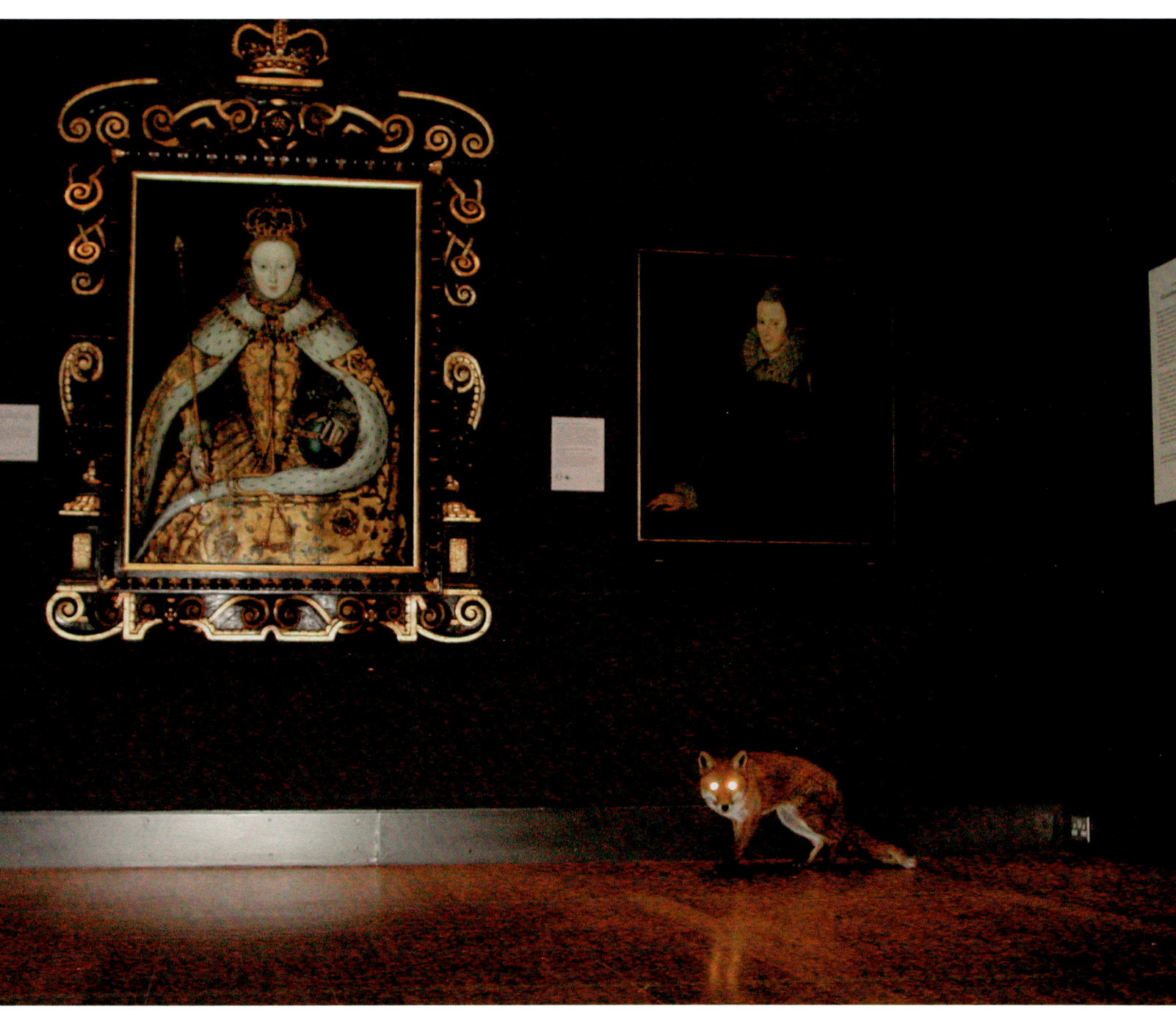

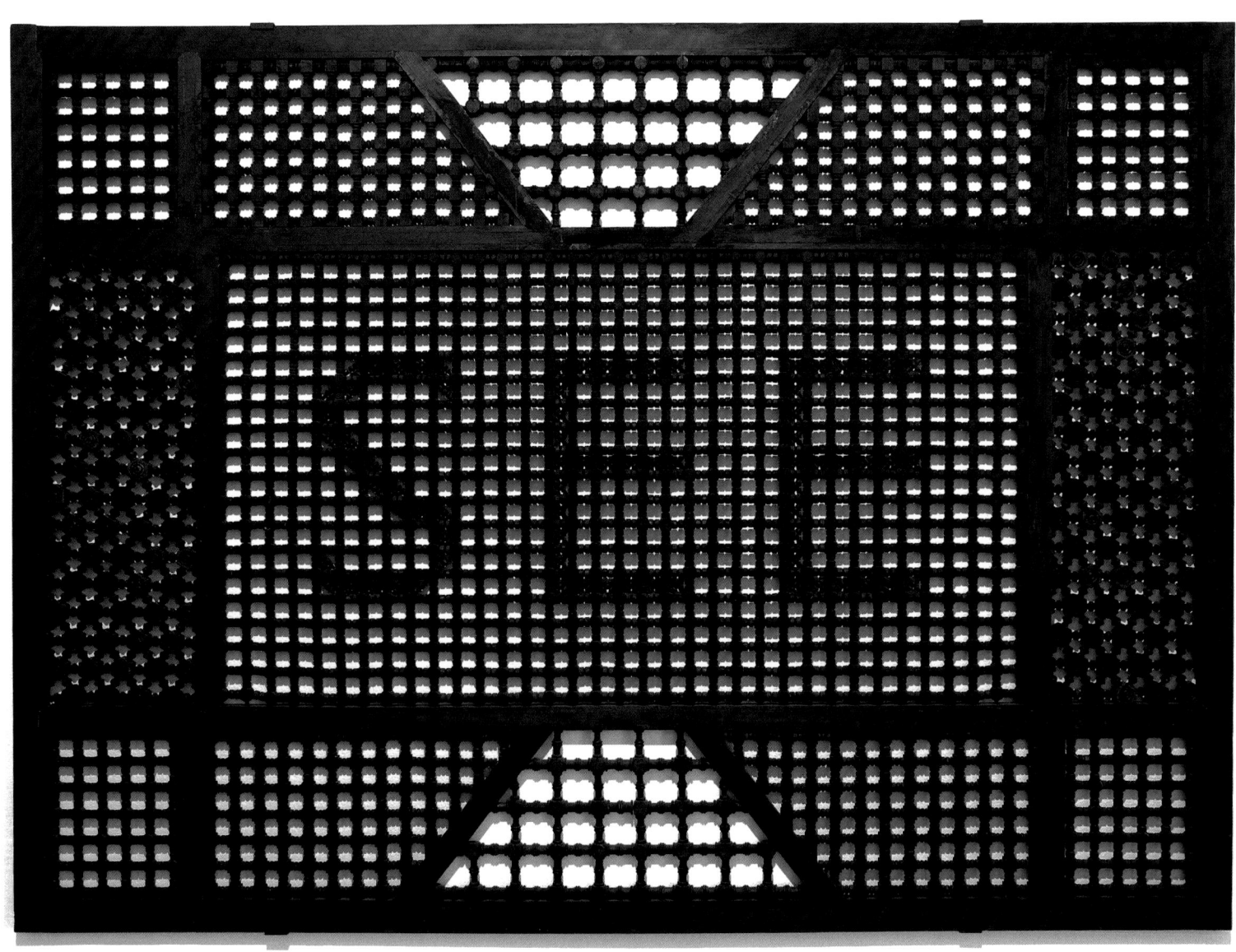

SUSAN HEFUNA

Egyptian/German, b. 1962
SEE
2006
Handmade wood carving, ink
55.12 x 3.54 x 77.5 in. (140 x 9 x 200 cm)
Courtesy of the artist and The Third Line, Dubai
Photography by Randy Batista

SUSAN HEFUNA

Egyptian/German, b. 1962
Knowledge is Sweeter than Honey
2006
Handmade wood carving, ink
78.83 x 3.54 x 82.68 in. (185 x 9 x 210 cm)
Courtesy of a private collection, Zurich, and
Rose Issa, London
Photography by Randy Batista

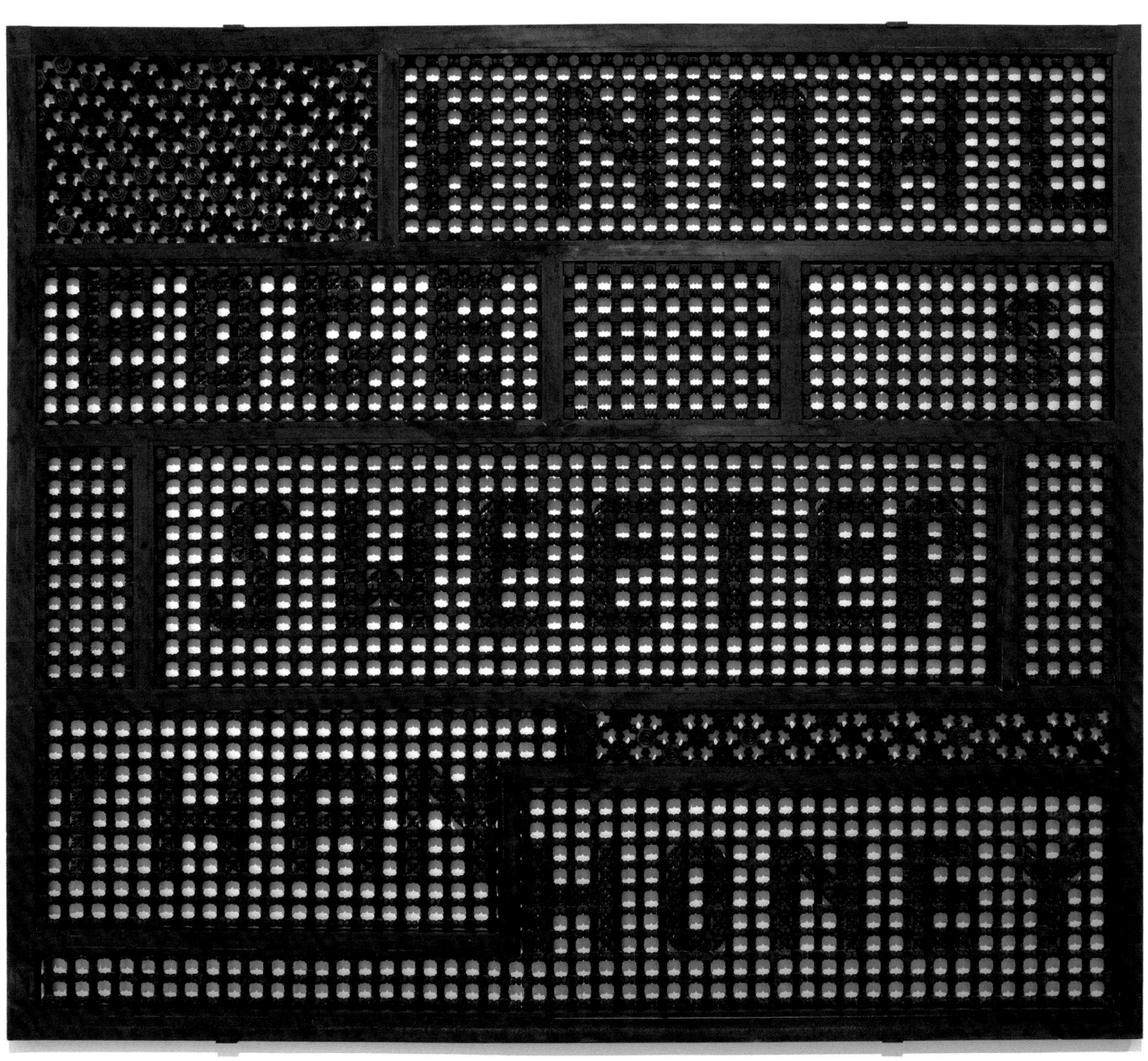

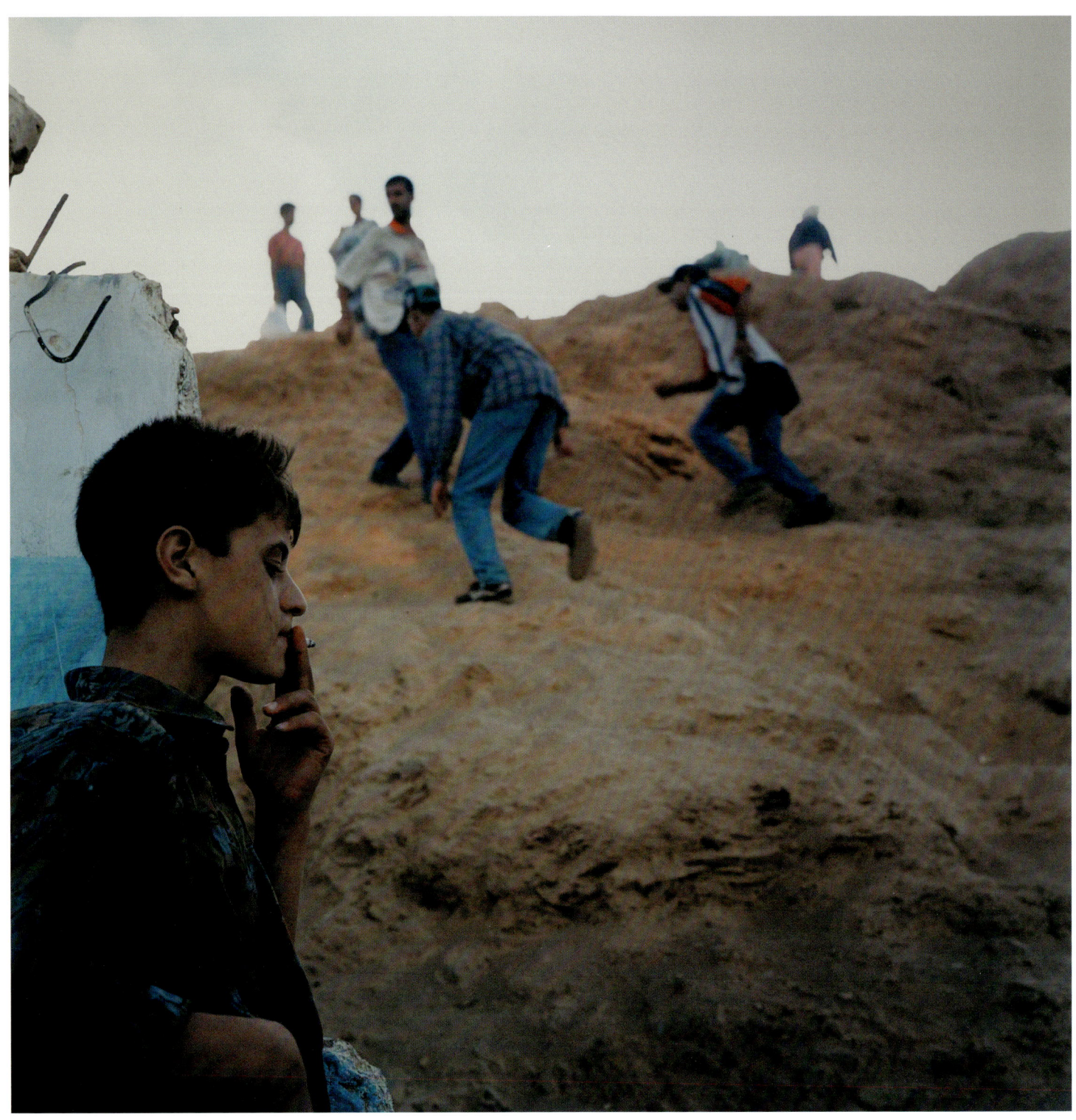

YTO BARRADA

French, b. 1971
Ceuta Border, Bab Sebta
A Life Full of Holes: The Strait Project
1999
C-print
31.5 x 31.5 in. (80 x 80 cm)
Courtesy of Galerie Polaris, Paris
Photography by Randy Batista

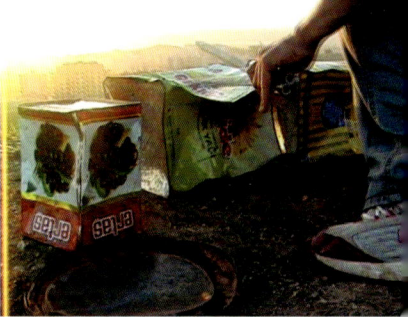

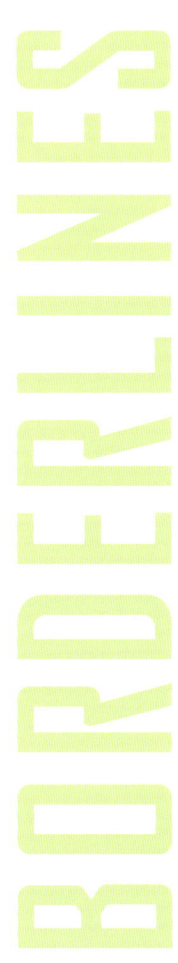

BORDERLINES

Yto Barrada, Bruno Serralongue, and Fikret Atay examine the threshold conditions existing at the intersection of continents, borderlines where people seek, wait, and fight for a better life. For French philosopher Étienne Balibar, these borders exist as the "non-democratic condition of democracy" (Balibar 2001, 16). Balibar, like the artists themselves, considers these as sections of "a great Wall of Europe" currently under construction (Balibar 2006, 3). He recognizes the use of borderlines in what Robert Kagan calls "frontier wars." This intricate operation of interlacing borders, walls, laws, and police control defines Europe and shapes its landscape. It is where the violence of democracy reveals itself most clearly. As Balibar tells us, violence rages in silence:

> "From the upper Adriatic to the Straits of Gibraltar, and all the zones of 'nonrights' surrounding ports, airports, and various land and water links between countries. These wars rage also in the 'suburbs' of the great European cities, illustrated once again by the lockdown of the Sangatte collection area for refugees in Pas-de-Calais. We have a true hunting-down of men here, compounded by a hunting-down of people with certain features" (Balibar 2003, 39).

Born in France of Moroccan parents, Yto Barrada lives and works in Tangier. Her photographs in the exhibition are from the series *A Life Full of Holes: The Strait Project*. This body of work focuses on the Straits of Gibraltar, the passage between Europe and Africa. Designating not only a separation of two continents, the Straits embody the dividing line between the north and south, Christianity and Islam, the Orient and the Occident. Barrada's aerial image, *The Strait of Gibraltar, Tangier,* represents the small stretch of land and water that paradoxically carries this historically weighted meaning. Her other photographs center on the city of Tangier, where hundreds of people endlessly wait to cross over to Europe. *Life Full of Holes* derives from stories of a Moghrebi adage: "Even a life full of holes, a life of nothing but waiting, is better than no life at all" (Hooper 2007, 34). Barrada captures the dichotomy of presence and absence, visibility and invisibility of an ephemeral experience.

Tangier, which still bears the mantle of Oriental exoticism, is anticipating ten million tourists in 2010. At the same time, poor and destitute Moroccans dream of Europe—their fantasy of Europe, El Dorado, shaped by the pictures beamed down by their satellite dishes. Barrada's photograph *Wallpaper, Tangier* reproduces a worn poster illustration of the German Alps.

Similar idealized images of Europe are common features in the city cafés. Barrada attempts to convey the longing, desire, and violence that confront a wall of resistance (Barrada 2006, 3). In her photograph *Advertisement Lightbox, Tangier,* Barrada depicts two young girls leaning dreamily against the advertising image of a cruise ship, gazing at a world that, although close, is utterly inaccessible to them.

Tangier is a launching site for illegal and dangerous attempts to enter Europe. The word used for crossing the border is to "burn," as the process requires burning your papers, past, and identity. Thousands die in the process. Tangier is a place of unemployment, boredom, deferred dreams, and endless waiting—a state of suspended animation for those wishing to escape. Barrada's photograph *Ceuta* reveals the vulnerability of youth, who stealthily approach the nearby Spanish enclave. The boys are emblematic of the early and incessant desire to leave. Some who have made the attempt to enter the enclave have been shot. For the young men who actually get to Europe, Barrada sees two tragic options: a "culture of death" associated with terrorism, or a life outside the law without rights and prey to gangs and recruiters (Tazi 2007, 91).

Barrada's work tells a story that escapes the mass media; simply, she focuses on the details of everyday life. A sense of emptiness and stasis is pervasive. In Barrada's square photographs, most of her subjects turn away; we see them obliquely, more often their backs rather than their faces. Nevertheless, their presence is unfailing and persistent.

The photographs of French artist Bruno Serralongue are part of his *Calais* series, which concentrates on the controversial and ongoing refugee crisis on the "border" between England and France. Migrants seek to cross the channel because of England's more flexible immigration and social policies. In a controversial move, Nicolas Sarkozy shut down the Sangette Red Cross shelter, near Calais, in 2002; this action did not stem the flow of migrants. In September 2009, bulldozers, backhoes, and chain saws cleared out the brush and tents where most of them lived. Nearly three hundred people were detained, almost half of them minors. In the previous year, twenty-eight thousand people had been stopped.

Serralongue documents conditions of the migrant. Most of the refugees are fleeing from the wars in the Middle East, mainly from Afghanistan and Iraq. In his photograph *Passer en Angleterre,* massive trucks rush by as lone figures stand and wait, looking for an opportunity to cross. A burst of yellow spring flowers lends a wistful and ironic note to their relatively hopeless quest. *Abri #6,* which shows the remains of a shelter in the woods, conveys desperate conditions for those who pass through. A shadow world of makeshift tents emerged in the "jungle," a wooded area of sand dunes. The woods have been regularly and ruthlessly raided. Hundreds live in conditions plagued by lack of sanitation, illness, and the threat of traffickers and smugglers. Serralongue's critical focus targets the same events that attract mass-media coverage, yet his approach is quite different. Like Barrada, Serralongue challenges the uniformity of the mass-media message to reveal complex and ignored details and realities. His work is carefully considered and produced over time; he strives to convey an experience rather than a message.

Artist Fikret Atay is from Batman, Turkey. He highlights the economic and cultural divide between the East and West while reflecting on the potential of art to transcend the restraints imposed by poverty and isolation. Atay's work concentrates on Kurdish culture, a segment of society ostracized within Turkey, a country that, in turn, has been repeatedly excluded from the European Union. Testing Europe's acceptance of Islam, Turkey has long been a controversial site in the debate over what is and what is not European.

In Atay's film *Tinica,* a teenage boy arranges a variety of tin cans and begins to perform a Western-style drum solo, music from afar but likely channeled through the media. He sits on a cliff overlooking the bleak and impoverished city below. Abruptly, he stops and, in a fit of anger, tosses his sticks and kicks his drums over the cliff's edge. With the harsh conditions of his city as a backdrop, the young drummer's frustration highlights the impossible barriers he faces. Still, the bravado of his performance lingers and creates the space for hope.

Atay's film reflects the extraordinary obstacles to art practice and cultural expression for a Kurd in Turkey. The Kurdish population has suffered punishing persecution from the state and operations of terrorism, and counterterrorism. The majority of the population lives under crushing poverty and unemployment. Until recently, speaking Kurdish in public was a crime. Despite these seemingly insurmountable conditions, Atay's work manages to transcend the sociopolitical isolation of his culture. By using the low-tech, accessible, and mobile features of video, he is able to distribute and communicate his work, not only to a growing Kurdish diaspora but to an international audience. In addition, he concentrates on everyday moments that extend beyond the borders of geography and the limitations of language. Dialogue is not central to Atay's work; instead, he focuses on young people who in some way connect to performance and art. In subtle but profound ways, the subjects reveal the underlying Kurdish experience. From a locus of severe repression, he succeeds in asserting and circulating Kurdish culture worldwide.

Romanian artist Dan Perjovschi confronts the contradictions of a new Europe with incisive and satirical humor. Drawing directly on the museum wall, he creates simple and quickly rendered images that challenge political and cultural assumptions. He focuses not only inside Europe's borders but also on global phenomena and the local events of his site-specific work.

Perjovschi combines everyday observations with reflections on such issues as religious conflict, surveillance, terrorism, militarization, capitalism, and climate change. He also reflects upon the art world and his own role as an artist. Because his drawings cover vast areas of a museum's walls, their apparent transgression of museum practice provokes a slight shock on initial viewing. Humor provides the next surprise, a seemingly lighthearted, yet subversive veil for an underlying and serious interrogation of social and political norms.

Dan Perjovschi trained as a painter, but bridled at the constraints of the rigid and moribund academy of Romania. He and his wife, Lea, explored and inspired alternative art practices while serving as mentors and leaders of the emerging avant-garde. Perjovschi has worked extensively with political journals and newspapers, continuing his involvement through the present. Working as a journalist has helped shape his role as a socially committed artist; it has also honed his ability to capture intensely complex situations in succinct form. His considerable research and the extensive preparatory drawings he records in his sketchbook enable him to work quickly. His art takes on a performative aspect through the gestural quality of his drawings and the openly public production of his work.

Perjovschi provides a unique perspective on the juncture of the East and the West. First heralding the liberating infusion of capitalism into the postcommunist East, he now finds reason to critique its more destructive effects. While continuing to see capitalism's potential as an economic system, he supports the responsibility of the state to its citizens. One satirical statement reads, "Let's bail out the rich people then beg them for sponsorship and charity." A drawing shows a large hamburger with text reading, "I'm too big to fail." In wry visual and verbal commentaries on Europe, he examines the economic disparity between the East and the West. He also targets Europe's relationship with the United States. In another drawing, a European tank following an American one underscores Europe's passive complicity with U.S. military directives. In addition, Perjovschi is keenly aware of cultural and religious extremism worldwide, rendering three similar shapes that represent, in turn, a church, a mosque, and a gun, in a rendering titled *Beliefs*. Subversive scrutiny and humor invite a reassessment of our political and social reality.

YTO BARRADA

French, b. 1971
The Strait of Gibraltar, Tangier
A Life Full of Holes: The Strait Project
2003
C-print
23.62 x 23.62 in. (60 x 60 cm)
Courtesy of Galerie Polaris, Paris
Photography by Randy Batista

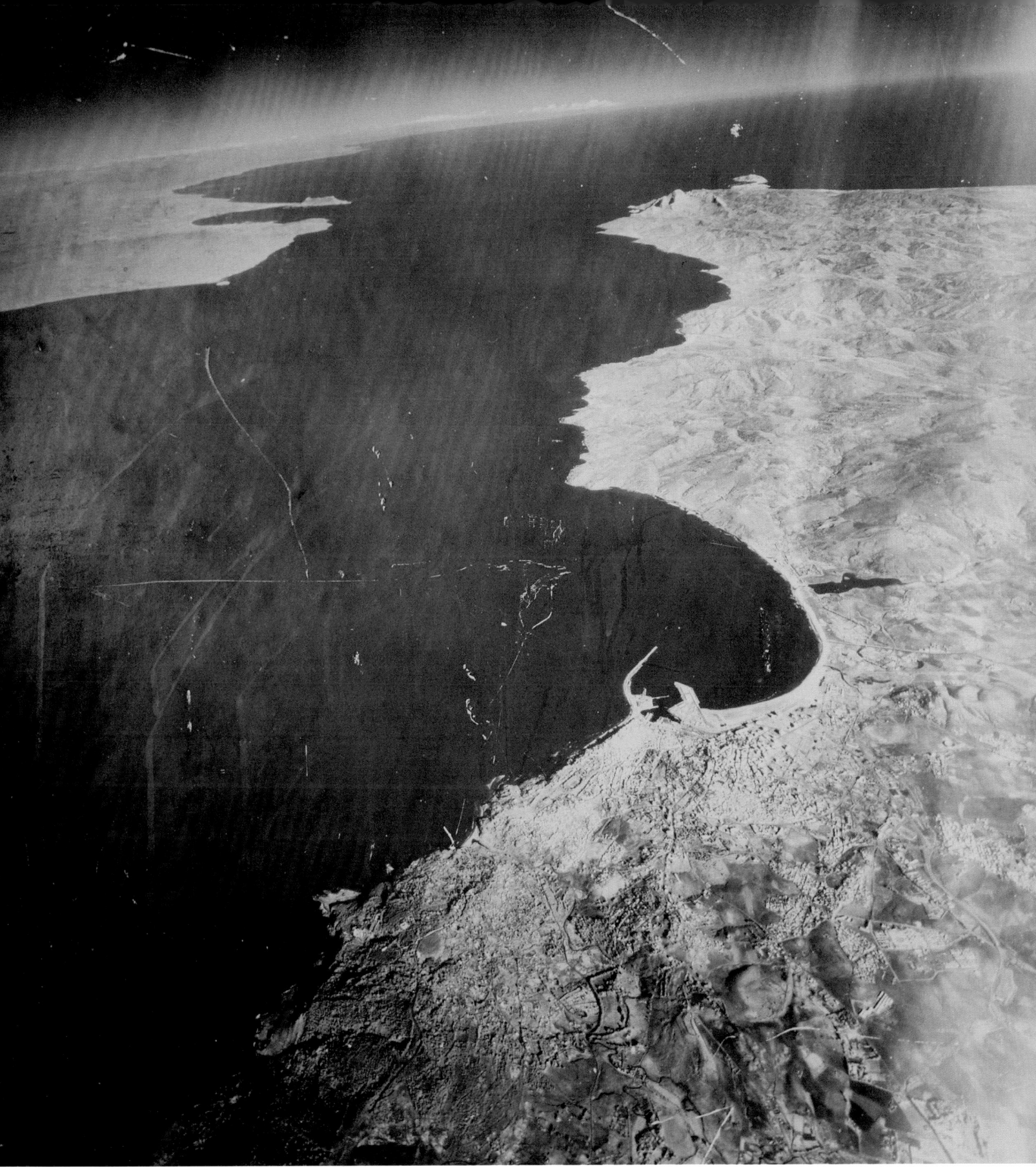

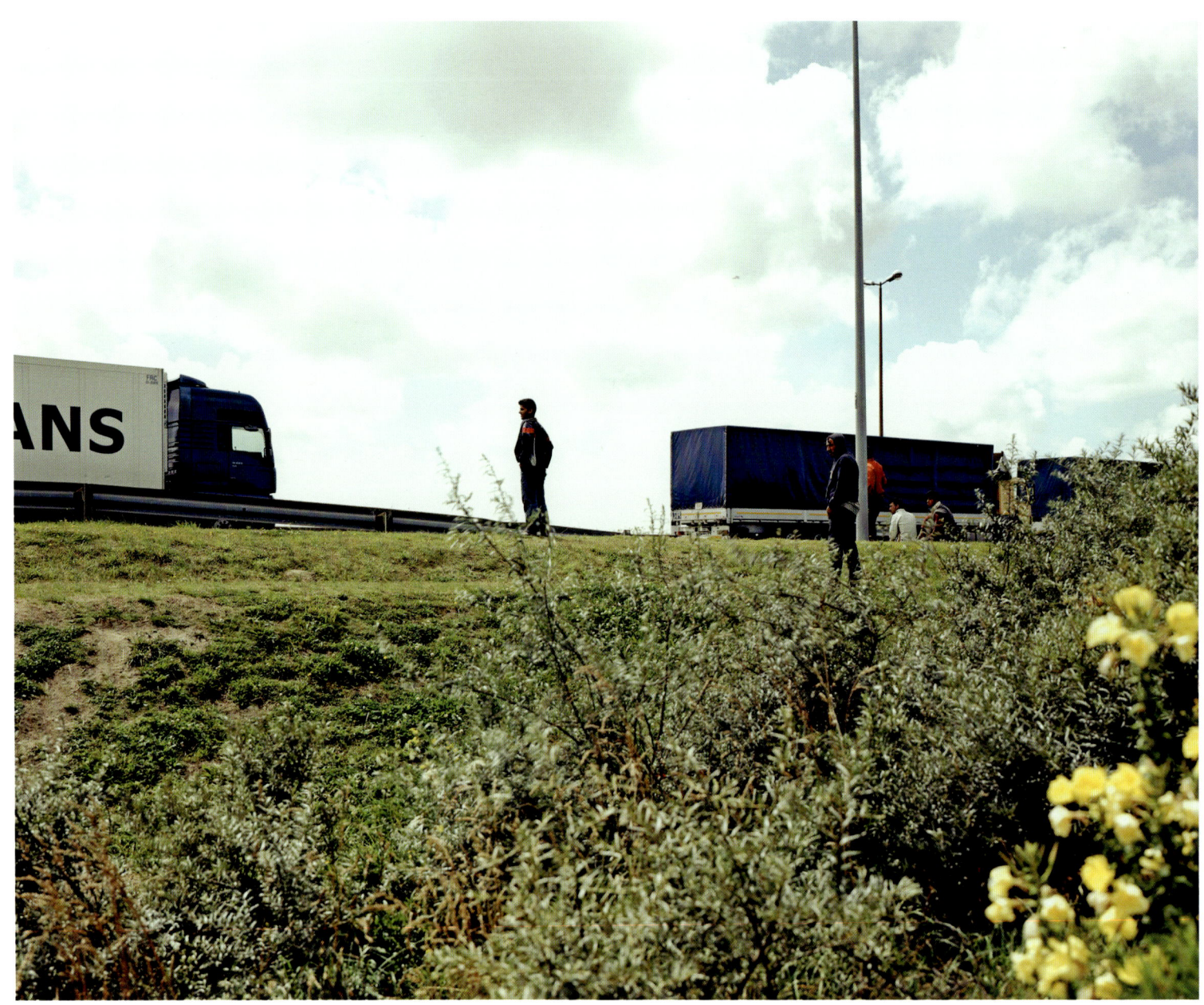

BRUNO SERRALONGUE

French, b. 1968
Passer en Angleterre. Accès terminal transmanche,
Calais, juillet 2007
2007
(from the series *Calais*, 2006–)
Ilfochrome mounted on aluminum with Plexiglas box
50 x 62.5 in. (127 x 158 cm)
Courtesy of the artist and Air de Paris Gallery, Paris

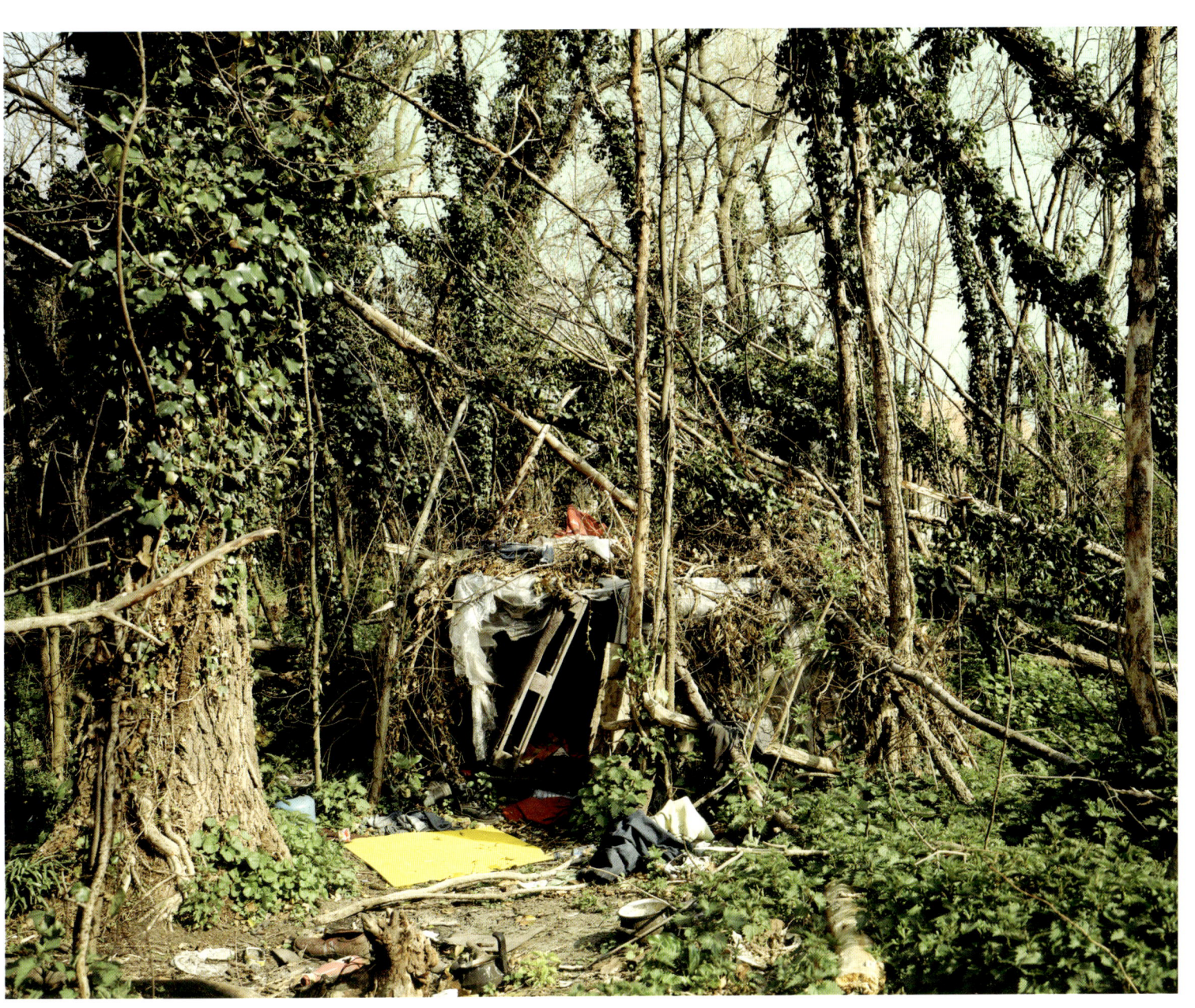

BRUNO SERRALONGUE

French, b. 1968
Abri #6, Calais, avril 2007
2007
(from the series *Calais*, 2006–)
Ilfochrome mounted on aluminum with Plexiglas box
50 x 62.5 in. (127 x 158 cm)
Courtesy of the artist and Air de Paris Gallery, Paris,
Collection Frac Île-de-France, Paris

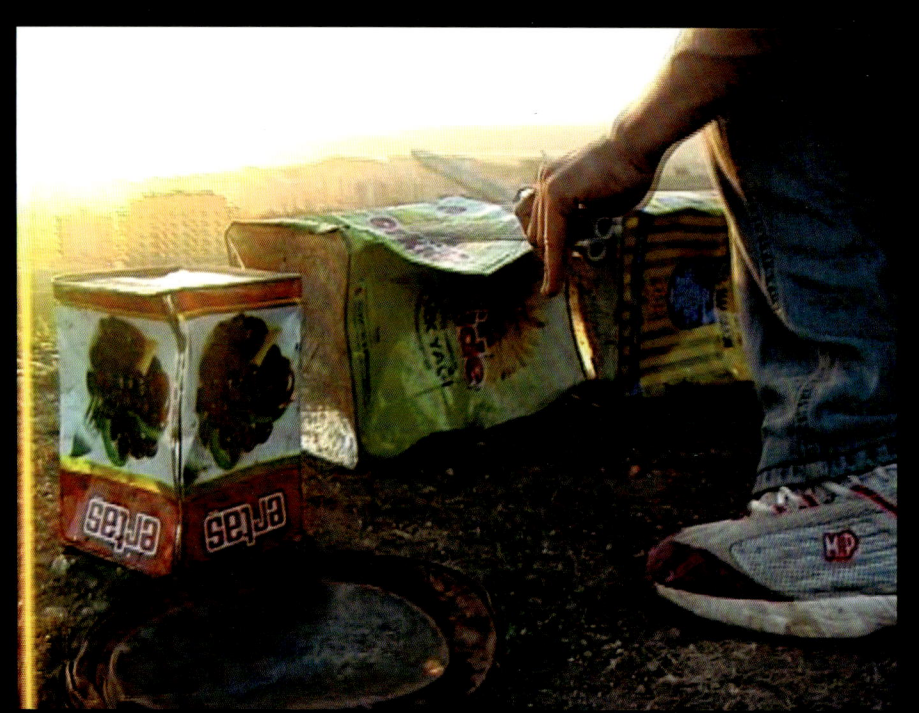

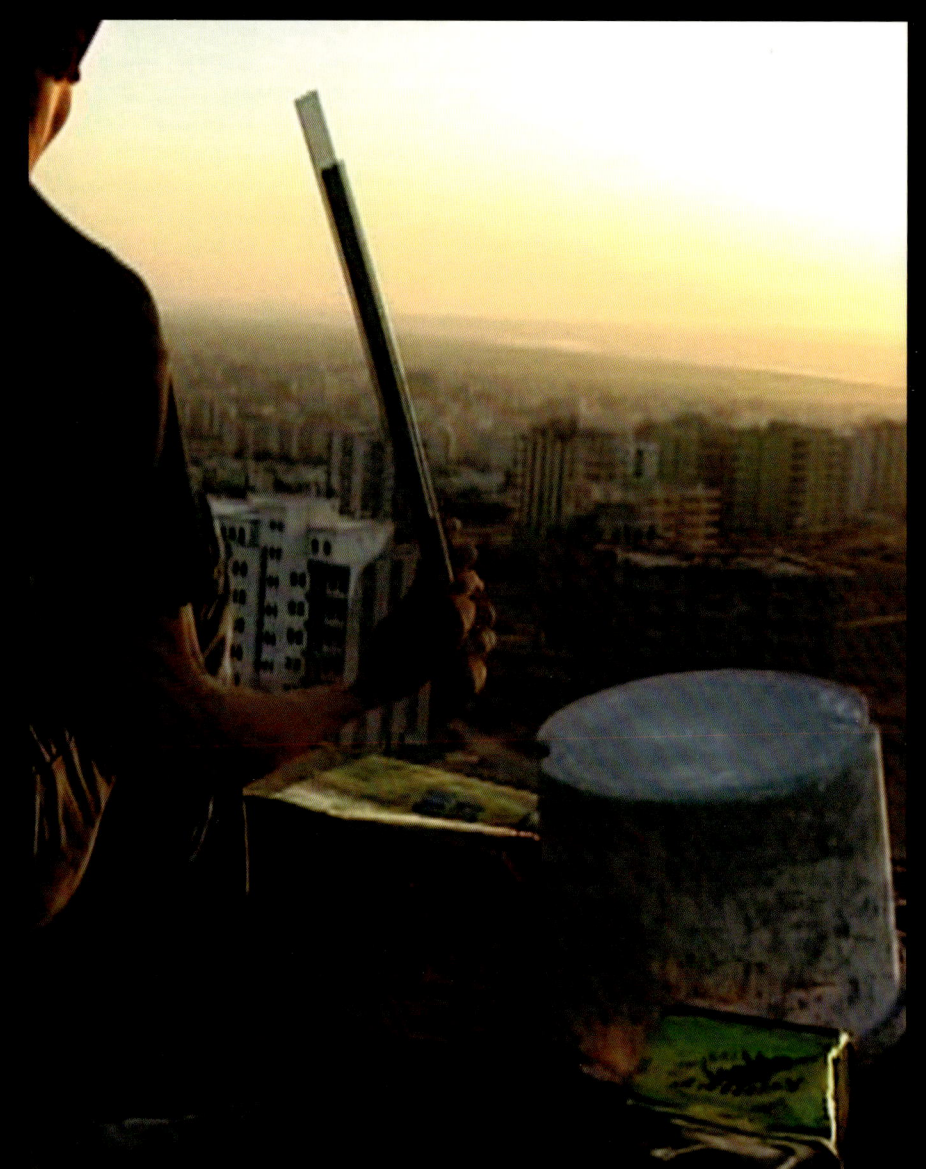

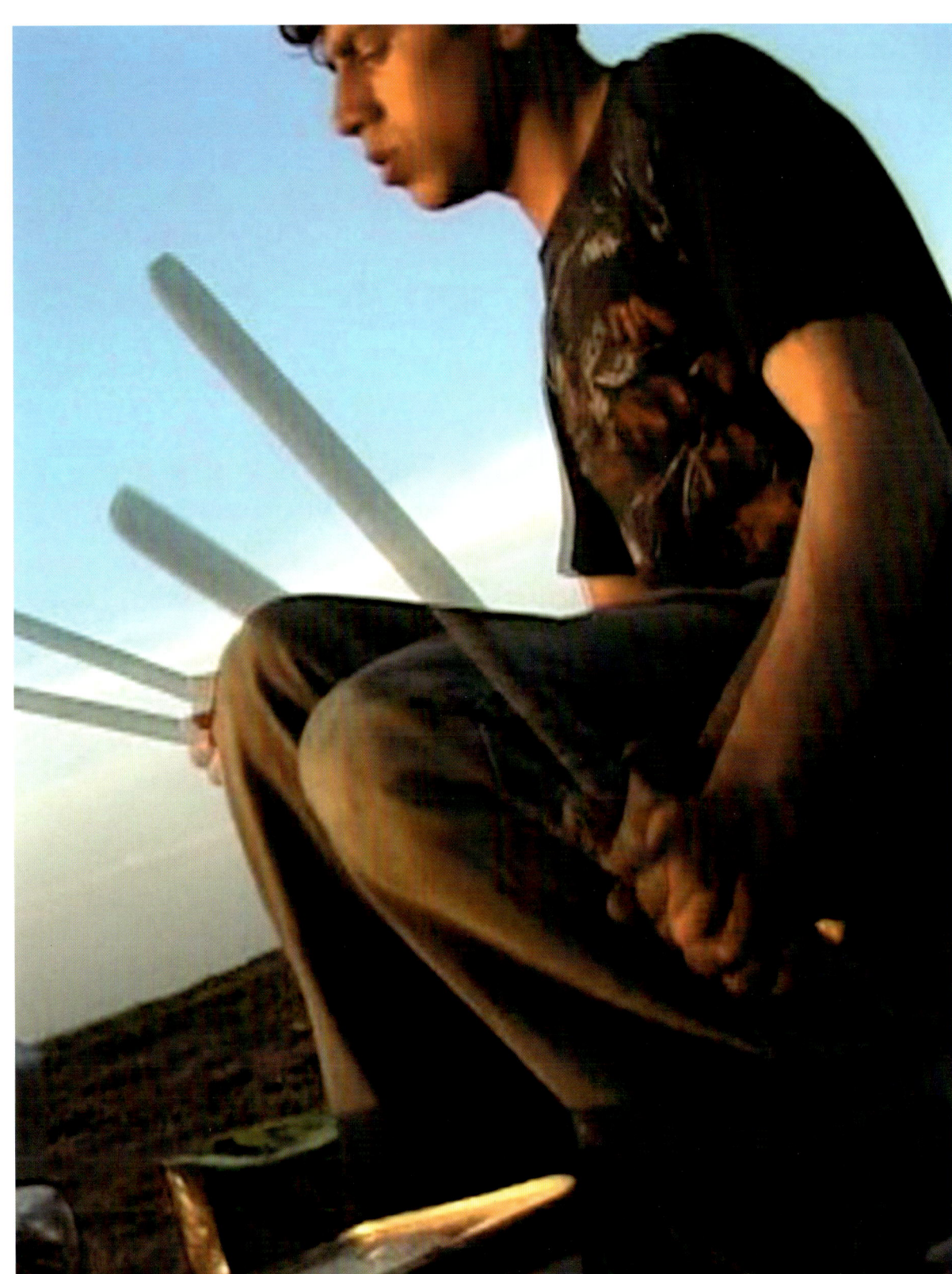

FIKRET ATAY

Turkish, b. 1976
Tinica
2004
Video projection
DVD, 7 minutes 32 seconds
Dimensions variable
Courtesy of the artist and
Galerie Chantal Crousel, Paris

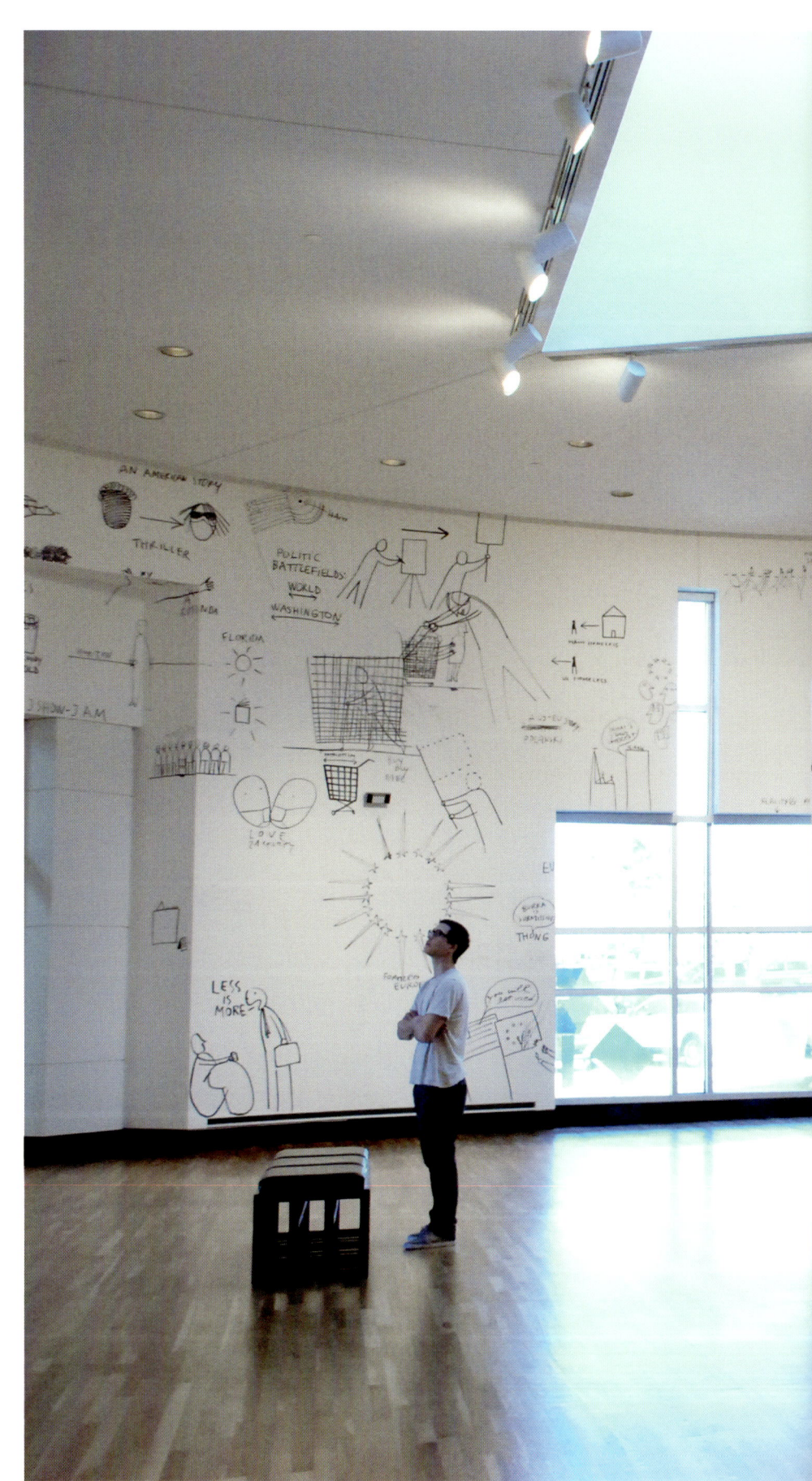

DAN PERJOVSCHI

Romanian, b. 1961
The Round Drawing
2010
Wall drawing, mixed media
16-ft. wall and rotunda walls
Courtesy of the artist and Lombard-Freid Gallery, New York

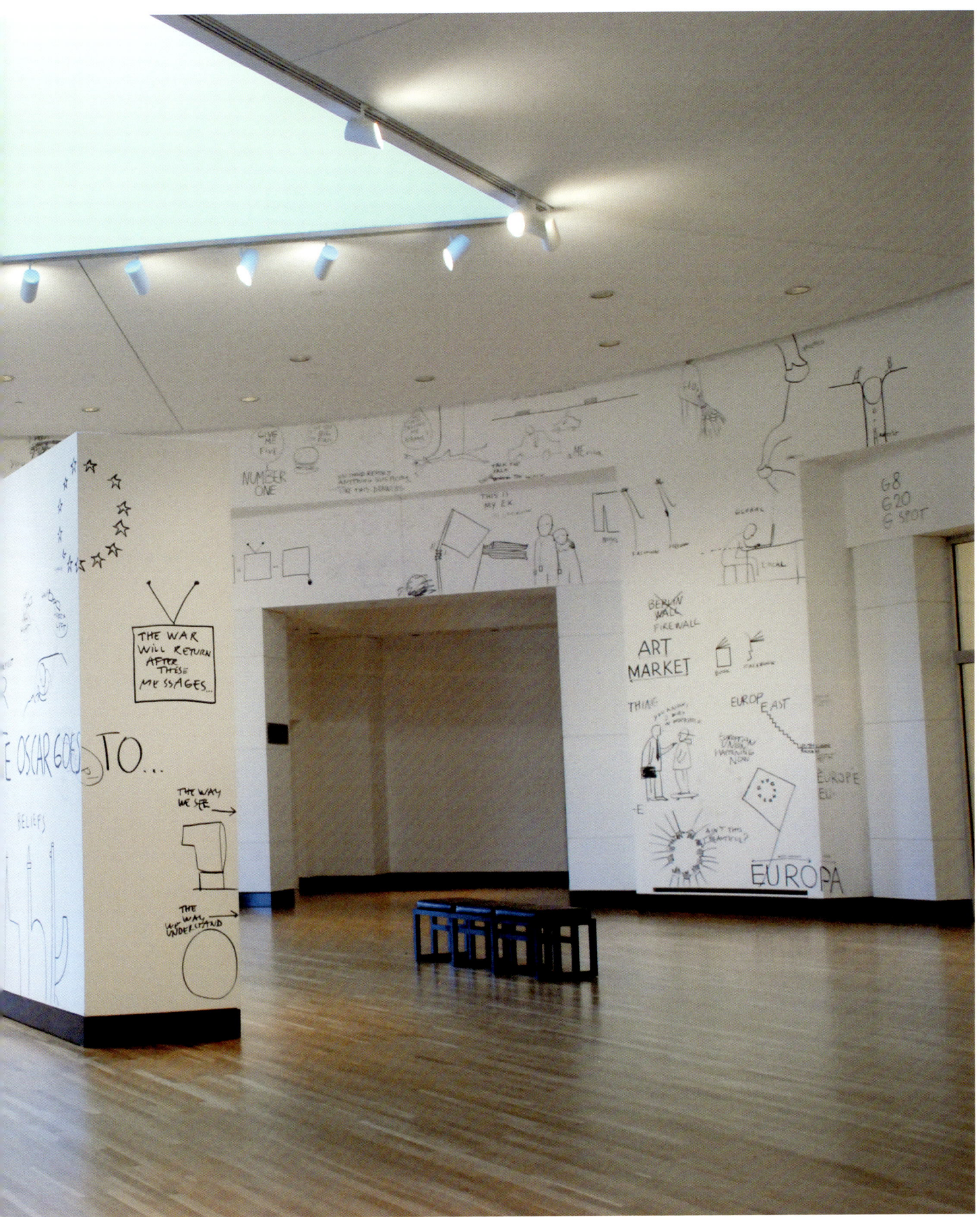

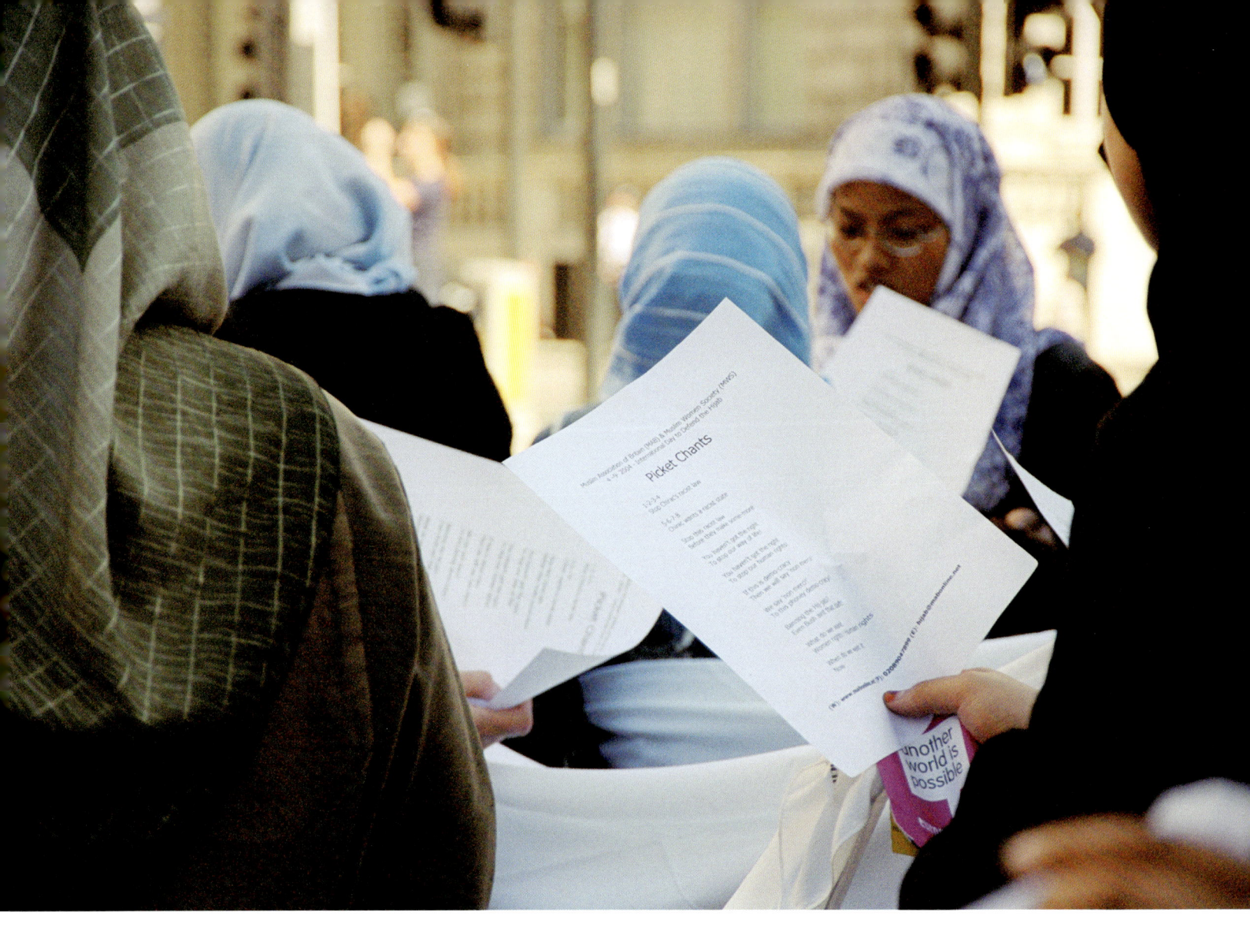

LIDWIEN VAN DE VEN

Dutch, b. 1963
London, 04/09/2004 (International Hijab Solidarity Day)
2007
Inkjet print on photo rag paper mounted on Dibond
59 x 88.5 in. (150 x 225 cm)
Courtesy of the artist and Galerie Paul Andriesse,
Amsterdam

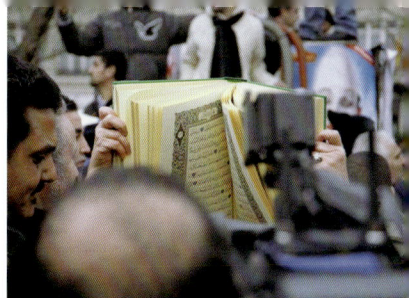

The pressures of globalization have created new forms of imperialism, exclusion, and police control, not only on the frontiers of Europe but within its cities. While Barrada, Atay, and Serralongue focus immigration issues along Europe's edge, others such as Lidwien Van de Ven, Eva Leitolf, and Kader Attia examine immigrant communities within urban communities. They look at issues of law, violence, and distortion of the media; they also explore how the immigrant is seen as the radical Other, one not indoctrinated by European values. These values, perceived as universal, are based on concepts of rights, equality, and democracy. The aporia evident in this equation is the implication that non-European cultures are antidemocratic, antihumanistic, and even antihuman. As Boris Groys notes, "Because the dominant discourse on European identity asserts both things—namely, that humanistic values are universal and that they are particular to Europe—the European psyche is incurably torn between moral superiority and paranoid fear of the other" (Groys 2008, 175). The fear and subsequent violence that the immigrant endures underlies the images represented in this section.

Dutch artist Lidwien Van de Ven considers politics and religion, with a special focus on the presence of Islam in Europe. Increasingly, there has been a shift; the terms "inclusion" and "exclusion" are being directed more toward religion than ethnicity. Religion, especially Islam, is seen by many in the media and population as premodern, deviant, and threatening to the heritage of freedom and tolerance (Dasgupta 2009, 2). Conflicts emerging from these distorted perceptions have been the subject of high-profile and sensational mass-media coverage. Although Van de Ven's subjects often coincide with those covered by the media, she distances herself from sensationalism and the need to persuade; instead, she concentrates on a poetic process and sustained reflection. Her work encompasses what is not seen as much as what is, recognizing that there are meanings to be found in the absences, in what is refused or erased.

Van de Ven's work *Paris, 11/02/2006* (*demo Danish cartoons*) concerns the release of cartoons in the Danish newspaper *Jylland Posten* that depict Mohammed as a terrorist. When the cartoons were eventually distributed worldwide, they violated a religious taboo, as Islam's interdiction against images applies particularly to the depiction of Mohammed. The incident reinforced the West's conflation of Islam with terrorism and resulted in a great controversy, the loss of several lives, and a major trial in Paris on freedom of the press. Van de Ven's photograph shows us a complex and fragmented image of a demonstration held on February

11, 2006, in Paris, organized to protest the republication of Danish cartoons in the French magazine *Charlie Habdo*. The image depicts a woman in the Paris demonstrations defiantly holding up a Koran to a camera held by a man. The viewer sees neither face, nor do the subjects see each other. Paradoxically, both objects that they hold in their hands function as transmitters of cultural truth. At this tense moment of impasse, it is not clear if either side can translate its message to the other; however, translation, as the capacity to understand despite gaps in common meanings, still may remain possible (Bauman, in Balibar 2006, 6).

Van de Ven's image *London, 04/09/2004* (*International Hijab Solidarity Day*) depicts the gathering of young, veiled women preparing to protest against the prohibition of wearing veils in French schools. Investigating 1905 laws on the separation of politics and religion, the Stasi Commission recommended passing a new law forbidding students to wear religious or political signs or symbols, including the Islamic headscarf, the Jewish skullcap, and large Christian crosses. The law passed in February 2004. The controversy polarized people across the continent, fueling misconceptions and antagonism. Some claimed the veil was a sign of fundamentalism and the suppression of women. For many Muslims, who often experience the rule of France's law in the form of oppression, this case was directed by bias, hate, and prejudice against Islam. Secular freedom was seen as a way to exclude and discriminate against ethnic and religious communities from North Africa, Turkey, and the Middle East (Butler 2009, 111). Van de Ven's photograph focuses on a quiet interlude as the young, veiled women get ready to take their voices and protests into the street. Their concentration reveals a certain serenity and sense of purpose. Van de Ven's image challenges the stereotype of the suppressed Muslim female. At the same time, she shares intimate moments seldom seen or recognized, closing the culture gap in a subtle and powerful way.

The work of German artist Eva Leitolf depicts the failure of tolerance and civility as it yields to insidious violence directed against immigrants, refugees, and asylum-seekers. Her photographic series *German Images—Looking for Evidence* (1992–94/2006–8) concentrates on specific attacks and hate crimes perpetrated in Germany. Like other artists, Leitolf's work counters mass-media methods that give momentary and sensational coverage to brutal events promptly forgotten. Leitolf's photographs record the location of the crimes after the event, offering the events for deeper and more nuanced consideration. Accompanying the image are papers that record factual accounts of hate crimes, including battery, robbery, and murder, along with the jurisdictional outcome of each event. Leitolf's quiet images and text act as memorials that invite our contemplation and mourning.

Paradoxically, the scenes where the crimes have occurred appear extraordinarily benign. An idyllic village is a neo-Nazi haven, a shaded café is a meeting place for right-wing extremists, a picnic area is the site of racist attacks, and a pristine city plaza is covered with posters for "whites only." Counter to stereotypes, the locations are not dark corners of inner cities or slums but prosperous areas that are often beautiful and bucolic. The unsettling juxtaposition between the place and the crime underscores the equally disturbing contradictions in Europe's image. Some Europeans identify themselves as modern,

LIDWIEN VAN DE VEN

Dutch, b. 1963
Paris, 11/02/2006 (demo Danish cartoons)
2007
Inkjet print on photo rag paper mounted on Dibond
47 x 71 in. (120 x 180 cm)
Courtesy of the artist and Galerie Paul Andriesse,
Amsterdam

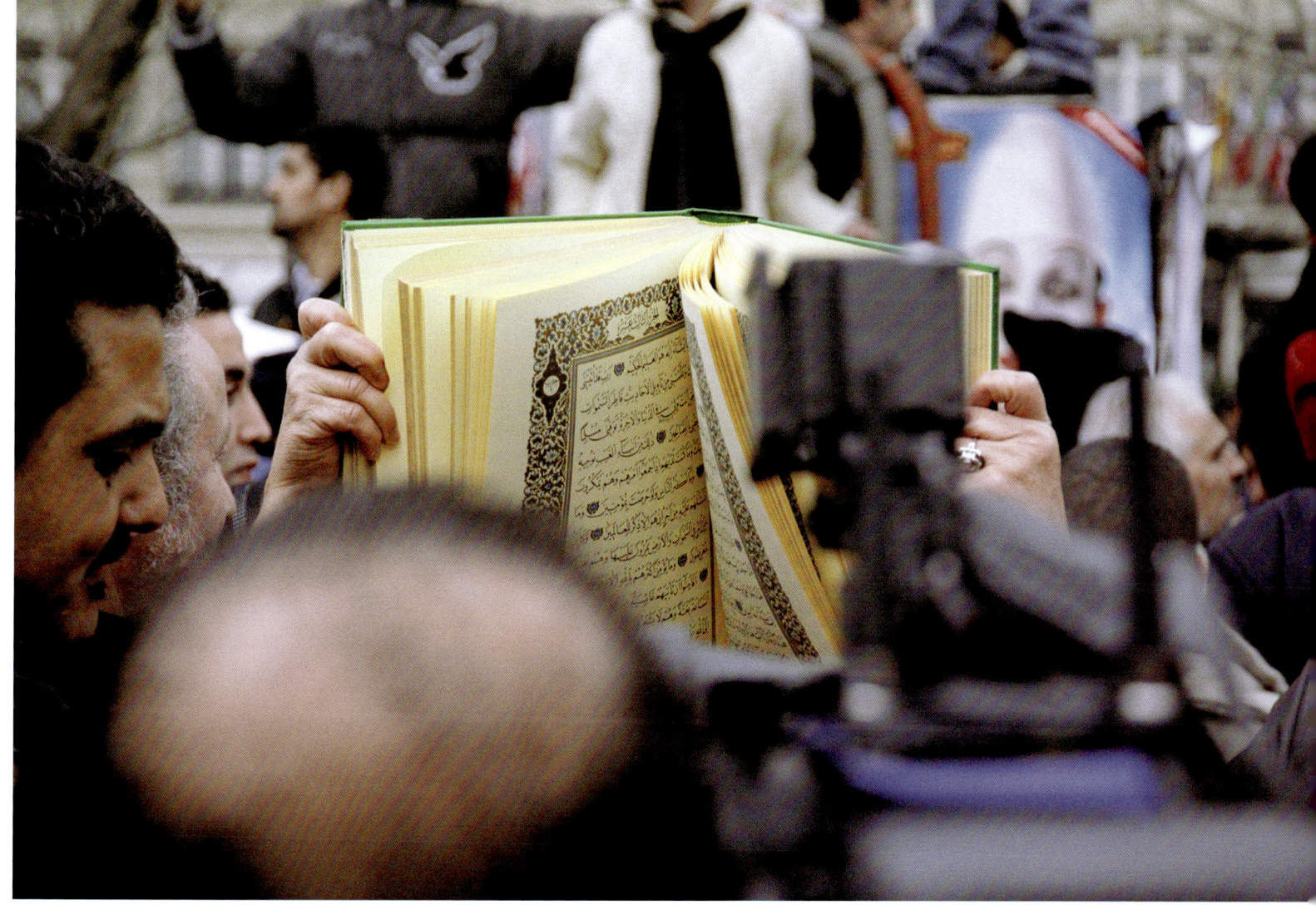

progressive, and liberal while considering foreigners to be reactionary, fundamentalist, and antimodern. Deep hatreds and prejudices lurk beneath the surface, sentiments that fester from unresolved histories of racism and fascism. A process of denial and hypocrisy allows this suppressed and hidden violence to erupt. Leitolf's work exposes social and cultural undercurrents that often remain hidden and unacknowledged.

The violence in Europe is often fueled by nationalism, paradoxically diminished and increased by the creation of the European Union. National identity is still the defining condition for EU membership and the criterion for inclusion and exclusion. While the line separating citizens and noncitizens is sharp, even immigrants with citizenship are subjected to a neoracism largely based upon cultural difference (Balibar 1991, 21). For instance, North African Muslims, or Maghrebians, are negatively stereotyped as Arab and linked with terror. They are not only stigmatized but find themselves forced to live in segregated residential zones under poor and stressful living conditions.

Kader Attia was born in France of Algerian parents. He is a multidisciplinary artist whose media and work is determined by each specific project. In his work, he avoids dogma and embraces poetry. Attia grew up in the crowded immigrant community in the suburbs of Paris, banlieues, where high-rise apartments, initially conceived in a utopian spirit of modernist architecture, have turned into segregated cities for a large, low-income community of primarily Muslim but also Christian and Jewish immigrants. For many, the Paris housing projects represent a no-man's-land cut off from cultural and economic life. Chronic unemployment, poverty, discrimination, and police brutality contribute to the strain and to increasing violence. The antiracist demonstrations and riots that erupted in 2005 went on for three months and spread throughout France. For the most part, cars, buses, and businesses were burned. They took aim at property, not people, but, nevertheless, lives were still lost.

The Paris banlieues are the subject of Kader Attia's large-scale wall painting in the exhibition. The intense crowding of the buildings signals the impossible pressures on a community with few resources and opportunities. The somber black color suggests the lack of hope, the black of charred remains, or a mantle of dripping oil representing a resource going to waste.

In these neighborhoods, Attia has witnessed the complex encounter between the East and West. Impoverished and unemployed youth are seduced by the dream of Western consumerism and the desire for the symbols of achievement and power. In the banlieues, such consumer brands as Nike, Lacoste, or Vuitton correlate with gang identification and social survival. The alternative is religious proselytizing. In this arena, the symbols of purity are especially valued, and, even here, Attia sees the incursion of consumerism. Singular objects and symbolic signs of religion serve as yet another kind of logo (Attia 2003, 112).

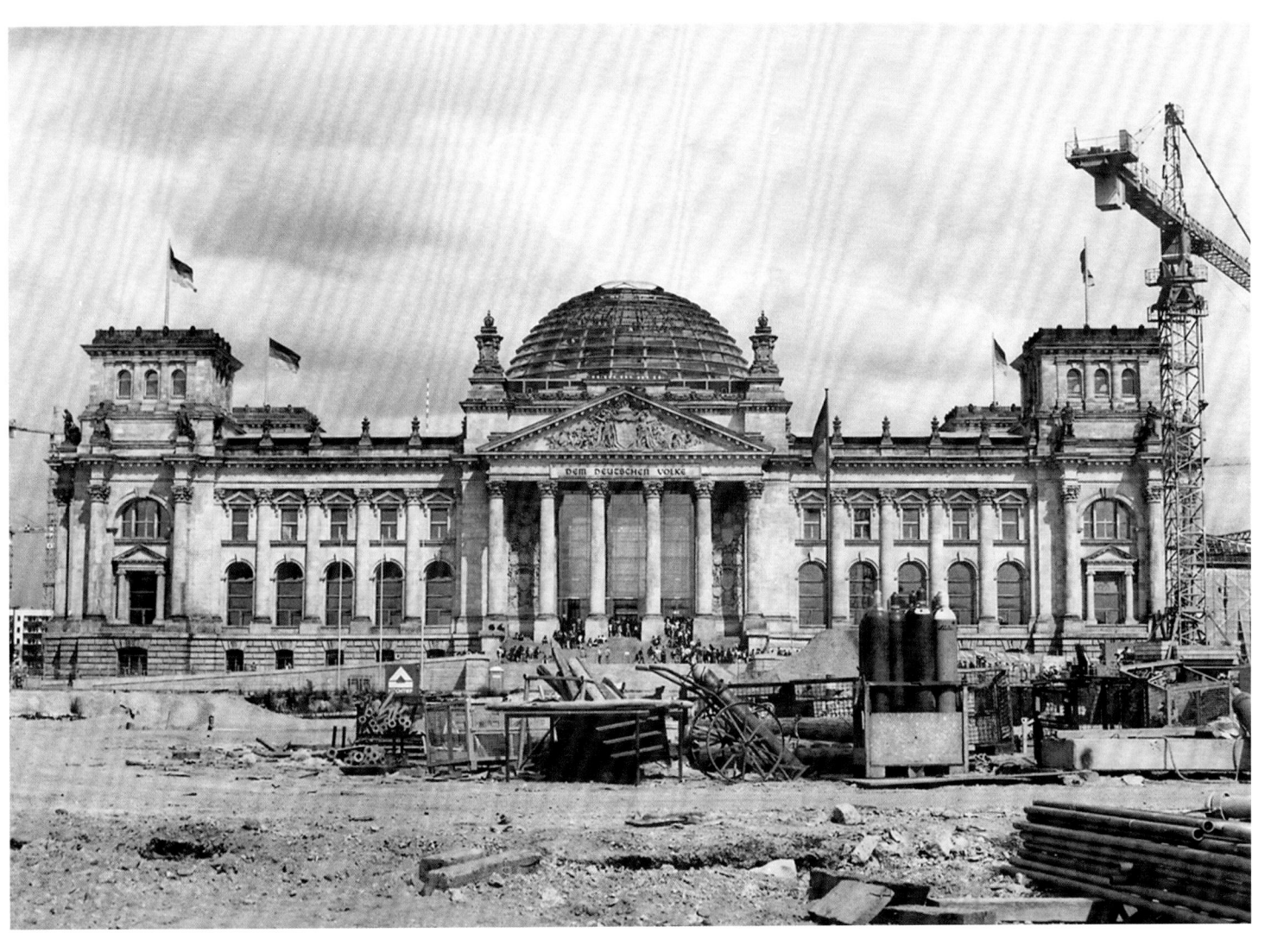

[page 67]

EVA LEITOLF

German, b. 1966
Althaldensleben ("Olln")
German Images—Looking for Evidence
2006
Color photograph
31.89 x 27.17 in. (81 x 69 cm)
Courtesy of the artist

[page 68]

EVA LEITOLF

German, b. 1966
Tramstop, Potsdam (Haltestelle, Potsdam)
German Images—Looking for Evidence
2006
Color photograph
31.89 x 27.17 in. (81 x 69 cm)
Courtesy of the artist

[page 69]

EVA LEITOLF

German, b. 1966
Disused Concrete Works (Ehemaliges Betonwerk)
German Image—Looking for Evidence
2006
Color photograph
31.89 x 27.17 in. (81 x 69 cm)
Courtesy of the artist

[page 70]

EVA LEITOLF

German, b. 1966
Schöna, Sächsische Schweiz
German Images—Looking for Evidence
2006
Color photograph
31.89 x 27.17 in. (81 x 69 cm)
Courtesy of the artist

[page 71]

EVA LEITOLF

German, b. 1966
Lake Schwerin, near Berlin (Schweriner See, bei Berlin)
German Images—Looking for Evidence
2006
Color photograph
31.89 x 27.17 in. (81 x 69 cm)
Courtesy of the artist

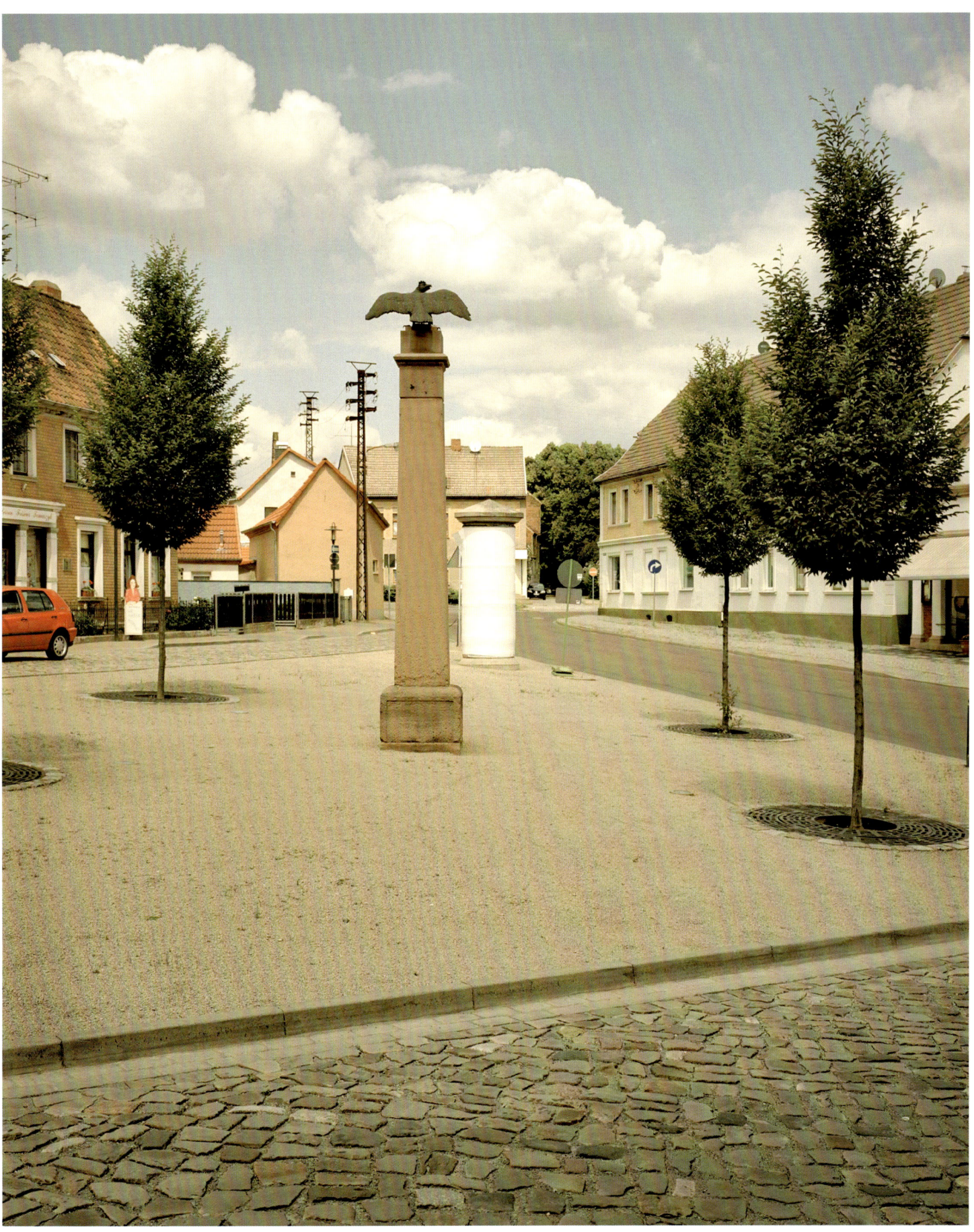

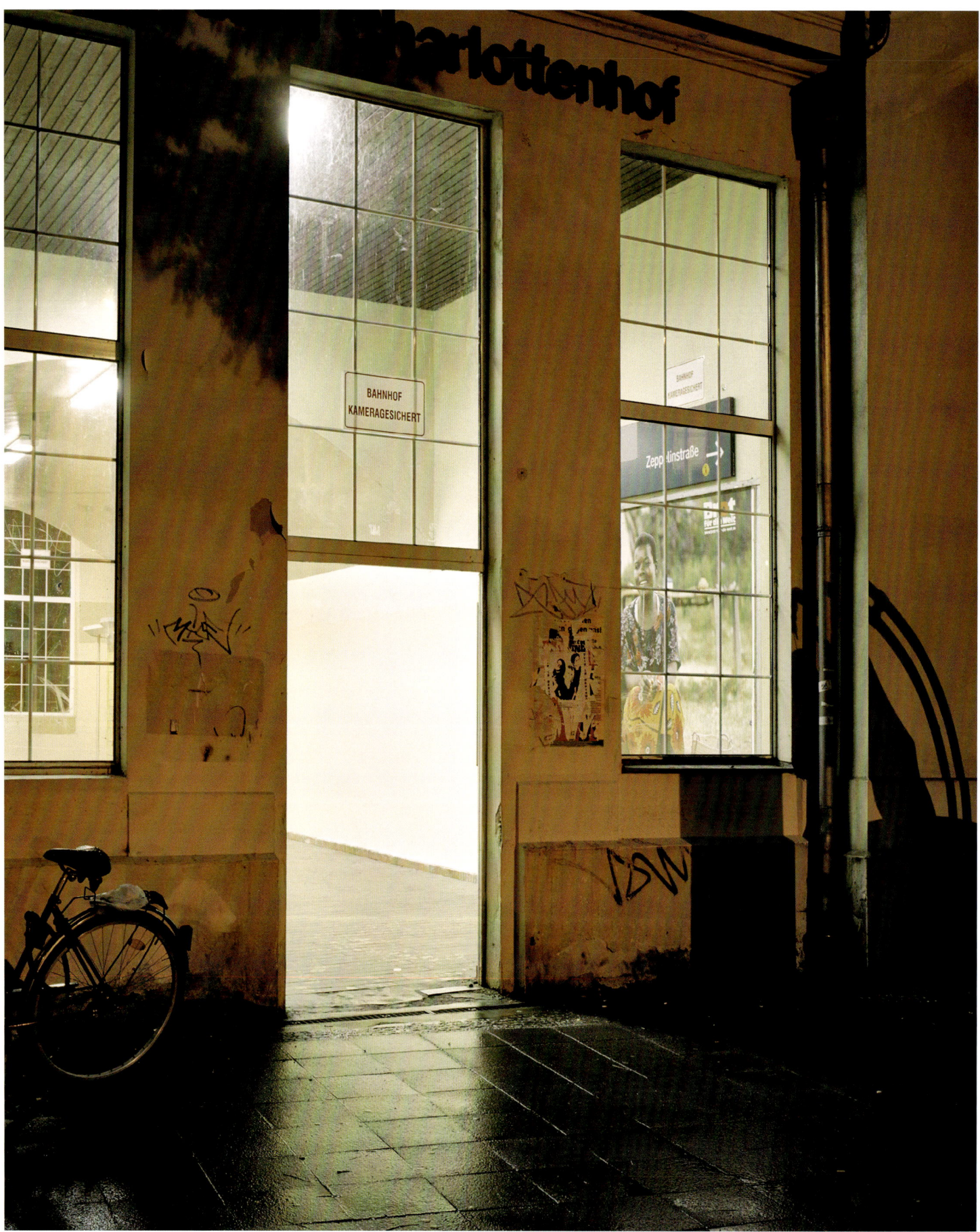

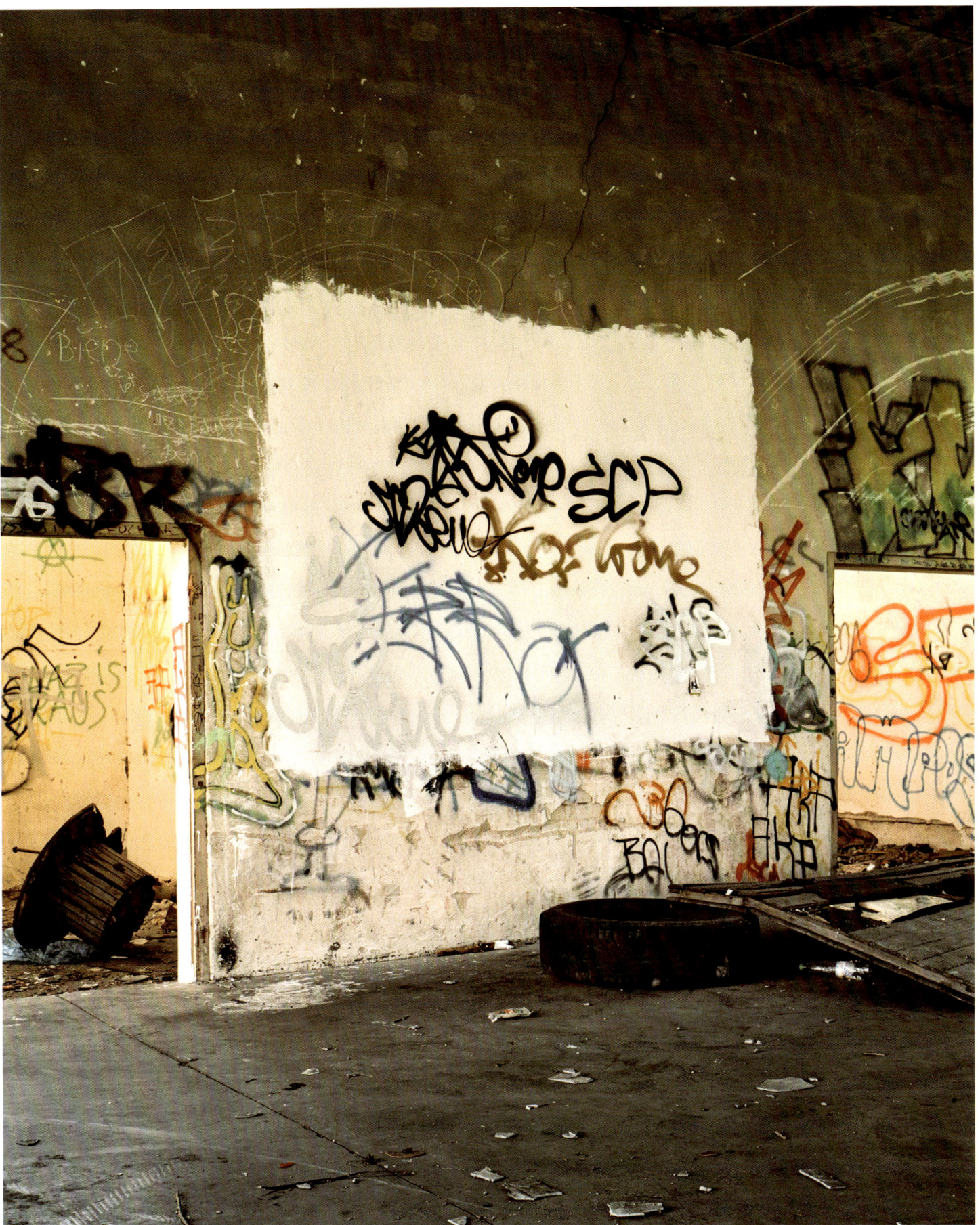

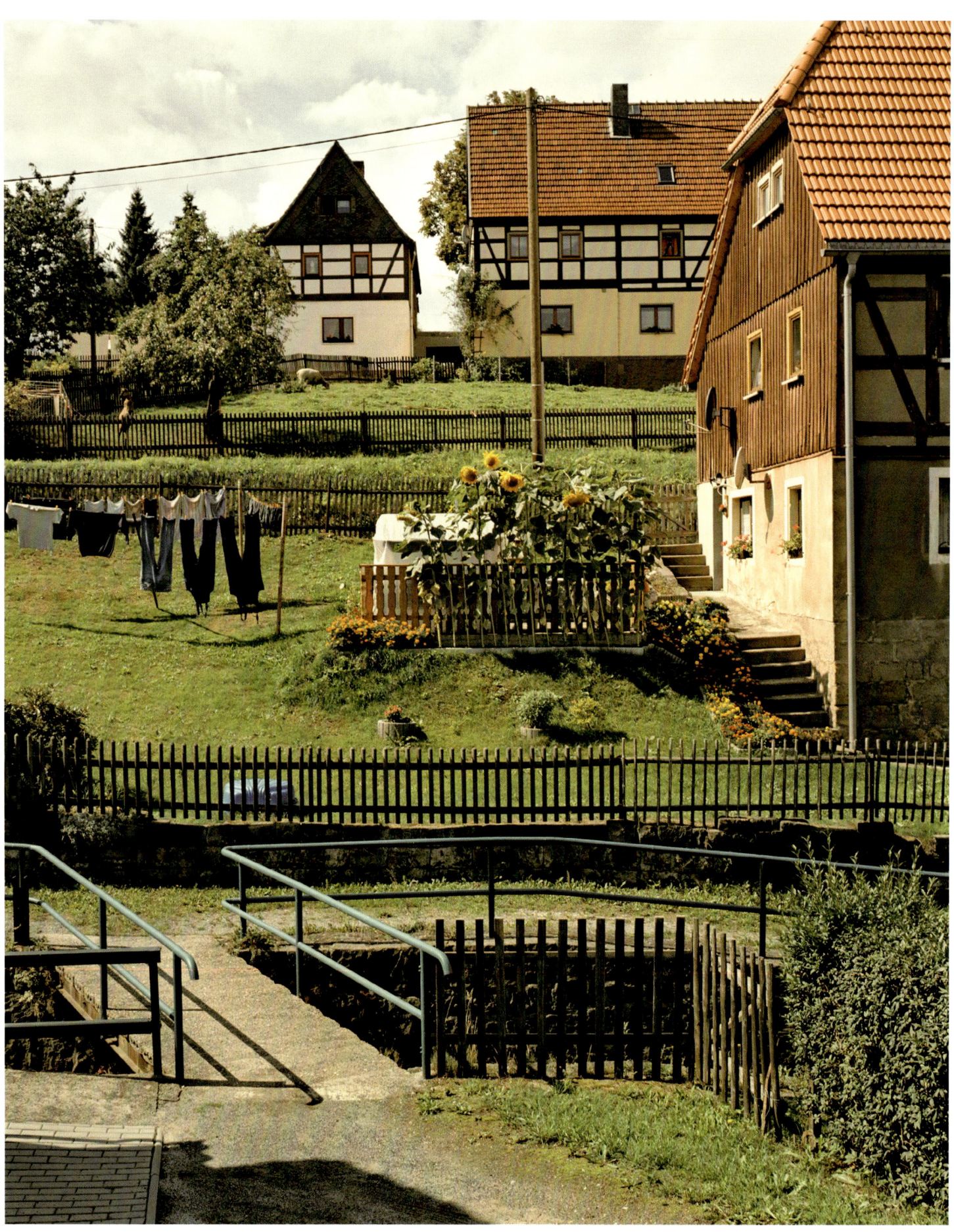

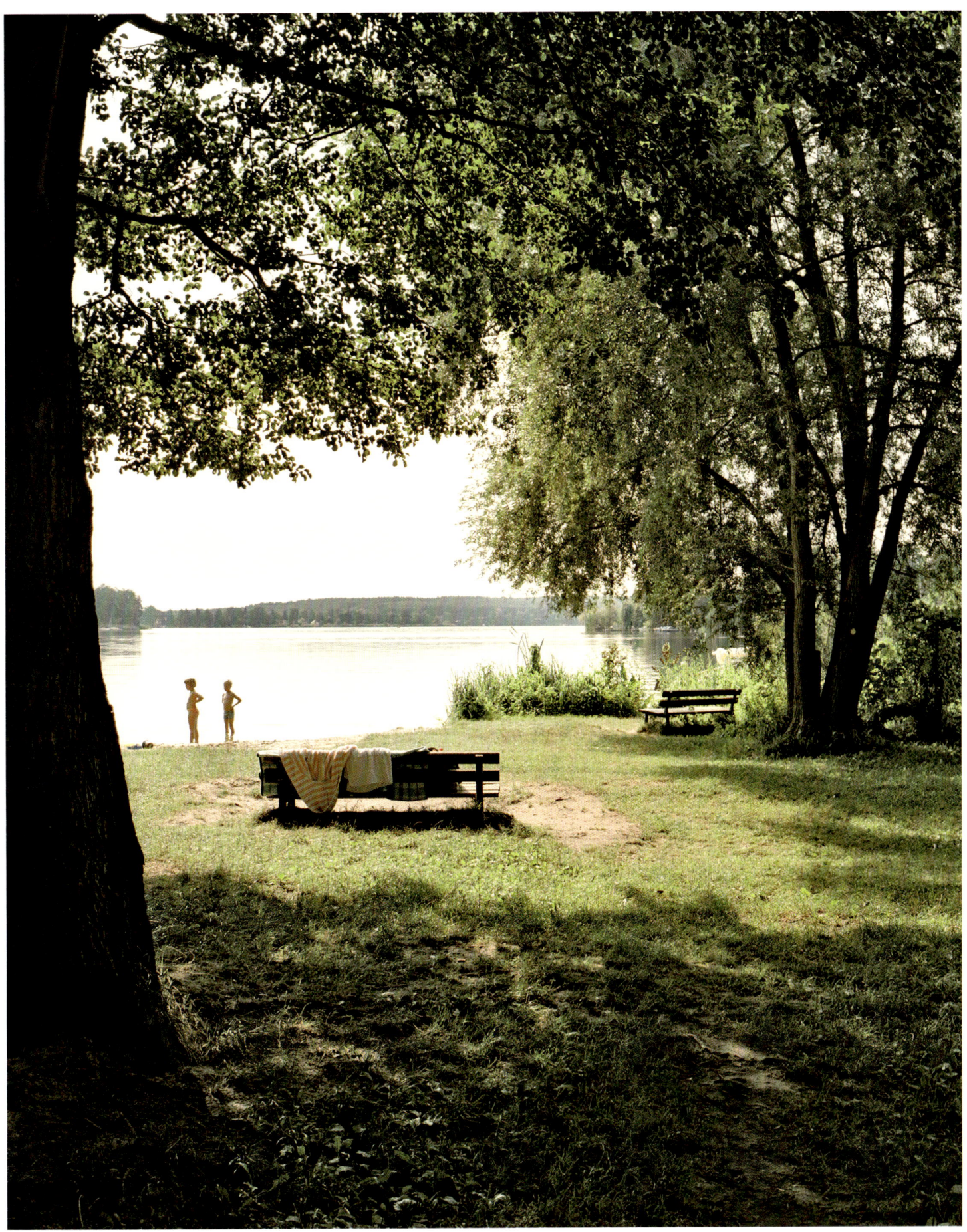

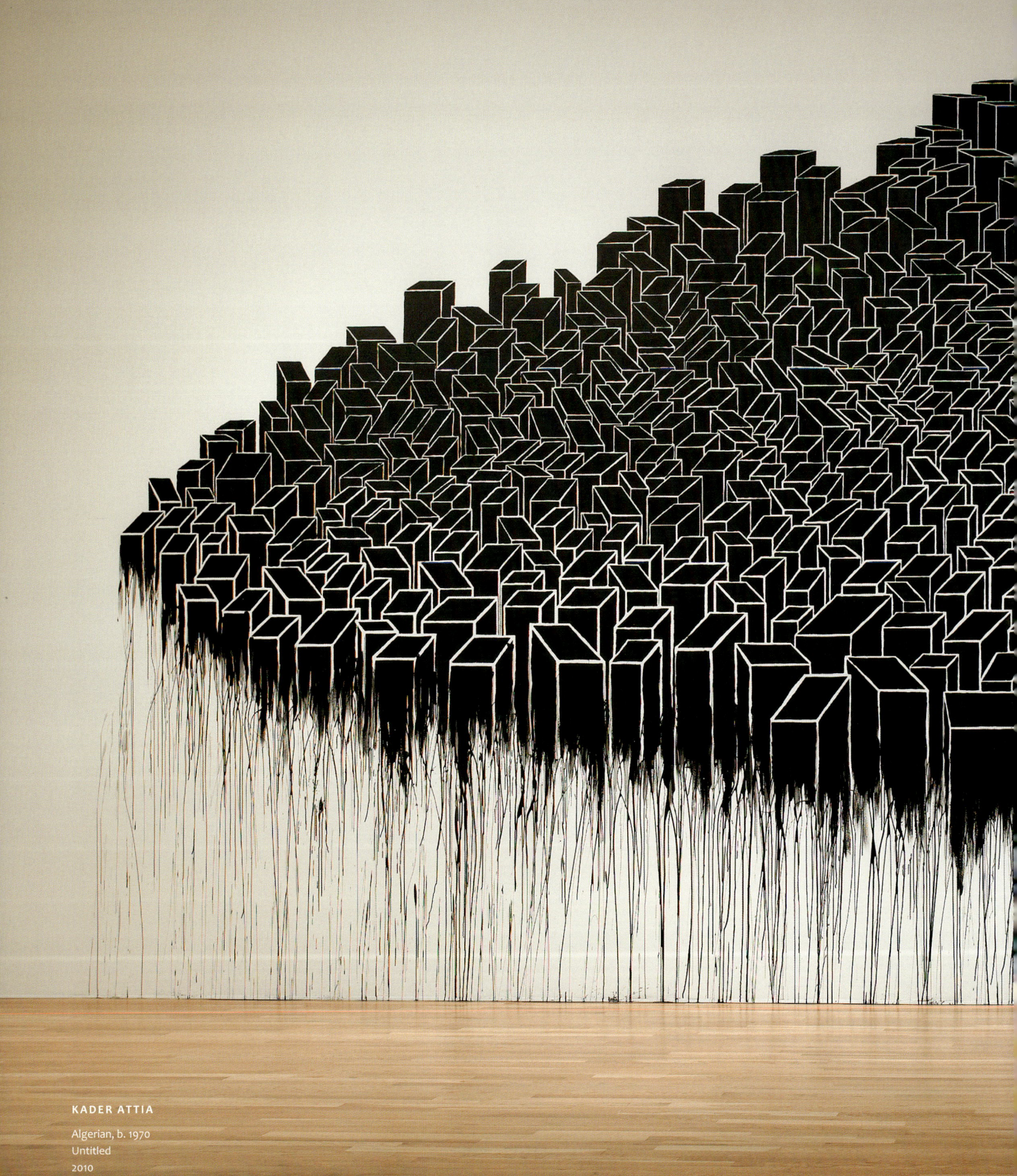

KADER ATTIA

Algerian, b. 1970
Untitled
2010
Wall painting
Dimensions variable
Courtesy of the artist and Christian Nagel Gallery,
Berlin and Cologne
Photography by Randy Batista

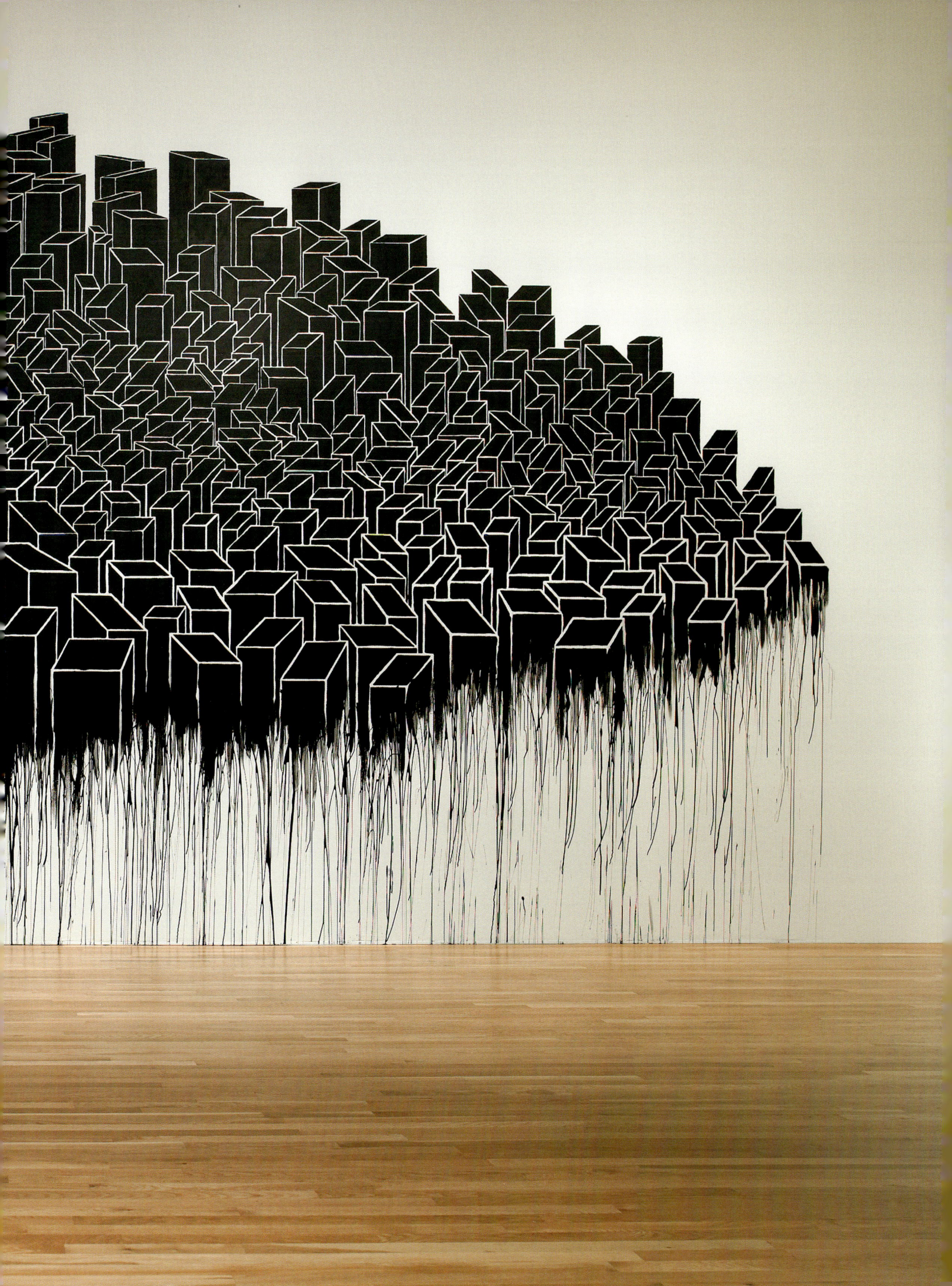

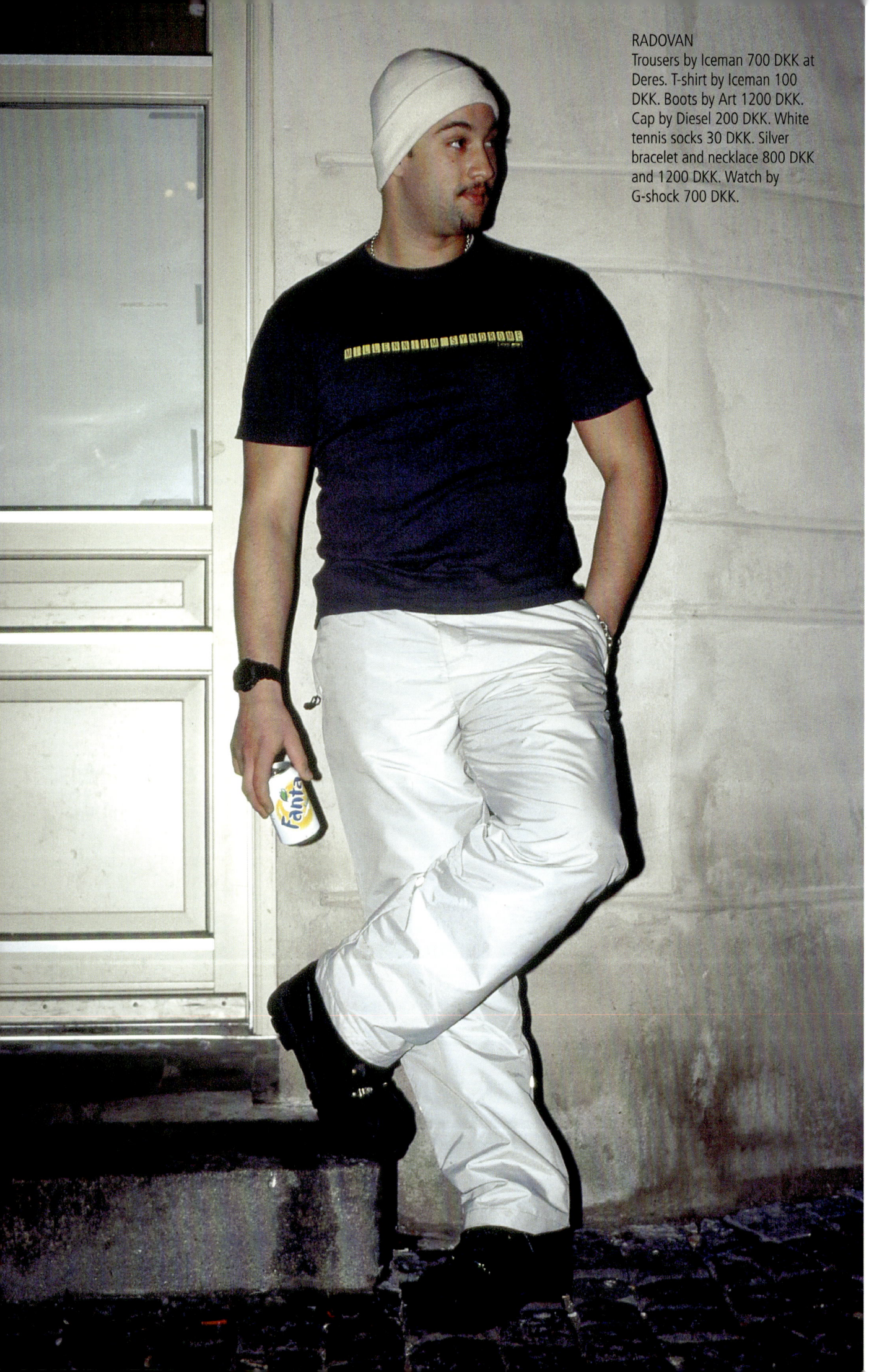

RADOVAN
Trousers by Iceman 700 DKK at
Deres. T-shirt by Iceman 100
DKK. Boots by Art 1200 DKK.
Cap by Diesel 200 DKK. White
tennis socks 30 DKK. Silver
bracelet and necklace 800 DKK
and 1200 DKK. Watch by
G-shock 700 DKK.

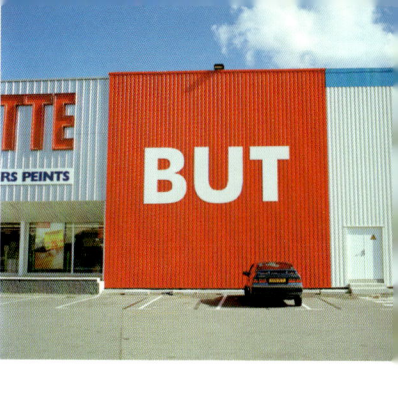

THE MARKET

Artists Andrea Robbins and Max Becher, Jens Haaning, and the collective Superflex challenge the Western economic model. They examine its manifestation in Europe, where it has created new forms of imperialism and exclusion. The model is reinforced by the policies of the European Union, which restricts the mobility of populations it is exploiting for cheap labor. On the basis of economic necessity, EU policies have also contributed to the dismantling of social welfare and the concentration of resources in a few hands, primarily in the West. Perry Anderson claims that the EU is governed "not by democracy, or welfare, but capital" (Anderson 2007, ref #17). Artists in this section offer an astute critique of globalization even as they extol the system's potential for emancipatory action. In subversive ways, these artists usurp and reinvent capitalist strategies for their own alternative purposes.

Andrea Robbins and Max Becher examine the effects of globalization in France with five photographs from their series *Strip Malls of Toulouse*. The photographs depict storefronts and massive box stores that brandish garish signs and are surrounded by vast and empty parking lots. The buildings are brightly colored and set against cheerful blue skies. Bold logos and letters, most in English, announce store and inanely comical product names: Jardiland, BUT, and Toys 'Я'Us. The Toys 'Я'Us image fills the picture frame, a fragment of its name sufficient to identify it. Box stores depicted in other images appear massive in scale. The closely cropped images emphasize a bleak environment devoid of nature and social space.

The locations in *Strip Malls of Toulouse* look decidedly American and create a sharp contrast to the typical picturesque images of a European city. Robbins and Becher disrupt the stereotypes of both America and Europe, presenting the viewer with the totalizing and global reach of American-style capitalism. Robbins and Becher are interested in the transportation of place, the uncanny simulation of one community by another because of overlapping historical and cultural influences. Their work records the present reality while revealing what is normally overlooked, ignored, suppressed, or denied. Unexpected juxtapositions provoke a new way of thinking and seeing. The contradictions that Robbins and Becher uncover challenge a vision of Europe as an alternative site to the hegemony of the United States. To the contrary, the images indicate the assimilation of one-dimensional mass communication reduced to a single language, culture, and economy. Perry Anderson and Andrew Moravcsik claim that the European Union is less about democracy and overwhelmingly about the promotion of free markets and multinational firms (Anderson 2007). The photo-

JENS HAANING

Danish, b. 1965
Radovan
2000
Lightjet print on photographic paper
27 x 19 in. (48 x 68 cm)
Edition of 5
Courtesy of the artist and Galleri Nicolai Wallner,
Copenhagen, Denmark

graphs of Robbins and Becher highlight the rift between Europe's utopian projection of self-determination and the undeniable alignment with the United States.

Danish artist Jens Haaning examines the relationship of the immigrant to the economy and subverts normative codes of identification. The individual immigrant is the subject of ten photographs from a series by Haaning. Each photograph is a full-length portrait of first-generation immigrant man living in Copenhagen. The subjects are identified by such first names as Hakan, Ömer, and Murat, signaling their Muslim heritage. Each man is also marked by the clothing and accessories he wears. As if part of a high-end or trendy fashion magazine spread, the brand names and cost of each item in Danish kroners (DKK) are detailed directly on the photograph. Shirts, trousers, belts, underwear, and even socks are identified with such names as Nike, Benetton, Levi's, and Calvin Klein. Cell phones, gold watches, rings, and chains are also noted. Through the ironic strategy of exchange, Haaning substitutes the role of refugee for the high-class model.

According to Haaning, foreigners are considered alien, and thus taboo, within the realm of positive representation (Pécoil 2003, 011). Jacques Rancière confirms this perspective, as he asserts that within the realm and distribution of the sensible, migrants are denied visibility. Haaning reverses the expected hierarchical order by positioning the migrant as a central figure in the economy, a place where possession is equated with power.

Haaning sees his work as a catalyst for social change and seeks to shift perception and patterns of looking. He avoids ideology, sloganeering, and agitprop. His work often takes place outside of museums and galleries, where he creates alternate systems of global exchange of information and goods.

Violence figures prominently in *Burning Car,* by the Danish art collective Superflex. The film focuses on the 2005 riots in the banlieues, where young men, mostly French citizens of North African descent, battled against their consistent exclusion from the benefits of society. Over several months, the riots received massive media coverage, with the picture of a burning car surfacing as the emblematic image of the conflict. For the most part, the media portrayed protestors as hooligans, providing spectacular images with little meaningful analysis. The protests were dismissed by the media and government officials as the violent acts of young men lacking firm paternal authority (Butler 2009, 115–16). Other sources compared the impact and cultural magnitude of the events to the riots in Detroit and Los Angeles in the 1960s and '70s.

For Superflex, the image of a car on fire serves as a symbol for the civil unrest and profound racism that plague contemporary Western Europe. Counter to sensationalism and short-lived attention given by the media to the subject, Superflex invites extended looking and consideration. At the same time, their methods appropriate commercial media strategies, using them for their own critical ends. In the film, the luxury car is replaced by the burning car as the iconic image of a new Europe. The film opens with a gleaming

Mercedes lit and staged against a dark background. Suddenly, the car erupts in flame. As the fire consumes the car, the camera circles it. Slow panning images are punctuated with close-ups of bubbling paint, ruptured tires, and cracked glass. In one long take, the film mimics the lingering gaze and format of a luxury car commercial. Here, however, the Mercedes stands for the brutal excesses and inequities of global capitalism.

Superflex has made *Burning Car* available to the public for free on the Internet site for *Pirate Bay*. The Swedish website is one of the world's largest distributors of illegal downloads. Along with *Pirate Bay,* Superflex takes a stand against the "excessive ownership and control of ideas and visual culture through copyright, trademarks and intellectual property legislation" (Christiansen 2009). Regarding this economy, political philosophers Michael Hardt and Antonio Negri believe that democracy of the multitude is possible because we share the "common" or "commonwealth" (Hardt and Negri 2009, 178). The common includes the material world of nature as well as the social production of knowledge, language, codes, and information. Like Superflex, Hardt and Negri assert that although globalization and capital can be destructive, these economic tools also can be harnessed for the common good.

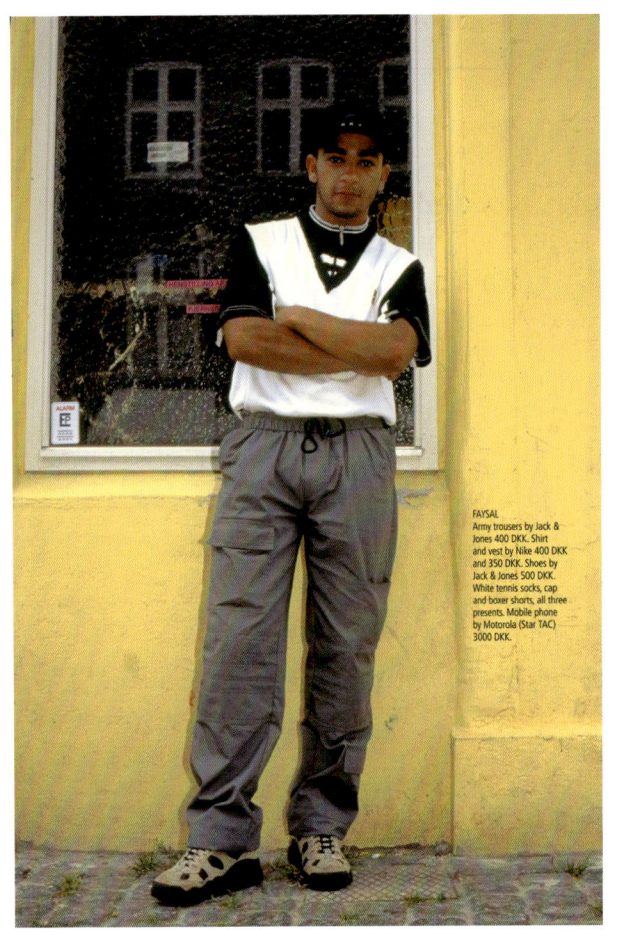

FAYSAL
Army trousers by Jack &
Jones 400 DKK. Shirt
and vest by Nike 400 DKK
and 350 DKK. Shoes by
Jack & Jones 500 DKK.
White tennis socks, cap
and boxer shorts, all three
presents. Mobile phone
by Motorola (Star TAC)
3000 DKK.

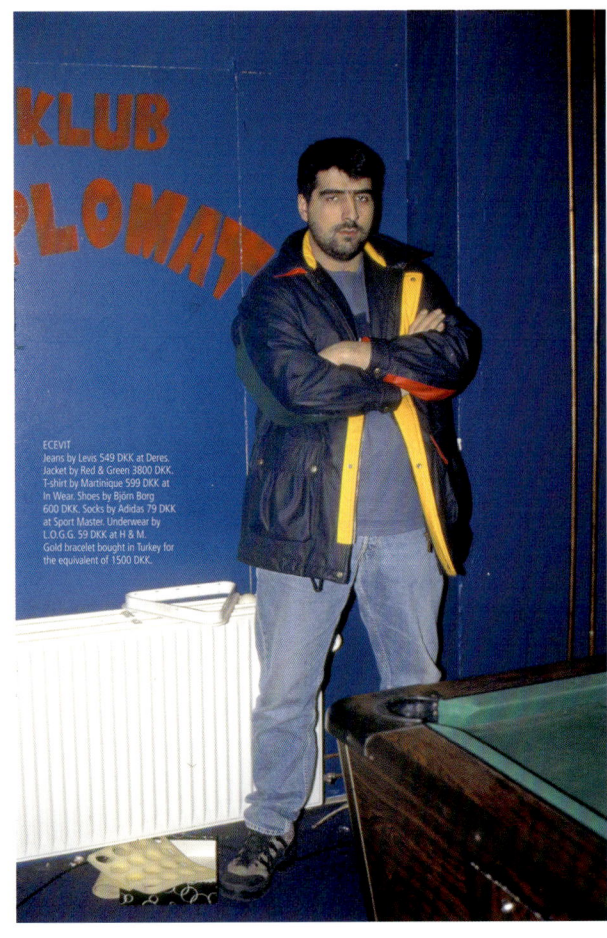

ECEVIT
Jeans by Levis 549 DKK at Deres.
Jacket by Red & Green 3800 DKK.
T-shirt by Martinique 599 DKK at
In Wear. Shoes by Björn Borg
600 DKK. Socks by Adidas 79 DKK
at Sport Master. Underwear by
L.O.G.G. 59 DKK at H & M.
Gold bracelet bought in Turkey for
the equivalent of 1500 DKK.

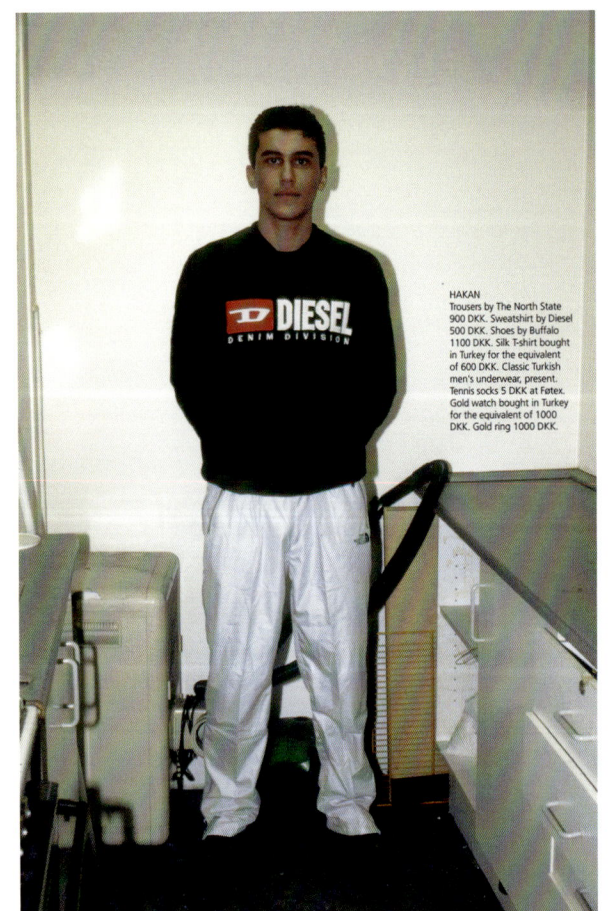

HAKAN
Trousers by The North State
900 DKK. Sweatshirt by Diesel
500 DKK. Shoes by Buffalo
1100 DKK. Silk T-shirt bought
in Turkey for the equivalent
of 600 DKK. Classic Turkish
men's underwear, present.
Tennis socks 5 DKK at Føtex.
Gold watch bought in Turkey
for the equivalent of 1000
DKK. Gold ring 1000 DKK.

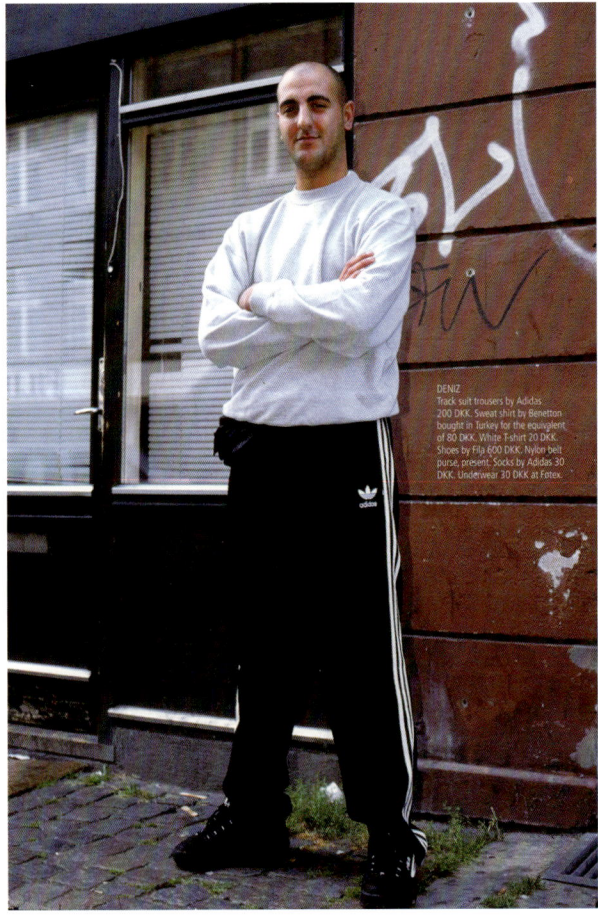

DENIZ
Track suit trousers by Adidas
200 DKK. Sweat shirt by Benetton
bought in Turkey for the equivalent
of 80 DKK. White T-shirt 20 DKK.
Shoes by Fila 600 DKK. Nylon belt
purse, present. Socks by Adidas 30
DKK. Underwear 30 DKK at Føtex.

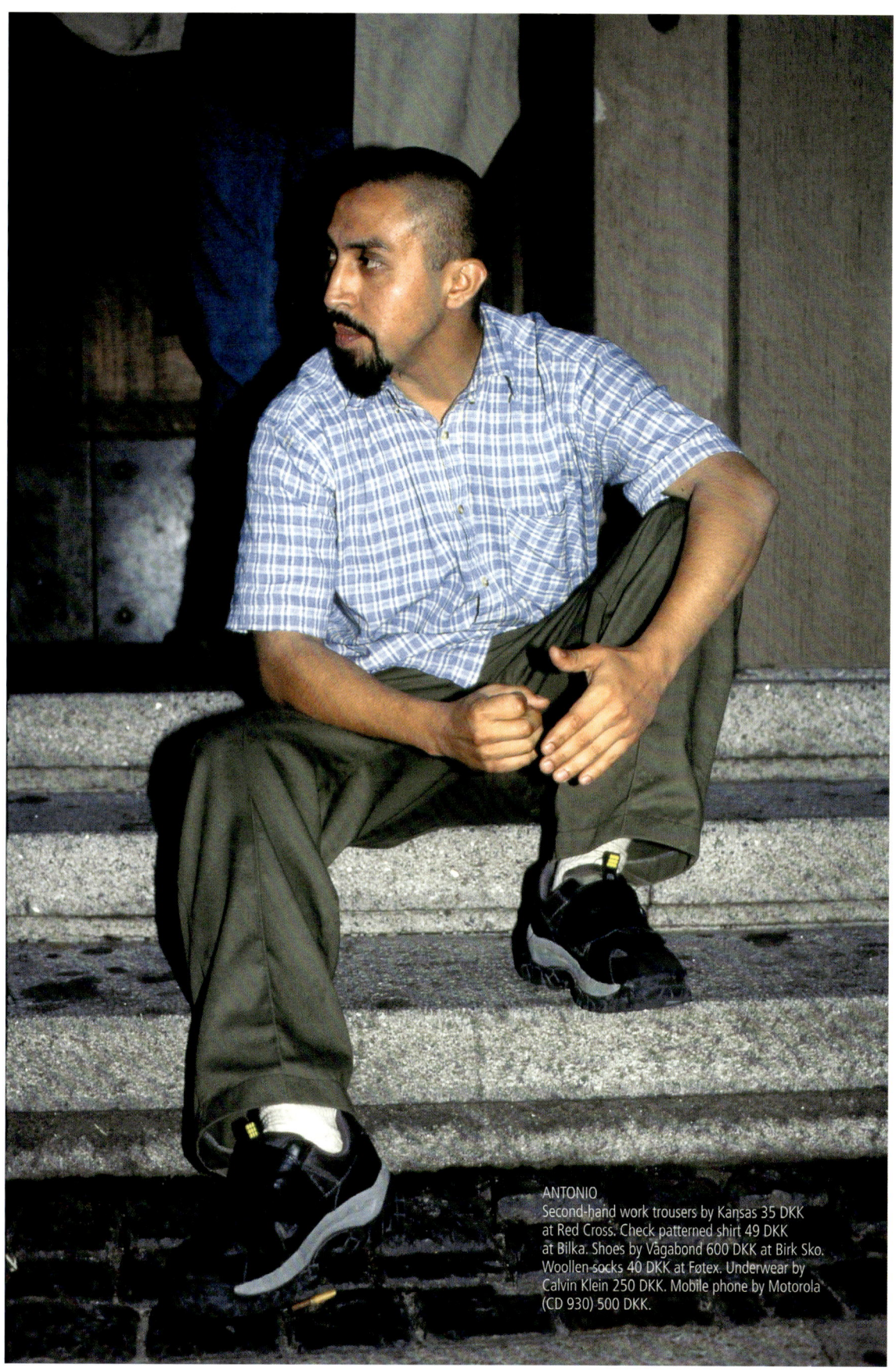

ANTONIO
Second-hand work trousers by Kansas 35 DKK
at Red Cross. Check patterned shirt 49 DKK
at Bilka. Shoes by Vagabond 600 DKK at Birk Sko.
Woollen socks 40 DKK at Føtex. Underwear by
Calvin Klein 250 DKK. Mobile phone by Motorola
(CD 930) 500 DKK.

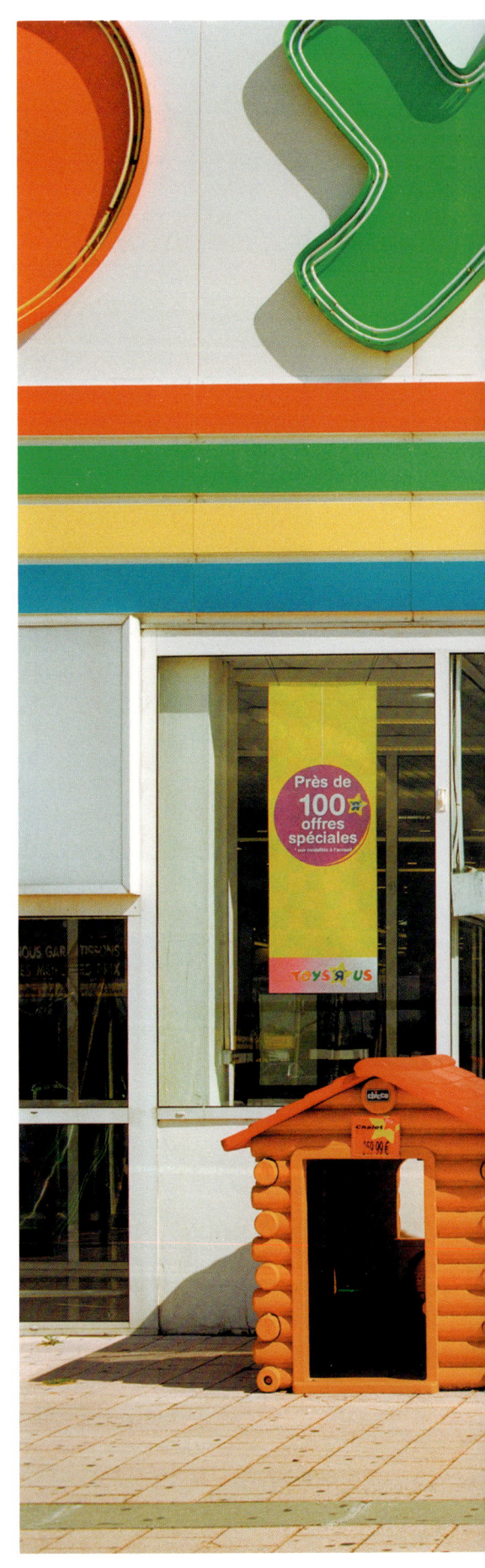

ANDREA ROBBINS AND MAX BECHER

American, b. 1963, and German, b. 1964
Toys 'Я' Us, America in France: Strip Malls of Toulouse
2003
Chromogenic print
30 x 34.75 in. (76.2 x 88.3 cm)
Courtesy of Sonnabend Gallery and the artists

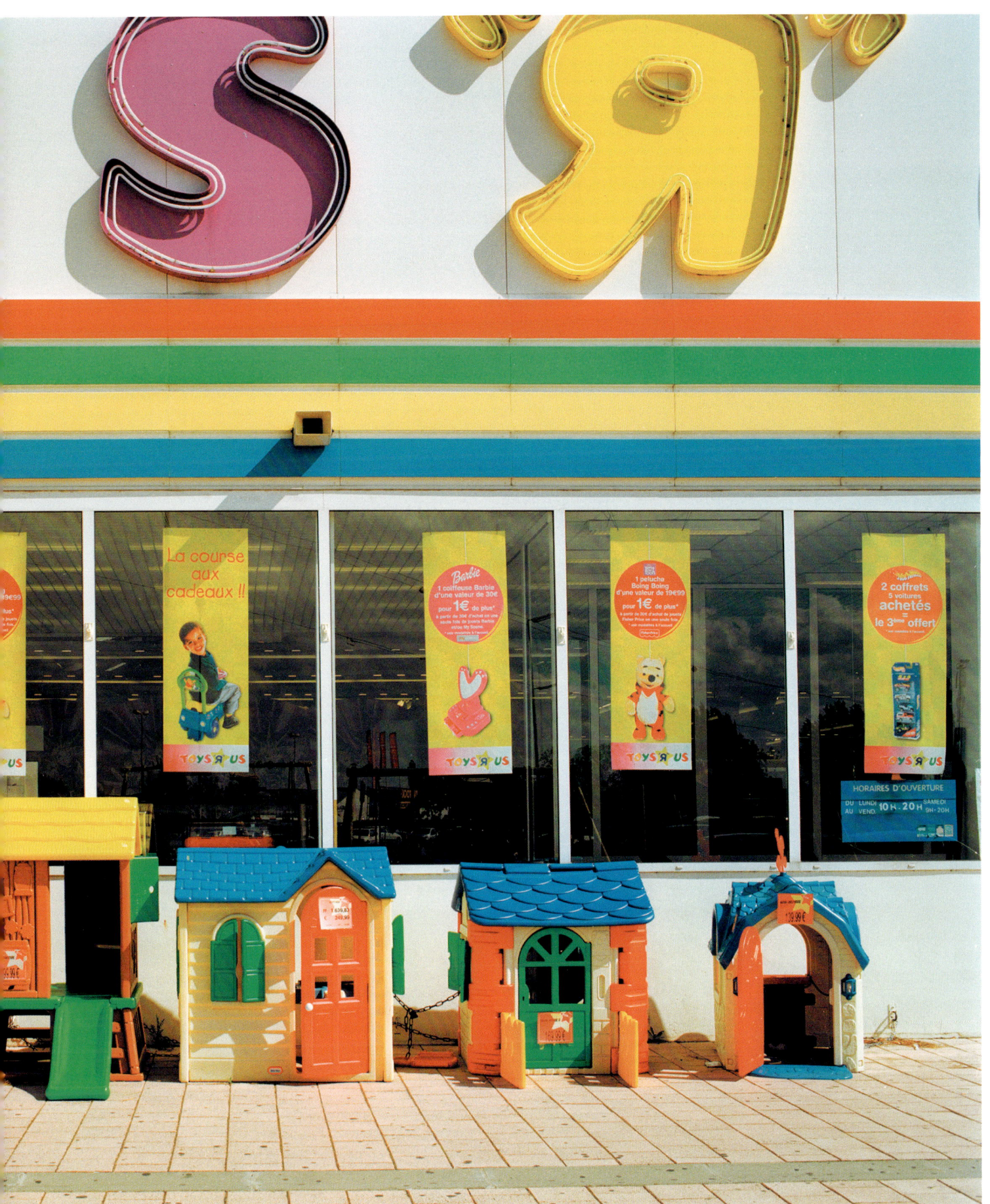

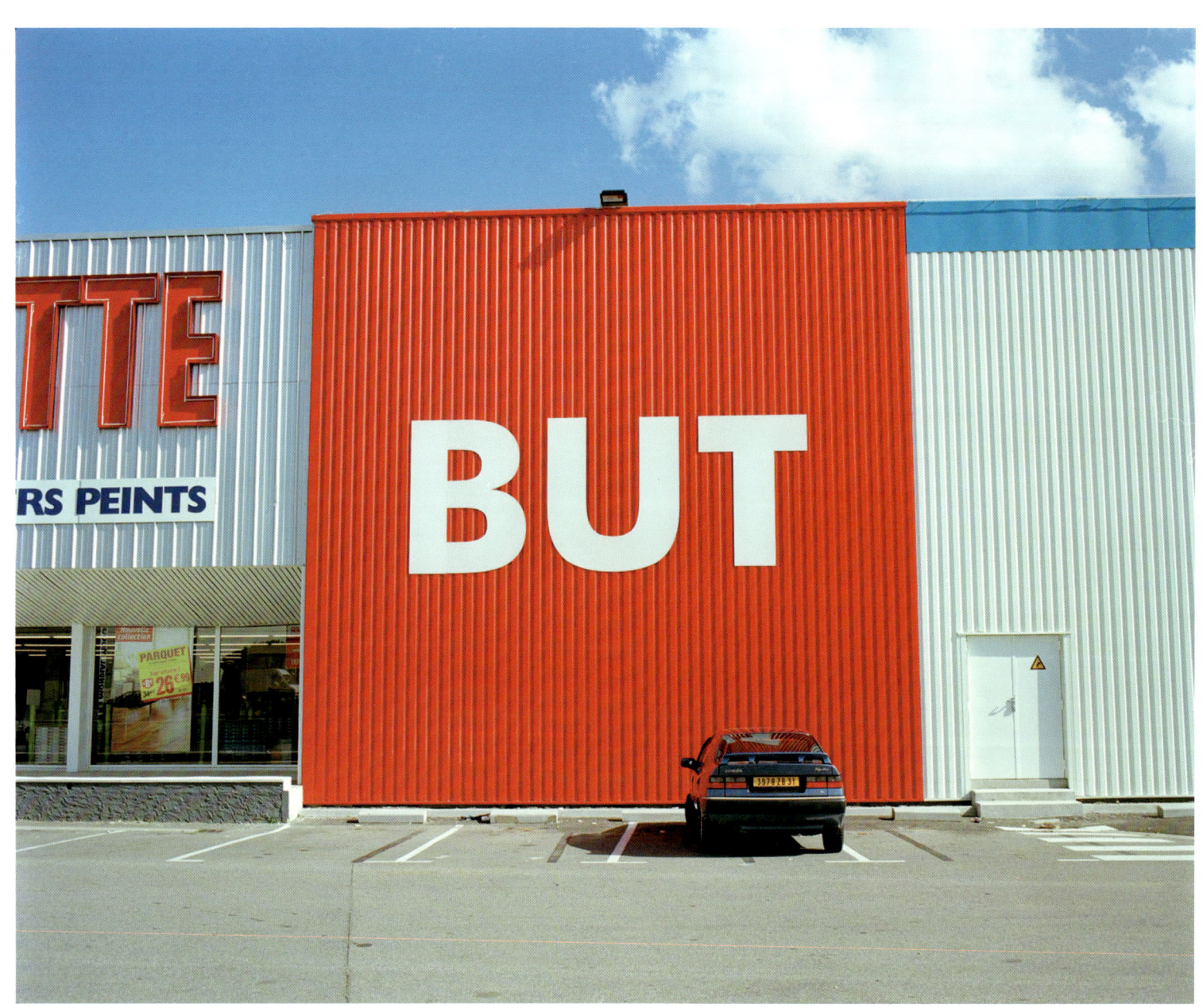

ANDREA ROBBINS AND MAX BECHER

American, b. 1963, and German, b. 1964
BUT, America in France: Strip Malls of Toulouse
2003
Chromogenic print
30 x 34.75 in. (76.2 x 88.3 cm)
Courtesy of Sonnabend Gallery and the artists

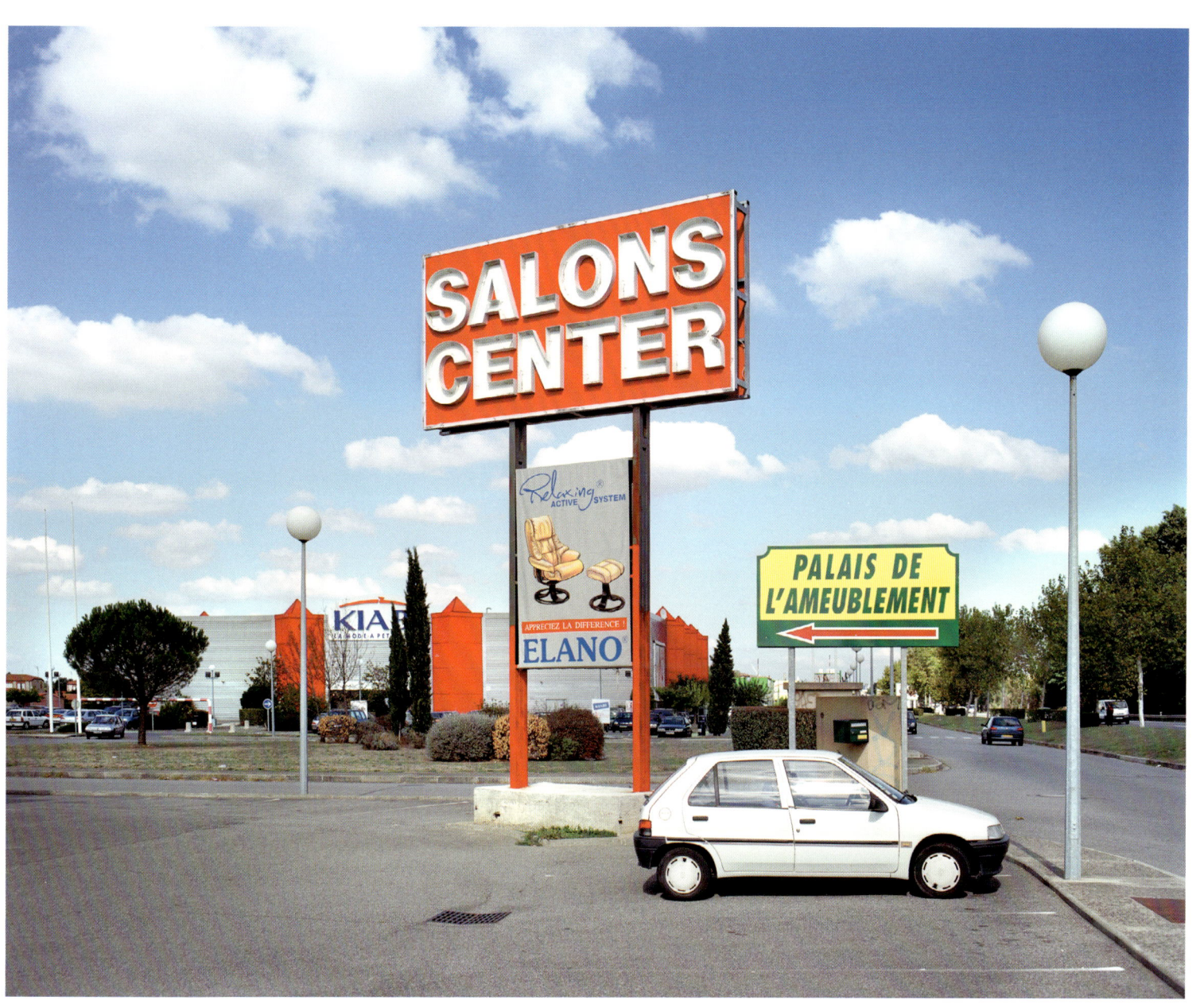

ANDREA ROBBINS AND MAX BECHER

American, b. 1963, and German, b. 1964
Salon Center, America in France: Strip Malls of Toulouse
2003
Chromogenic print
30 x 34.75 in. (76.2 x 88.3 cm)
Courtesy of Sonnabend Gallery and the artists

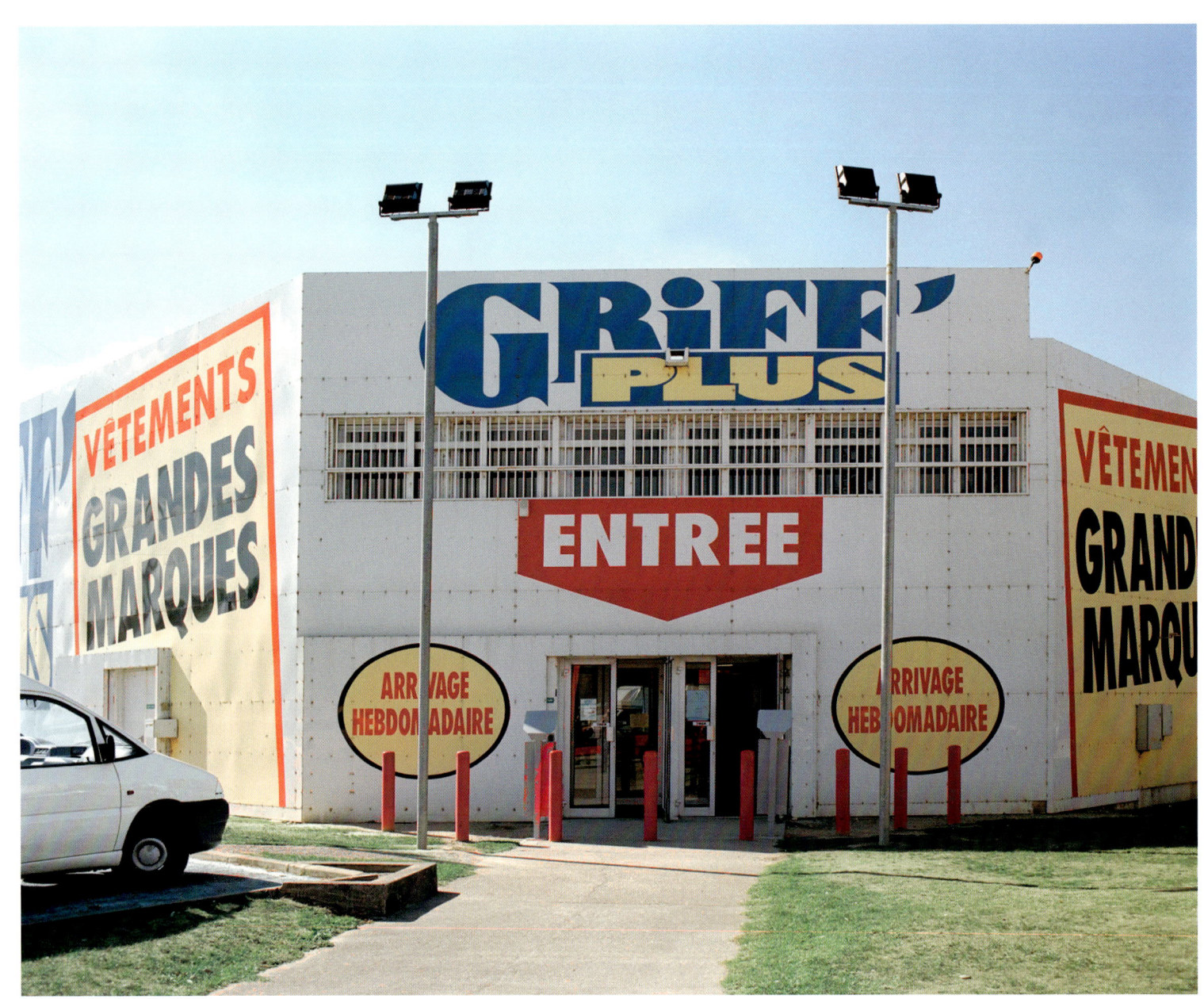

ANDREA ROBBINS AND MAX BECHER

American, b. 1963, and German, b. 1964
Griff Plus, America in France: Strip Malls of Toulouse
2003
Chromogenic print
30 x 34.75 in. (76.2 x 88.3 cm)
Courtesy of Sonnabend Gallery and the artists

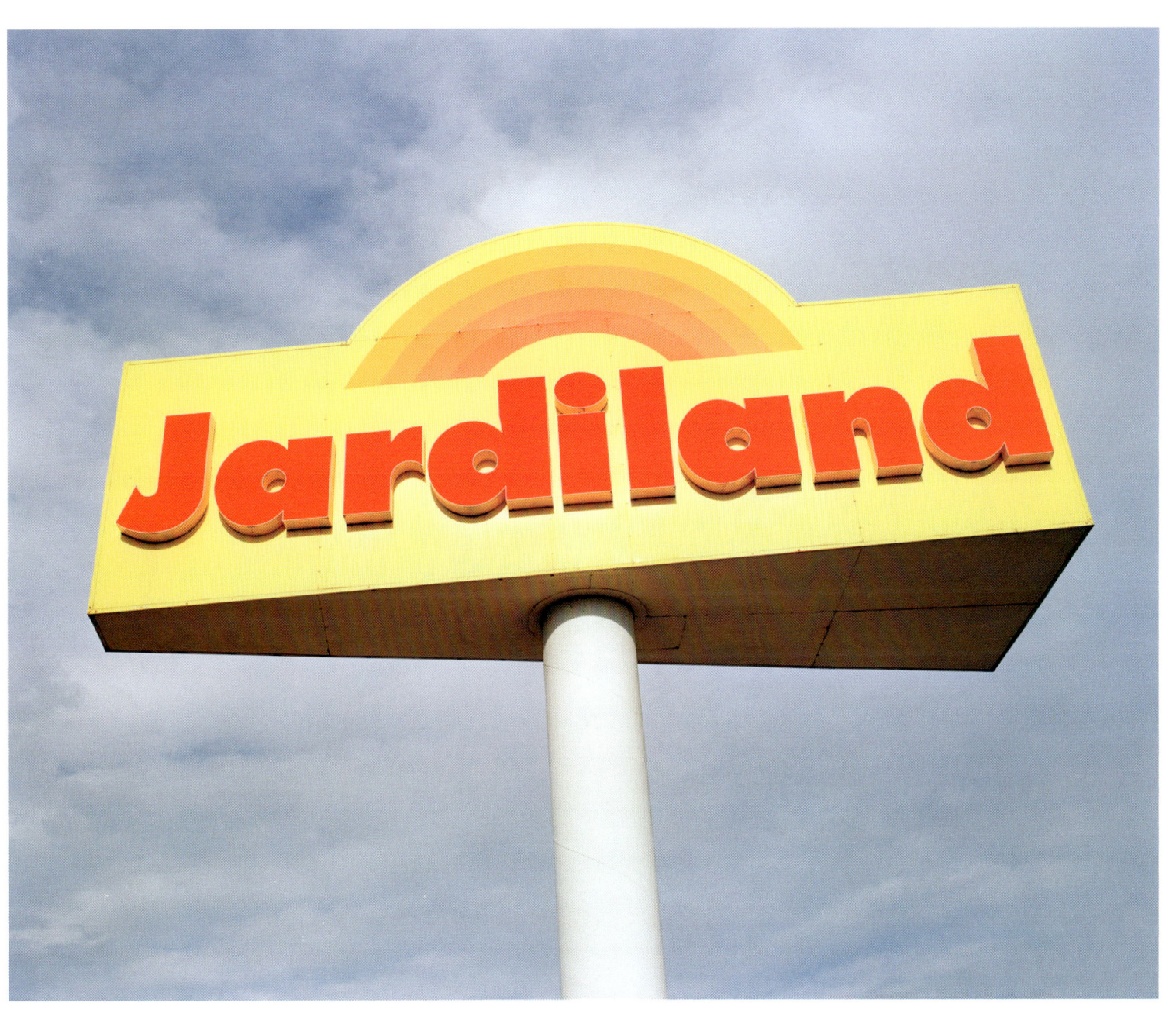

ANDREA ROBBINS AND MAX BECHER

American, b. 1963, and German, b. 1964
Jardiland, America in France: Strip Malls of Toulouse
2003
Chromogenic print
30 x 34.75 in. (76.2 x 88.3 cm)
Courtesy of Sonnabend Gallery and the artists

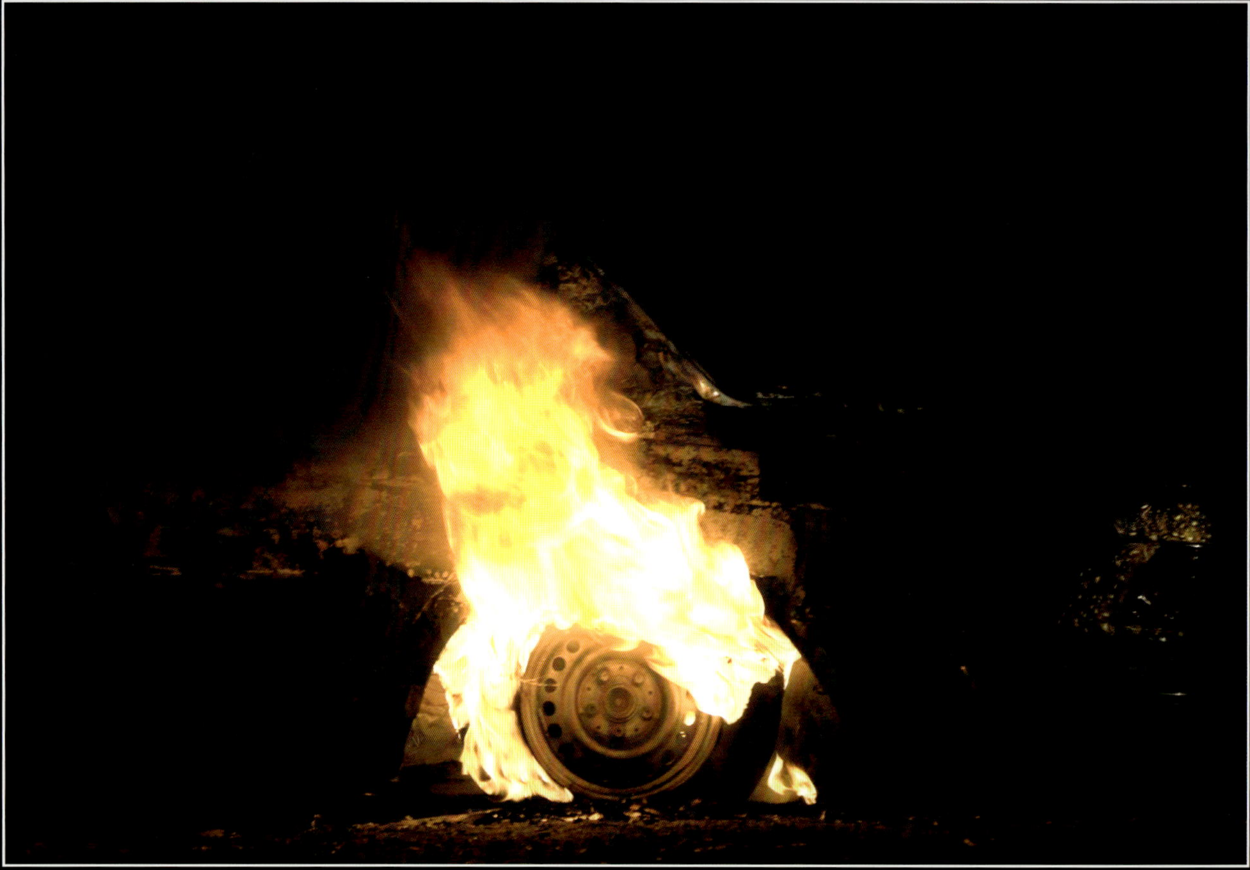

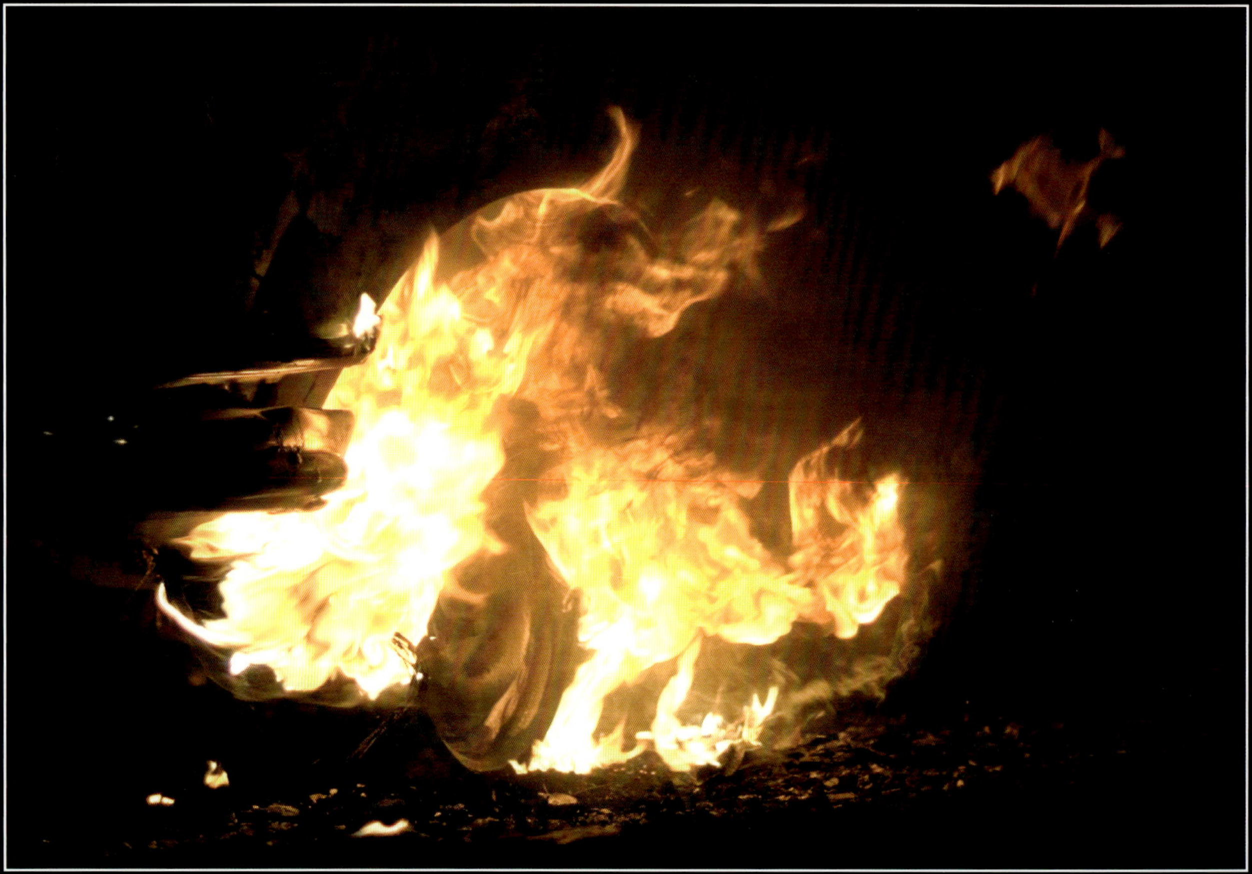

SUPERFLEX

Jakob Fenger, Bjørnstjerne
Reuter Christiansen, and
Rasmus Nielsen
Danish
Burning Car
2008
Blu-ray projection, 11 minutes
Produced by Propeller Group
(Ho Chi Minh City) and co-
produced by the Vleeshal,
Middelburg, Netherlands
Dimensions variable
Courtesy of the artists and
Nils Staerk, Copenhagen

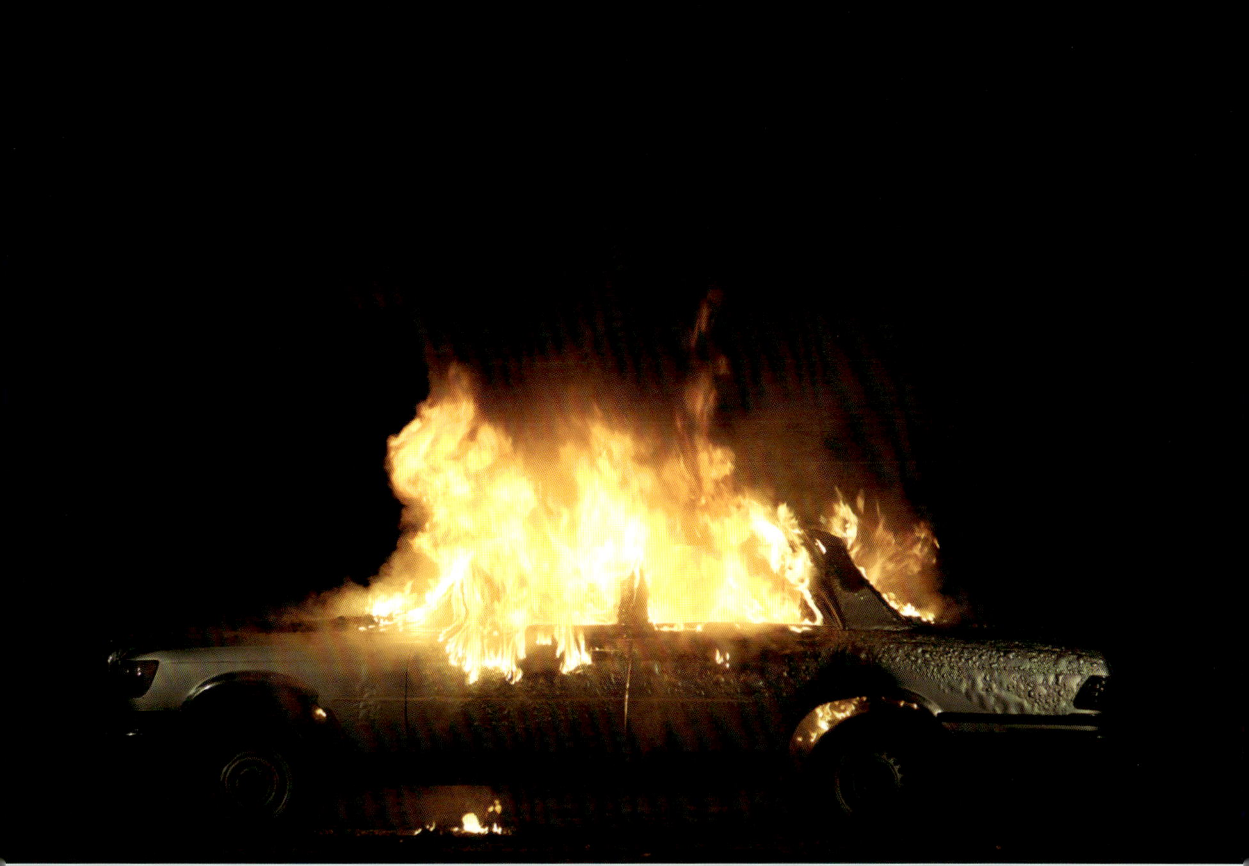

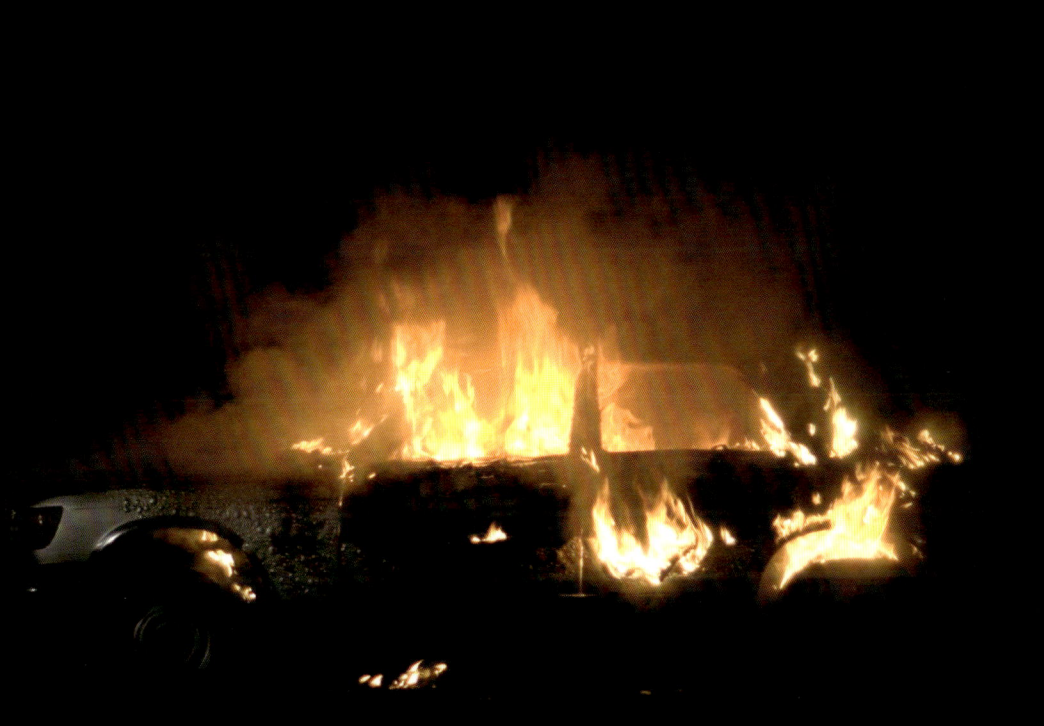

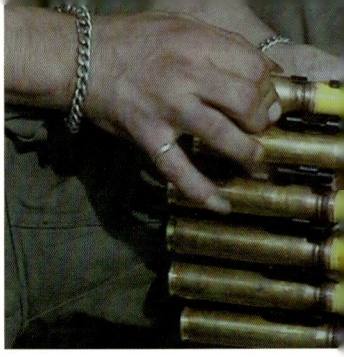

Europe's "frontier wars" create institutional segregation and blur the distinction between police control and military operations. Civil wars have also proliferated worldwide, particularly in the Balkan region. These conflicts obscure the difference between stranger and enemy (Balibar 2006, 8). Two artists, Maja Bajevic and Aernout Mik, look back to the Balkan wars as a way to understand the present and foresee the future. Civil war erupted in 1990; the war that ensued in Bosnia was considered the most brutal stage of the Yugoslavian disintegration. Campaigns of "ethnic cleansing," the siege of Sarajevo, the displacement of millions, human rights abuses, and systematic rape horrified the world. Bitter controversies over media manipulation and lack of European intervention erupted. The Bosnian conflict resulted in "the forceful separation of mixed populations and cultures and the terrorization of groups who refuse to bow down to ethnic and religious fundamentalism . . . " (Kaldor, in Balibar 2008, 378).

Bosnian artist Maja Bajevic confronts the hypocrisy, brutality, and politicization of religion in her film *Double Bubble*. As the single performer in the film, she stages herself in a variety of distinct architectural settings, primarily thresholds, doorways, windows, and stairwells. Architectural angles and details combine with the use of silhouette, angular lighting, and shadows to emphasize the uniqueness and performative setting of each site. For each station of her film, she takes on a different male character. The sequences recall the shape of religious medieval theater. At each stop, she makes declarative and contradictory statements from different religious perspectives, such as, "I free people from sins. They give me money"; "I do not drink during Ramadan, but I take ecstasy"; and "I have shot fifty-five people during prayer—in the name of God." The flat inflection of Bajevic's voice contrasts with the brutality of the messages, suggesting the banality of these acts for the perpetrators. Her gender provides a critical distance.

Bajevic's messages reflect what she calls the new forms of religion—"techno" religion, which is personalized, and "turbo" religion, which is based on nationalism, hatred, and exclusion. Her statements reflect the distortion of religious teachings to accommodate acts of aggression and violence (Bajevic 2008, 57). The echo of her words lends a sense of duration and endless repetition in a closed "bubble," cultural system, or hierarchical regime. Using the word "I" underscores the individuality usually denied under a fundamentalist regime; it also brings forth the subjectivity of the perpetrator, the absence of the victim,

[pages 89, 91]

MAJA BAJEVIC

Bosnian, b. 1967
Double Bubble
2001
DVD projection, 3 minutes 36 seconds
Dimensions variable
Courtesy of the artist and Galerie Peter Kilchmann,
Zurich

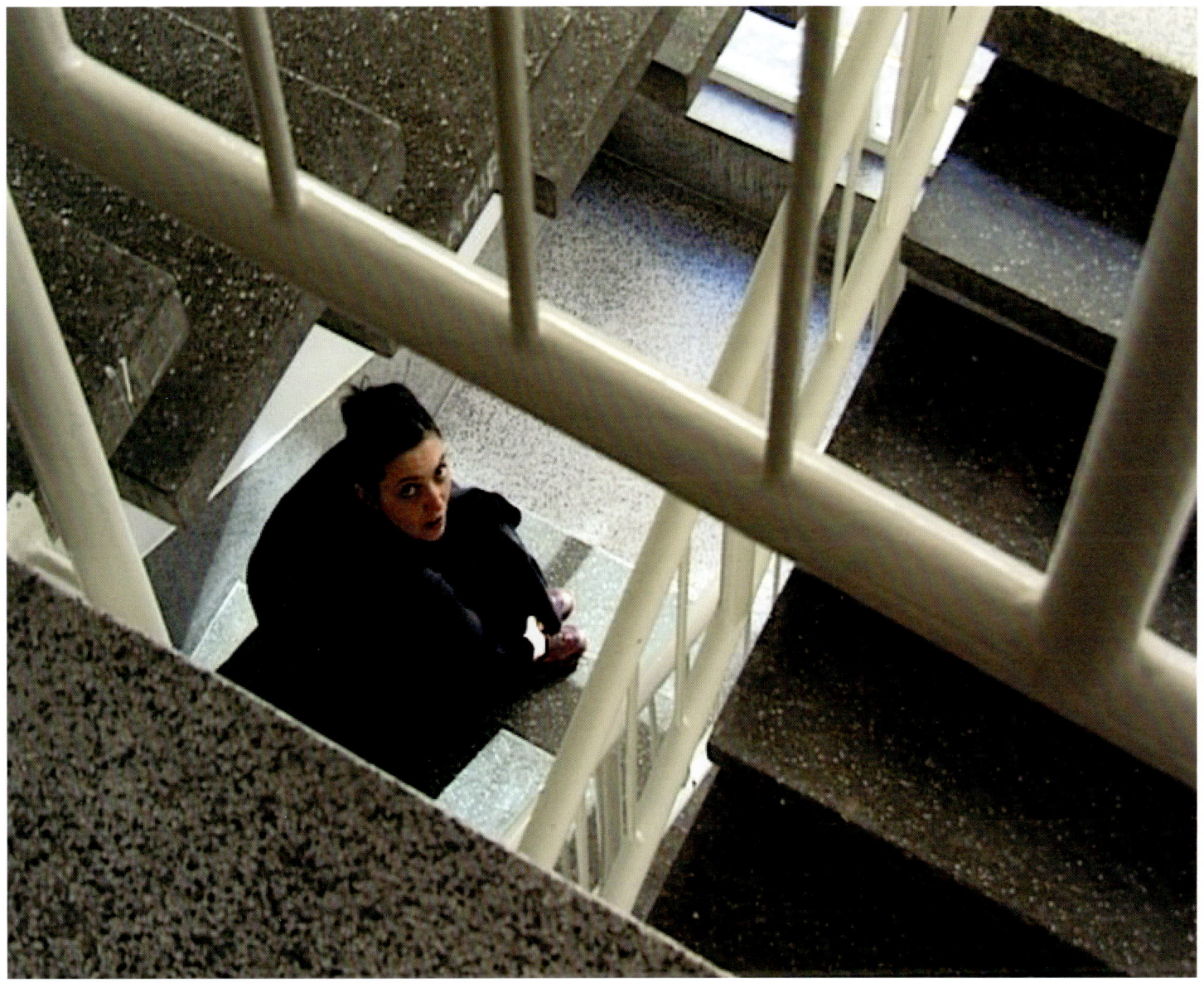

and the presence of the performer—and the witness or viewer who questions the position of each. Effective and precise, Bajevic's work refracts the harsh consequences of religious absolutism and fundamentalism in Bosnia.

In *Raw Footage*, Aernout Mik examines the effect of war as part of daily life. The film, carefully constructed from the archives of Reuters and Independent Television News (ITN), represents film footage from the television news coverage of the Yugoslavian war that was considered insufficiently dramatic for broadcast. Mik's film is projected onto two floating screens, where it interacts with the viewer's physical space as a form of sculpture. From the start, the film disrupts any conventional or passive relationship to the media; instead, the work demands the active looking and participation of the viewer. Mik alters our way of seeing and thinking.

Different from the dramatic spectacle covered by television film crews, *Raw Footage* shows interludes between fighting, waiting and waging intermittent battle. Soldiers filter through the countryside, streets, and parks. Tanks and snipers in the city form a backdrop for shopping, gathering at the local café, and jogging through the streets. Female soldiers walk by in black attire, their hair, makeup, and jewelry in place. Children carry real and toy guns. Bombarded buildings go up in smoke as neighbors pass in the street. It is not clear who is friend and who is foe, who is Bosnian, Croat, or Serb. Perpetrator and victim are indistinguishable. Nevertheless, the consequences of war are relentless and deadly.

Aernout Mik's film is an antidote to the numbing spectacle and stereotypes fashioned by the media, the "shock and awe" of conflict. Bizarre and surreal, the film captures a reality that escapes our view—what is not broadcast by the media industry. Mik exposes a normalizing of war and an adaptation to constant fear. It is the condition of fear that is repeatedly projected onto the other in the form of violence.

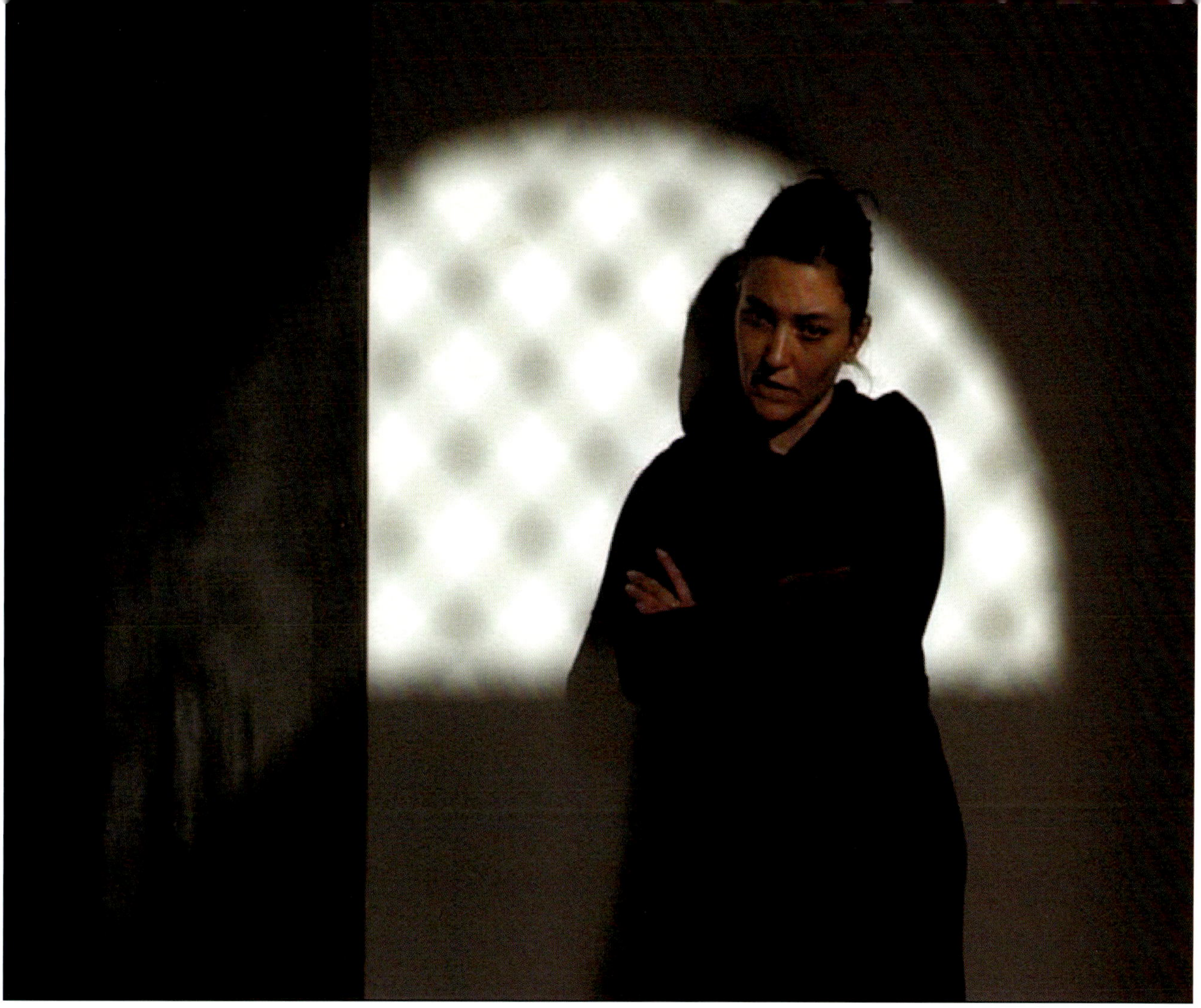

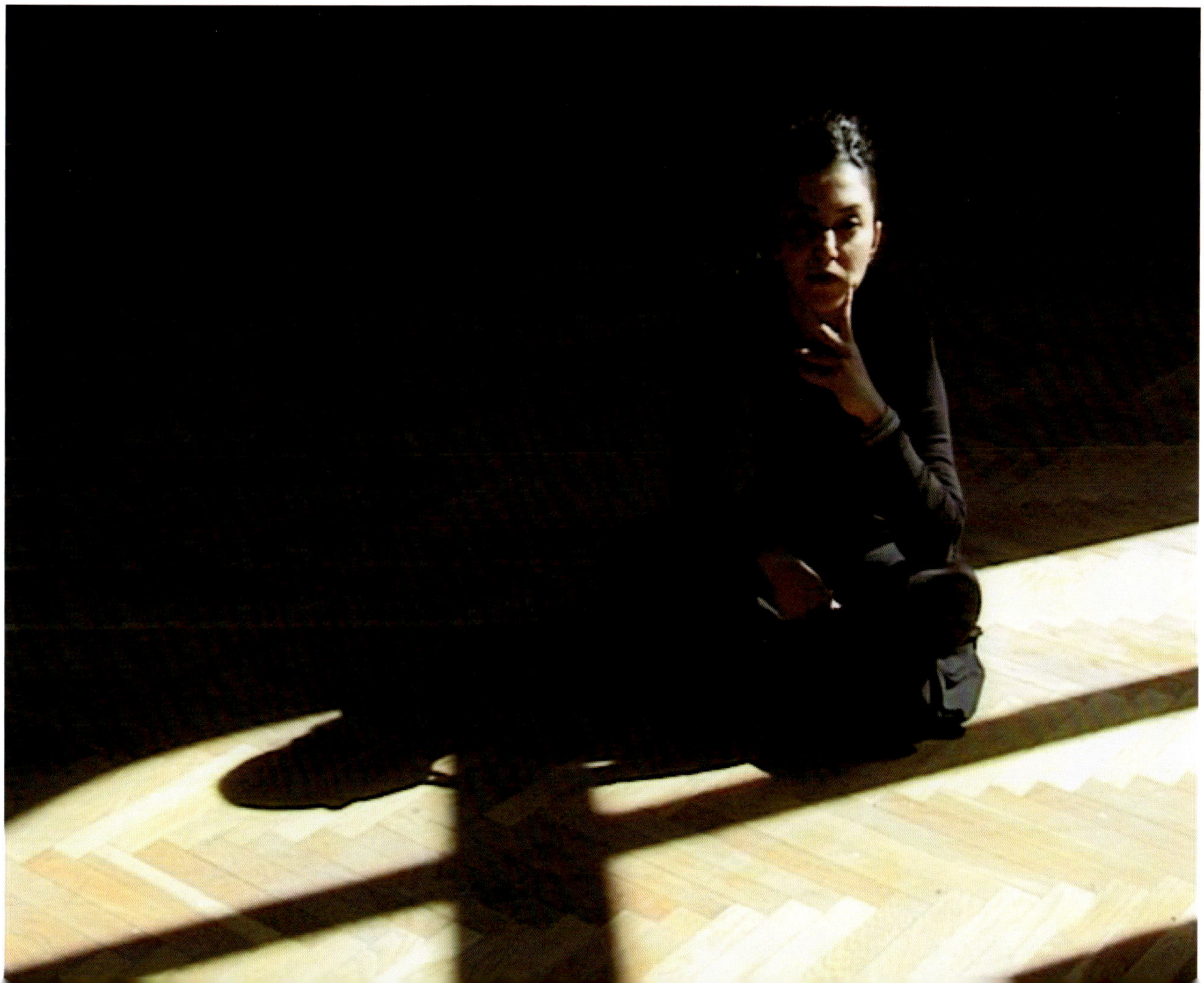

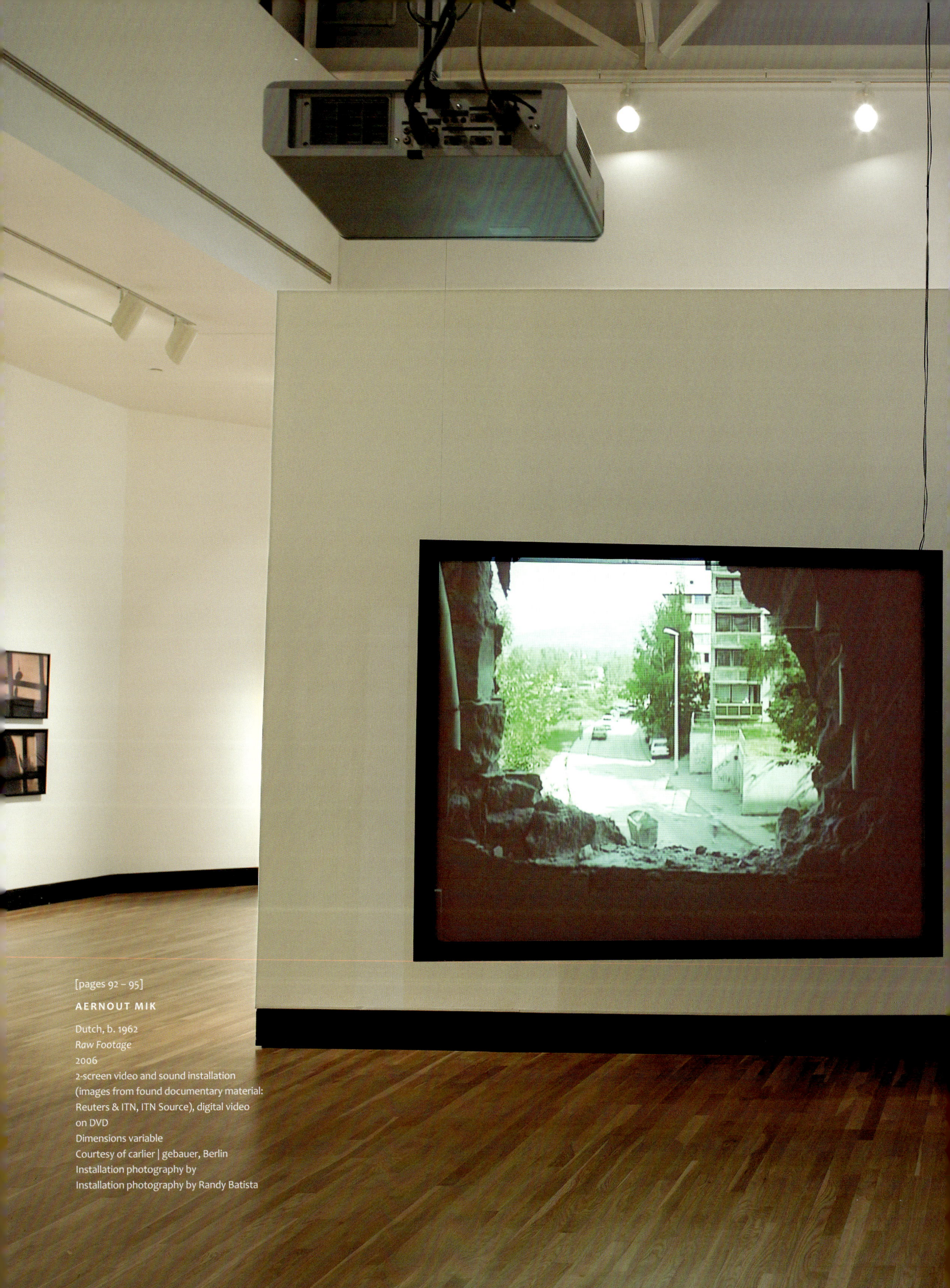

[pages 92 – 95]

AERNOUT MIK

Dutch, b. 1962
Raw Footage
2006
2-screen video and sound installation
(images from found documentary material:
Reuters & ITN, ITN Source), digital video
on DVD
Dimensions variable
Courtesy of carlier | gebauer, Berlin
Installation photography by
Installation photography by Randy Batista

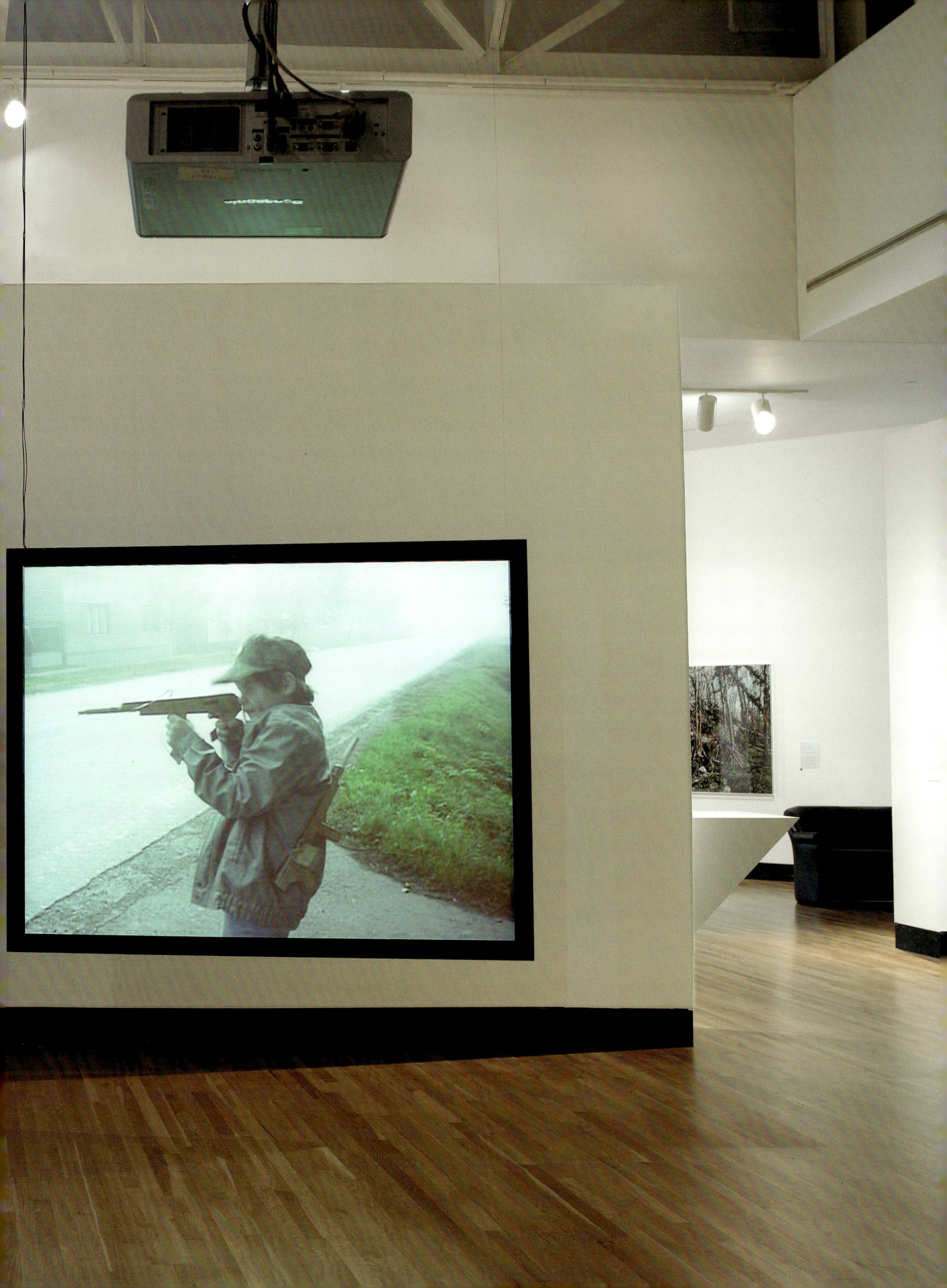

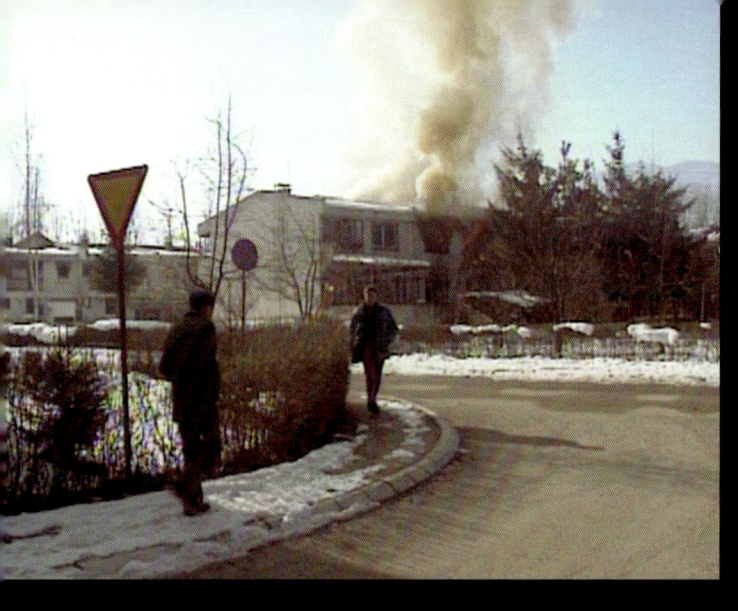
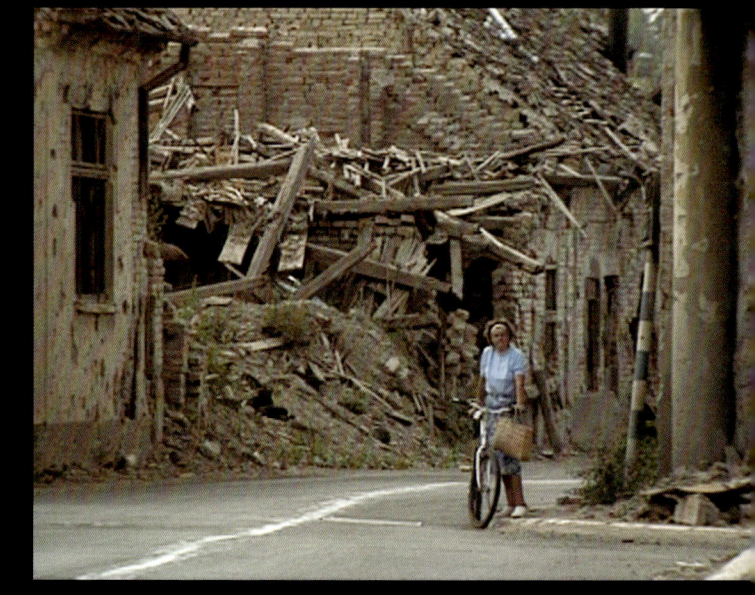
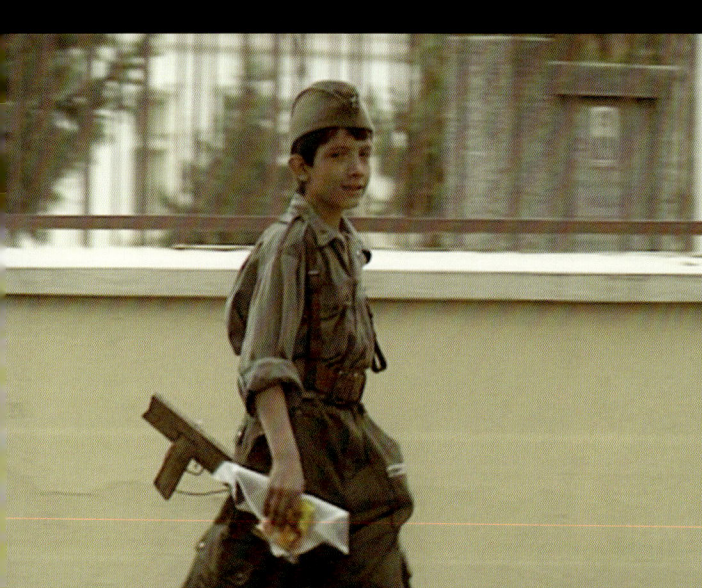
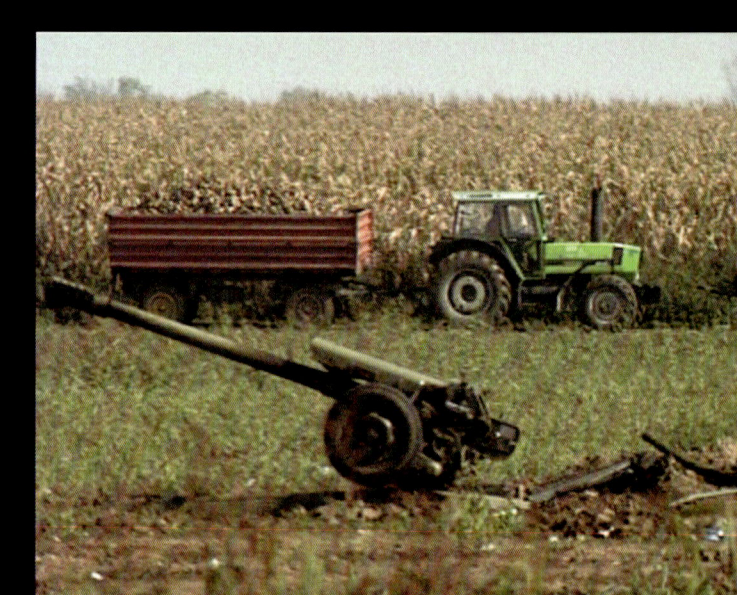

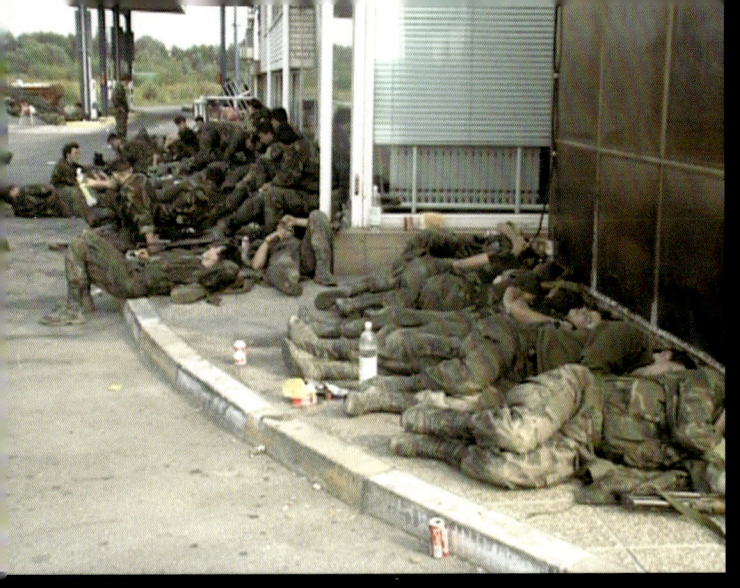
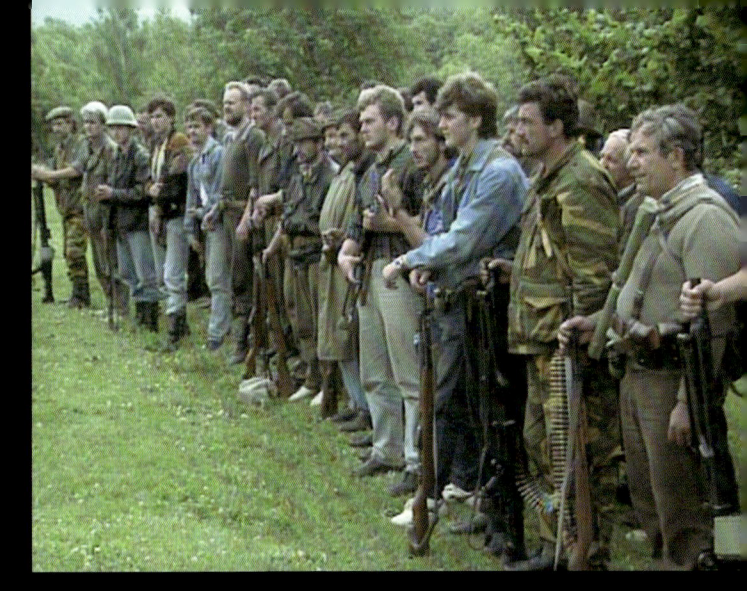
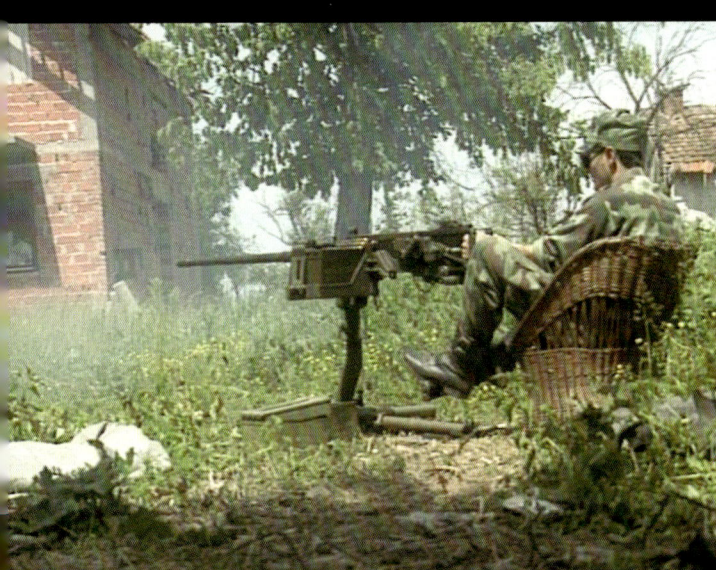
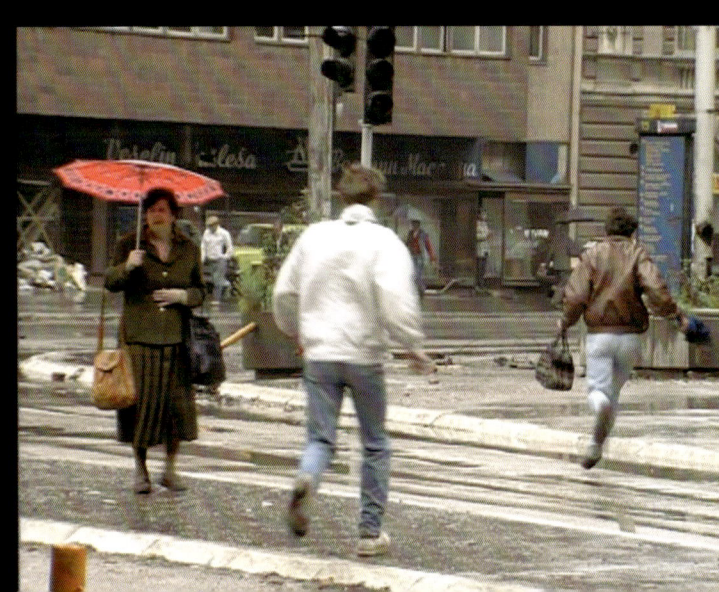

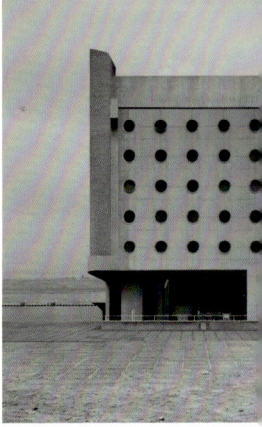

Evidenced by their work throughout the exhibition, artists have considered the impossible, the aporias that impede the workings of democracy. They have also found the possible within the impossible by expanding modes of perception and thought. Two artists, Beate Gütschow and Marjetica Potrč, look at the future from opposing perspectives of possibility. German artist Beate Gütschow presents a postapocalyptic vision of a world that suggests totalitarian rule. Her two black-and-white photographs in the exhibition are part of her S series. The letter stands for "*stadt*," the German word for city. In both cityscapes, monolithic buildings reveal an uncanny mix of modernist innovation, Soviet brutalist architecture, and corporate design. Evidence of life is spare. Gütschow's buildings reflect the failure of modernism and of twentieth-century utopian ideals. They also warn of a future characterized by displacement, conflict, and fear.

Gütschow's building in the photograph *S#31* stands alone in a stark setting. The exposed concrete and geometric relationships seem inspired in part by the designs of Le Corbusier. Institutional and forbidding, there are no windows to the outside world. Except for an adjacent and dead tree, the surrounding expanse is vast, bleak, and empty. This is a no-man's-land that seems to exist outside of place and time. Claudia Aradau notes how economy and security policies claim the urgent imperative of necessity overwhelming such other concerns as individual agency and democratic engagement (Aradau 2006, 6). In Gütschow's vision, it appears that necessity for security has eliminated most of nature and communal space. In *S#1(M)*, the viewer sees the remains of a helicopter that has crashed incongruously within a wedge of massive, corporate-style buildings, suggesting a recently aborted military operation. A few people in the distance appear to be retreating in fear to shelter. Her image suggests a perpetual state of war invading private and public space.

Gütschow's work seems to reflect our surface reality, but a closer inspection reveals it to be fiction. She exploits this tension between fact and fiction as she constructs her own version of reality: "It is a question of inclusion and exclusion—of what is visible and what exists but nevertheless remains invisible to us" (Gütschow 2007). Her black-and-white images deliberately refer to documentary photography of the 1950s and '60s, and are influenced by such artists as Lewis Baltz and Bernd and Hilla Becher. The black-and-white images also lend a credible appearance to her work. Nevertheless, her cityscapes are collaged from hundreds of analog photographs taken on her worldwide travels. She then rebuilds the images through digital collage in Photoshop and darkroom techniques.

In a very different vein, Marjetica Potrč focuses on new promises and possibilities for European communities, using architecture as a form of research and practice in her socially engaged art. Responding to areas of crisis and change around the world, she investigates and proposes possible solutions for urban problems. Potrč is keenly interested in the western Balkan area and sees it as a template for the future of the European Union. This idea is explored in her wall painting and installation *The Future Is Now*. As an alternative to the unilateral domination of global capitalism, grand utopian schemes, and religious fundamentalism, she advocates the growth of distinct communities based on a small-scale and local context. Potrč noted the shrinking of cities and the huge shift in population, borders, and territories after the war in Yugoslavia. It was then that she recognized the positive formation of smaller territories that cluster around diverse communities.

Potrč's drawing refers to a legacy of modernism and modern architecture founded on the ideal of "equality and justice for all"; however, she considers that modernism has failed in many ways. For instance, modernism embraces large-scale residential communities that often compress as many as ten thousand residents into crowded and inhospitable high-rises often serving as vectors for poverty and crime. In contrast, new models of residential communities are formed by as few as ten families.

Modernism works from the top down, but local communities work from the bottom up and are characterized by fragmentation and adaptability. Potrč perceives that these families are interested in privacy, security, and locally based solutions, with a preference for small-scale growth. For her, hybrid identities, flexible hierarchies, plural exchange, and a decentered organization provide for a vital and vigorous environment.

In *Project Europa,* artists reflect on the impossible obstacles and the promising potential for democracy in Europe, considering both the condition of war and the possibility of establishing equality, exchange, and understanding. Increasingly, artists and scholars comment upon the escalating violence in Europe and throughout the world. Border and ethnic and civil wars emerge as the signs of persistent conflict. The events of 9/11 and the War on Terror have radically expanded the nature of war itself by taking the entire world as its theater. More and more, war is a perpetual dimension of the societies we live in, posing one of the greatest threats to democracy in Europe as well as the rest of the world.

At the same time, artists and scholars have proposed new ways of imagining Europe. For instance, Balibar sees an alternative guarded space of singular nations. He asserts that Europe has the potential of being a transnational space of equality and liberty, where everyone has the right of circulation and residence (Balibar 2006, 14). According to Rancière, it is possible for Europe to conduct politics based not on war or consensus but through dissensus, where everyone has the freedom to debate and fight for his or her part of society (Rancière 2003). Instead of participating in war, Europe could serve as the "Vanishing Mediator"—a force that mediates conflict and then withdraws without imposing its own control (Balibar 2004, 2003, 235).

Artists in the exhibition imagine both the impossible and possible conditions for democracy. By confronting aporias of Europe, they heighten the potential for equality and inclusion. From their individual perspectives, they engage in the realities and particulars of social and cultural upheaval. Consistently, they work against the uniform and sanctioned messages of mass media, using strategies that involve the viewer in critical and active looking. By modifying and reorienting the given political and aesthetic regime, they encourage new modes of perception and thought. Artists embrace new ways to confront the challenges of our time and give us reason to hope.

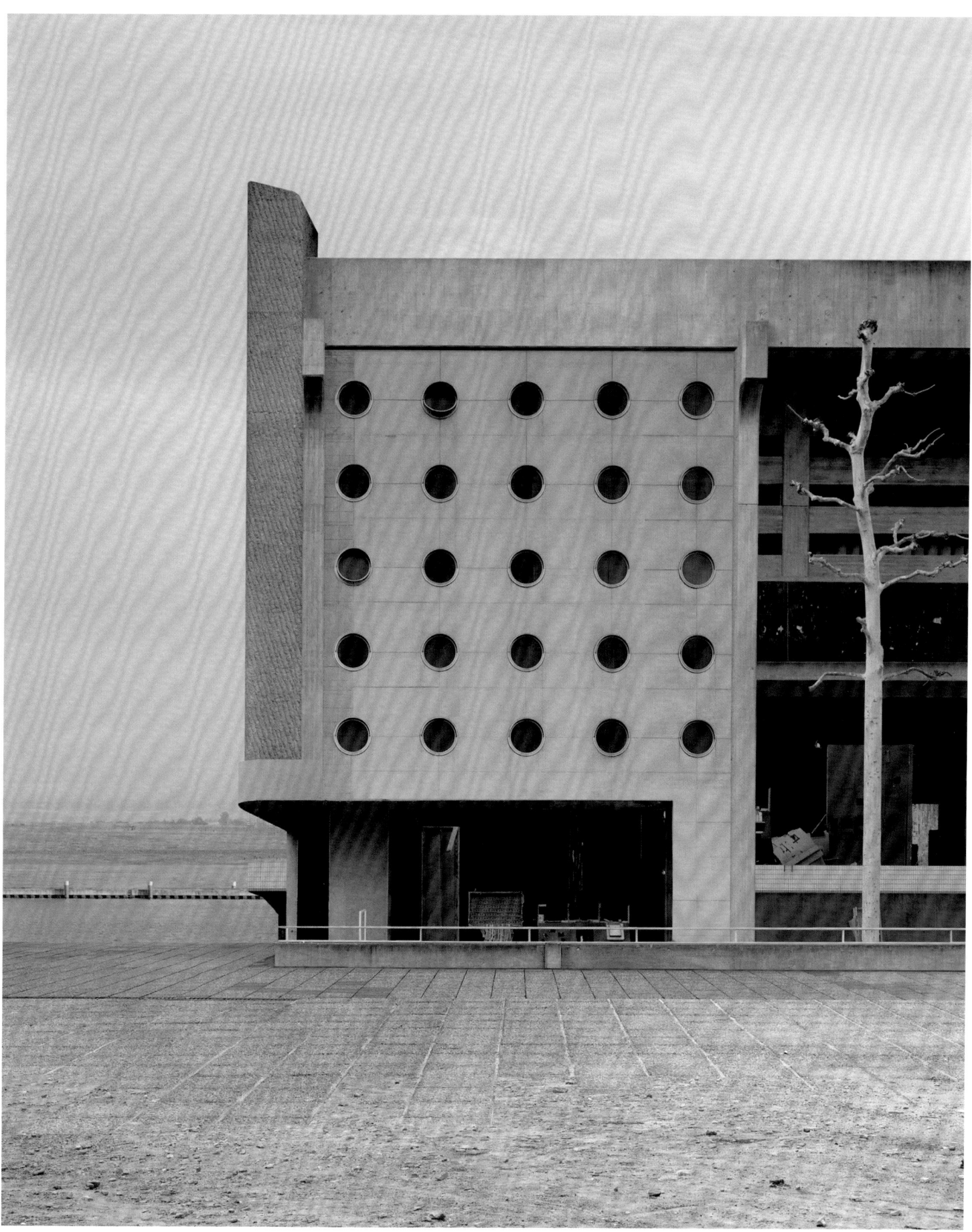

BEATE GÜTSCHOW

German, b. 1970
S#1(M)
2004
Lightjet print, mounted on aluminum Dibond
55.9 x 48 in. (142 x 122 cm)
©2010 Artists Rights Society (ARS), New York/VG
Bild-Kunst, Bonn
Courtesy of Beate Gütschow; Sonnabend Gallery,
New York; VG Bild-Kunst, Bonn

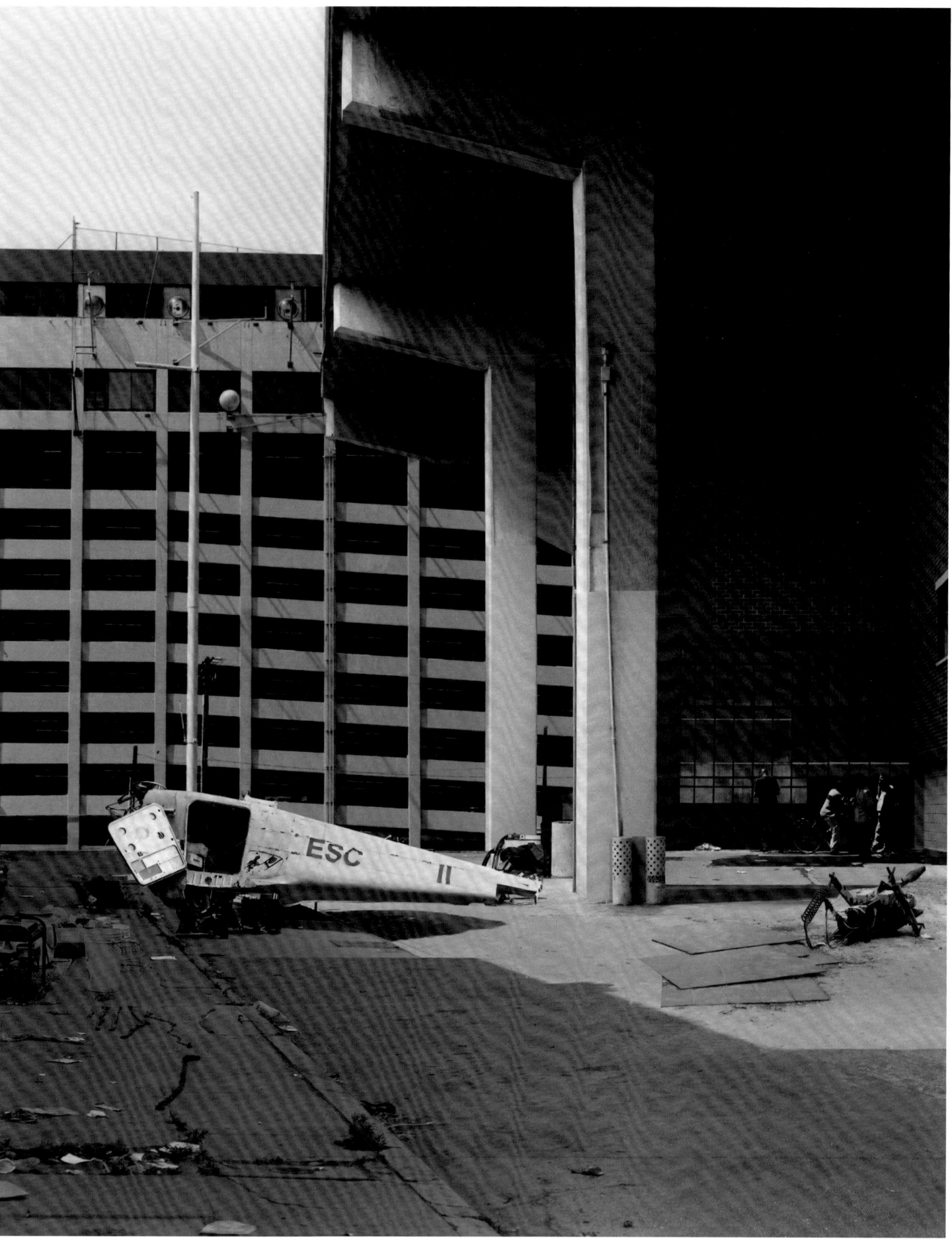

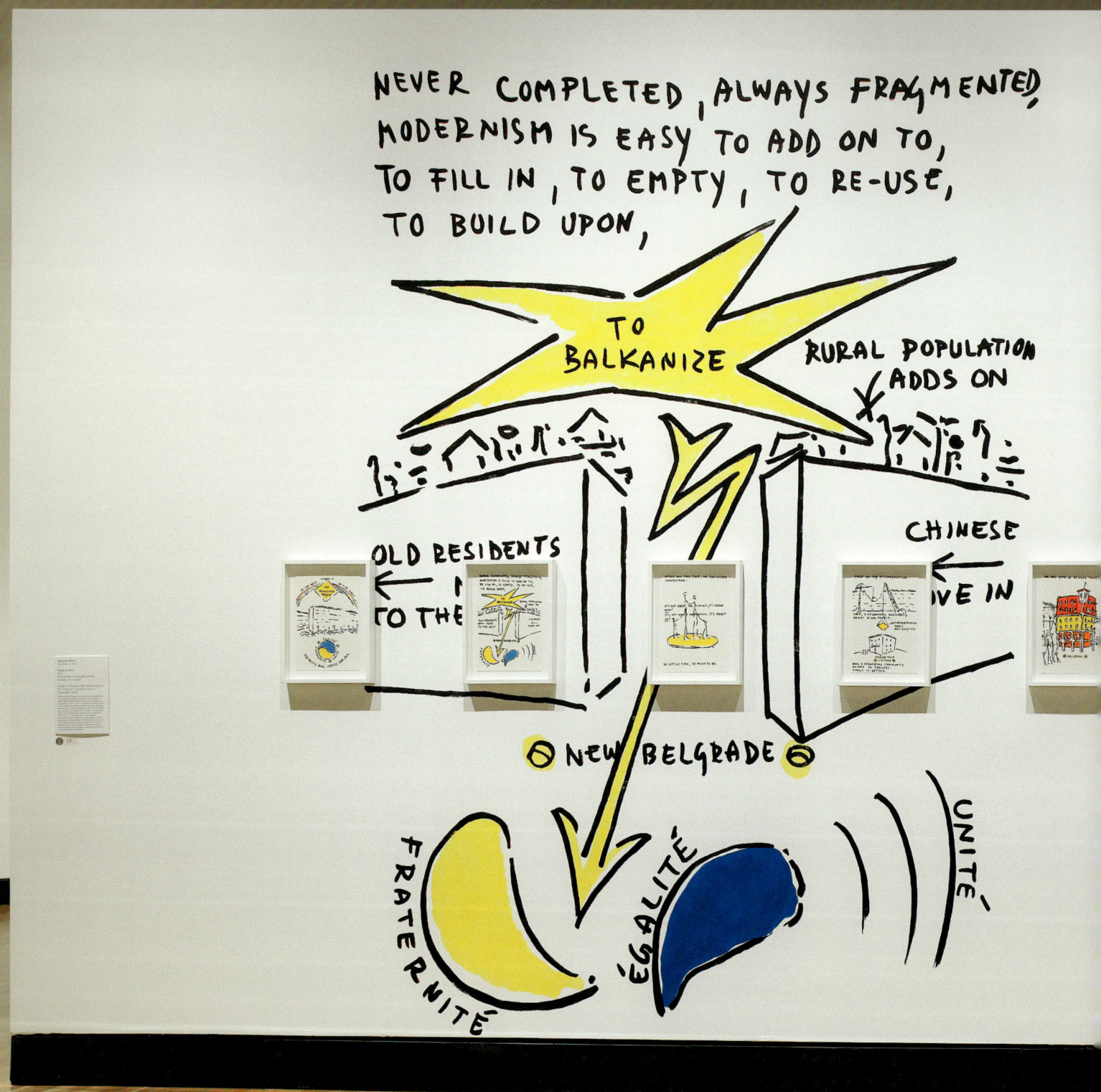

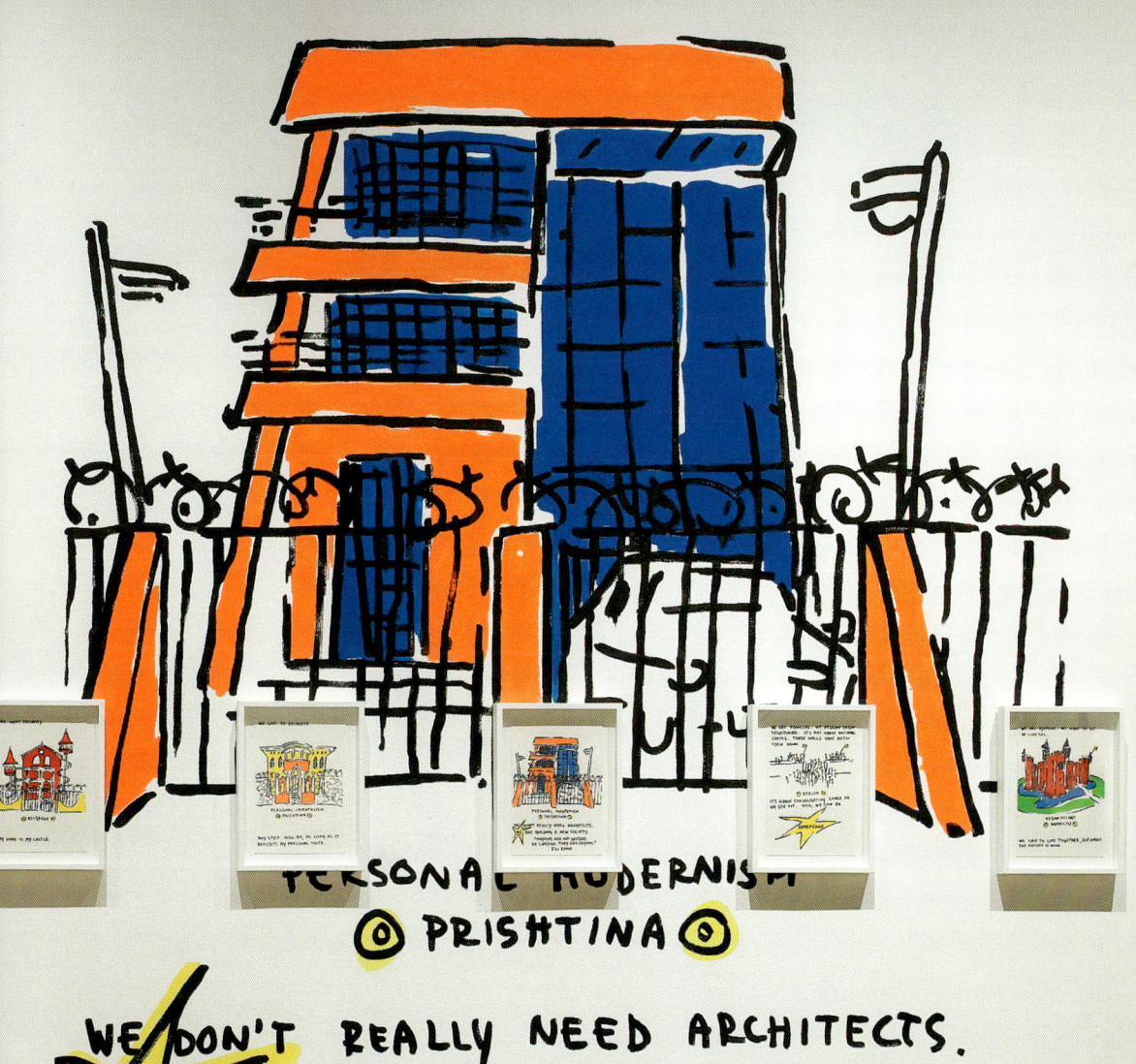

[pages 102 – 105]

MARJETICA POTRČ

Slovenian, b. 1953
The Future is Now
2003
Installation, wall drawing, acrylic paint, dimensions variable
10 drawings, ink on paper, each 8.27 x 11.69 in. (21 x 29.7 cm)
Courtesy of the artist, Max Protetch Gallery, New York, and Collection of Gary L. Wasserman, Naples
Installation photography by Randy Batista

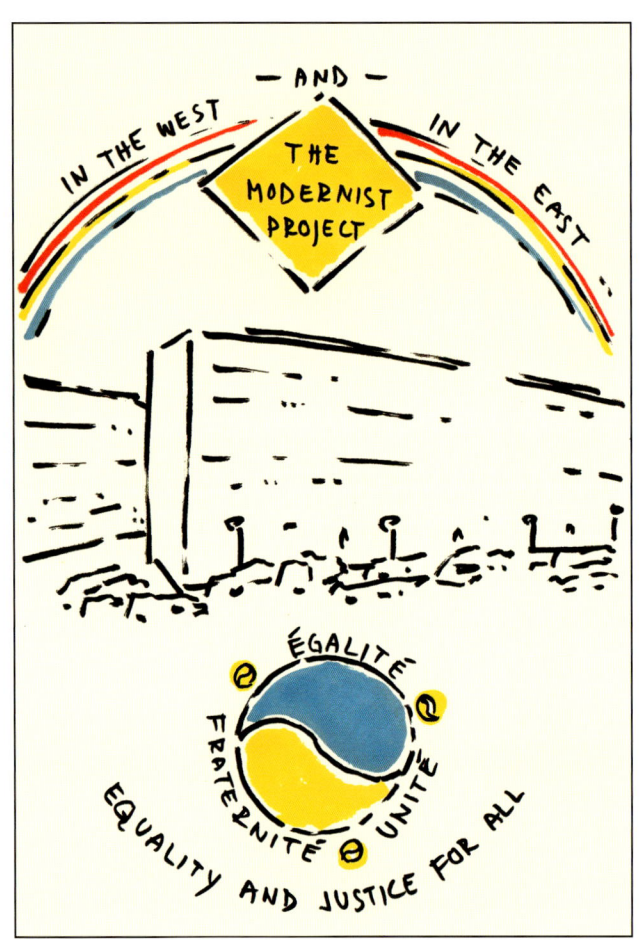

— AND —

IN THE WEST ... THE MODERNIST PROJECT ... IN THE EAST ...

ÉGALITÉ
FRATERNITÉ
UNITÉ

EQUALITY AND JUSTICE FOR ALL

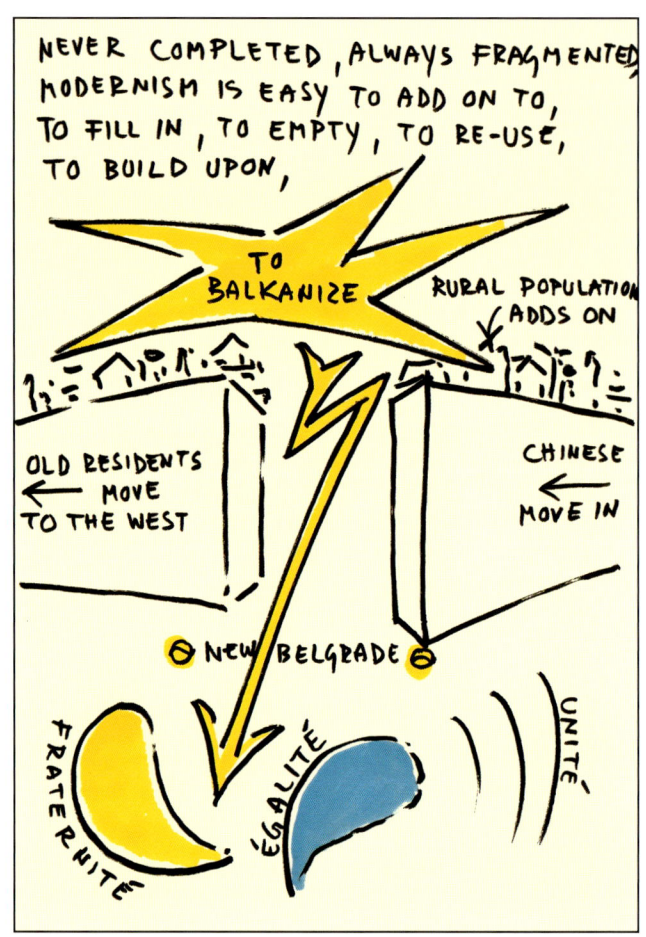

NEVER COMPLETED, ALWAYS FRAGMENTED, MODERNISM IS EASY TO ADD ON TO, TO FILL IN, TO EMPTY, TO RE-USE, TO BUILD UPON,

TO BALKANIZE

RURAL POPULATION ADDS ON

OLD RESIDENTS MOVE TO THE WEST

CHINESE MOVE IN

NEW BELGRADE

FRATERNITÉ   ÉGALITÉ   UNITÉ

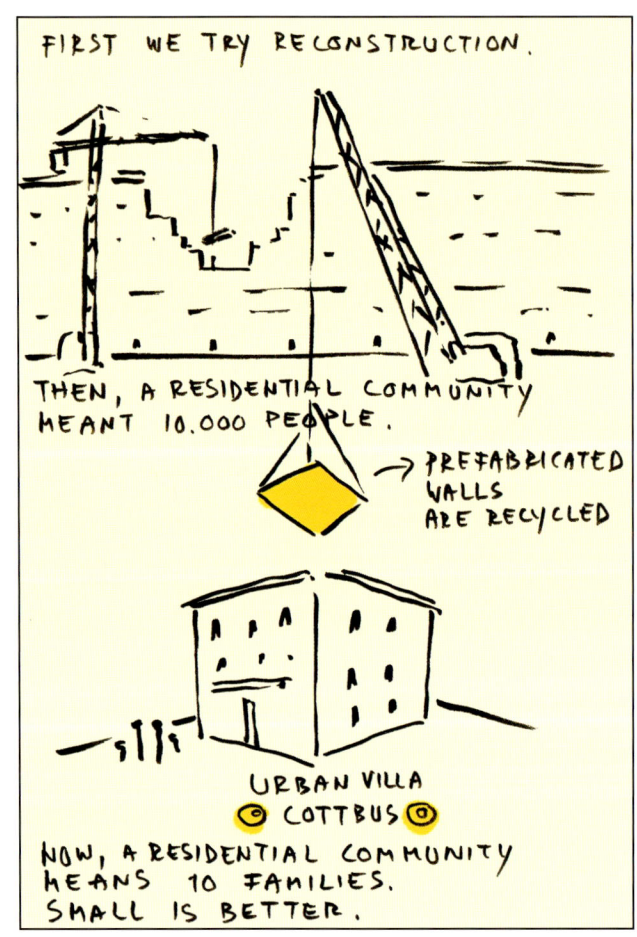

FIRST WE TRY RECONSTRUCTION.

THEN, A RESIDENTIAL COMMUNITY MEANT 10.000 PEOPLE.

→ PREFABRICATED WALLS ARE RECYCLED

URBAN VILLA
COTTBUS

NOW, A RESIDENTIAL COMMUNITY MEANS 10 FAMILIES. SMALL IS BETTER.

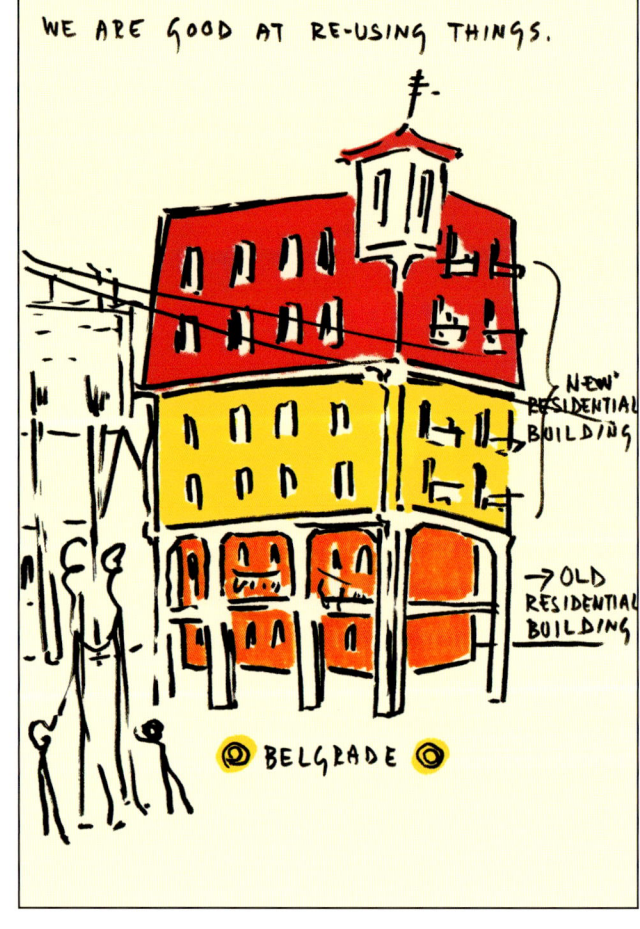

WE ARE GOOD AT RE-USING THINGS.

NEW RESIDENTIAL BUILDING

→ OLD RESIDENTIAL BUILDING

BELGRADE

WE LIKE TO DECORATE.

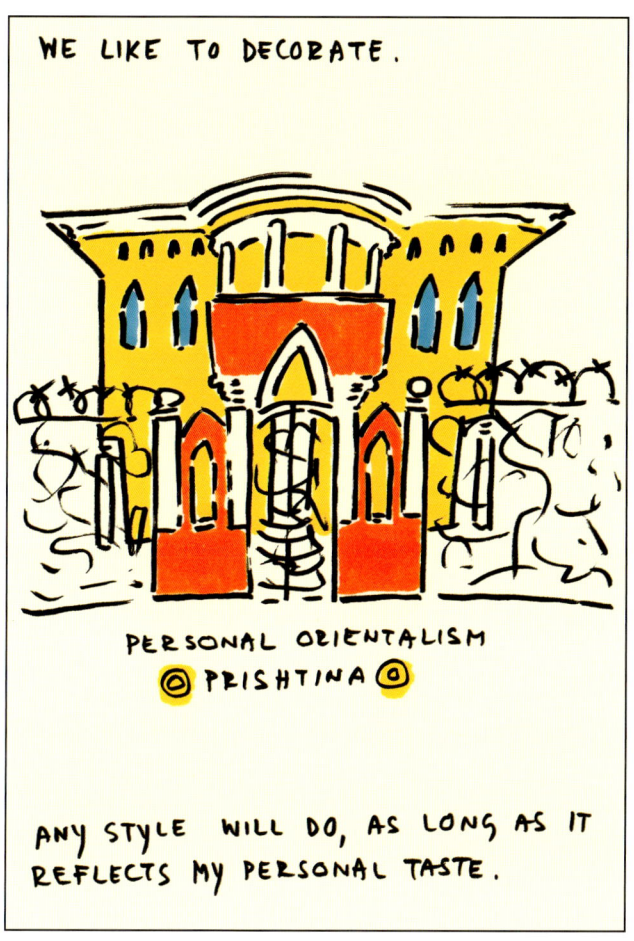

PERSONAL ORIENTALISM
◎ PRISHTINA ◎

ANY STYLE WILL DO, AS LONG AS IT
REFLECTS MY PERSONAL TASTE.

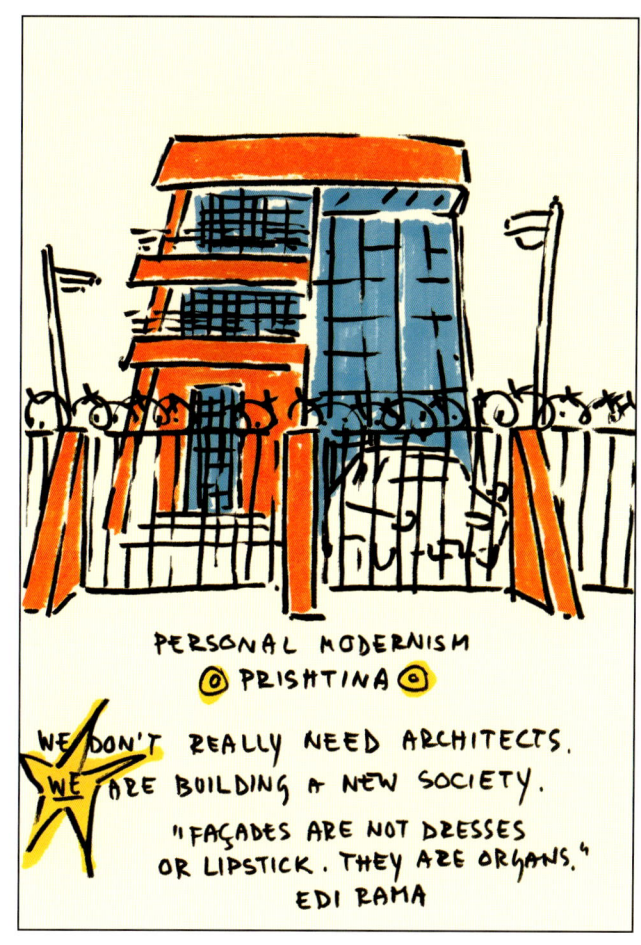

PERSONAL MODERNISM
◎ PRISHTINA ◎

WE DON'T REALLY NEED ARCHITECTS.
WE ARE BUILDING A NEW SOCIETY.

"FAÇADES ARE NOT DRESSES
OR LIPSTICK. THEY ARE ORGANS."
EDI RAMA

WE ARE PIONEERS. WE REDRAW URBAN
TERRITORIES. IT'S NOT ABOUT NATIONAL
STATES. THOSE WALLS HAVE BEEN
TORN DOWN.

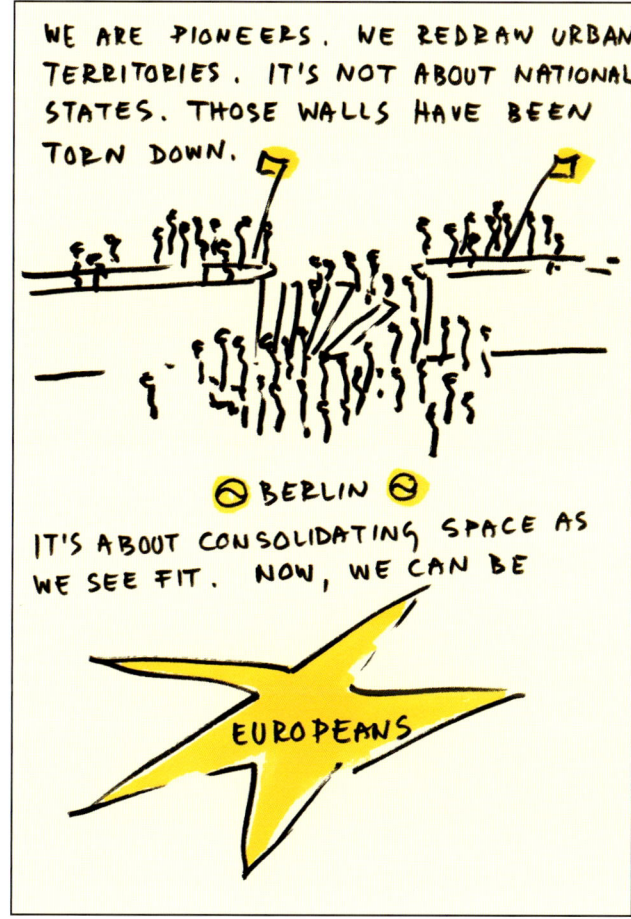

◎ BERLIN ◎

IT'S ABOUT CONSOLIDATING SPACE AS
WE SEE FIT. NOW, WE CAN BE

EUROPEANS

WE ARE DYNAMIC. WE WANT TO BE
IN CONTROL.

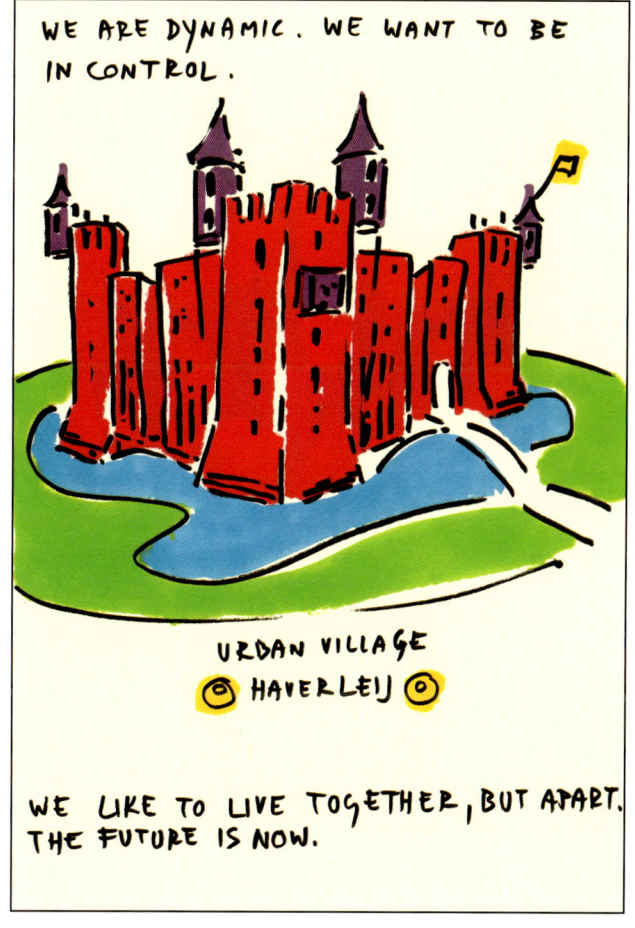

URBAN VILLAGE
◎ HAVERLEIJ ◎

WE LIKE TO LIVE TOGETHER, BUT APART.
THE FUTURE IS NOW.

Anderson, Perry. 2007. "Depicting Europe." *London Review of Books* 29, 18: 13–21. http://www.lrb.co.uk/v29/n18/perry-anderson/depicting-europe.

Aradau, Claudia. 2006. "Only Aporias to Offer? Étienne Balibar's Politics and the Ambiguity of War." *New Formations* 58: 39–46.

Attia, Kader, and Jérôme Sans. 2003. "The Right Position: An Interview with Kader Attia." In Gilane Tawadros, editor, *Fault Lines: Contemporary African Art and Shifting Landscapes*. London: Institute of International Visual Arts, in collaboration with the Forum for African Arts and the Prince Claus Fund, 105–17.

Bajevic, Maja. 2008. *Maja Bajevic*. New York: Charta Books Ltd.

Balibar, Étienne. 2008. "What's in a War? (Politics as War, War as Politics)." *Ratio Juris* 21, 3, (September): 356–86.

Balibar, Étienne. 2006. *Strangers as Enemies. Further Reflection on the Aporias of Transnational Citizenship*. Distinguished Visiting Lecturer address, Institute on Globalization and the Human Condition, McMaster University, March 16, 2006. http://www.ciaonet.org/wps/ighc/0007550/index.html (accessed May 7, 2009).

Balibar, Étienne. 2004. "Europe: Vanishing Mediator?" In *We, the People of Europe? Reflections on Transnational Citizenship*. Translated by James Swenson. Princeton, N.J.: Princeton University Press.

Balibar, Étienne. 2003. "Europe, An 'Unimagined' Frontier of Democracy." *Diacritics:* 33.3–4: 36–44.

Balibar, Étienne. 2001. "Outline of a Topography of Cruelty: Citizenship and Civility in the Era of Global Violence." *Constellations* 8, 1: 15–29.

Balibar, Étienne, and Immanuel Maurice Wallerstein. 1991. *Race, Nation, Class: Ambiguous Identities*. New York: Verso.

Barrada, Yto, and Charlotte Collins. 2006. "Morocco Unbound: An Interview with Yto Barrada." *openDemocracy Ltd*. http://www.opendemocracy.net (accessed February 24, 2009).

Butler, Judith. 2009. *Frames of War: When Is Life Grievable?* New York: Verso.

Christiansen, Bjørnstjerne, and William Shaw. 2009. Interview. *RSA Arts & Ecology*. http://www.rsaartsandecology.org.uk/magazine/features/superflex-flooded-mcdonalds (accessed May 5, 2009).

Dasgupta, Sudeep. 2009. "Trouble in the Contact Zone: Culture and Art in the Age of Identity." *Museum as Hub: Be(com)ing Dutch at a Distance* 5 (January–March 2009): 1–5.

Dillon, Brian. 2006. "Back to the Future: Tacita Dean and the New Nostalgia." *Modern Painters,* (June): 76–79.

Groys, Boris. 2008. "Europe and Its Others." *Art Power*. Cambridge: MIT Press: 172–81.

Gütschow, Beate. 2007. "Interview with Natasha Egan, Lesley Martin, and Akiko Ono." *Beate Gutschow: LS/S*. New York: Aperture. http://www.beateguetschow.net/texts.html?&cid=73&cHash=44819e1074 (accessed July 10, 2009).

Hardt, Michael, and Antonio Negri. 2009. "The Becoming—Prince of the Multitude." *Artforum,* (October).

Hooper, Rachel. 2007. "Complicated Desires: Yto Barrada." *Brave New Worlds*. Minneapolis, Minn.: Walker Art Center.

Martha, Samar. 2007. "Susan Hefuna." *In Focus*. http://www.infocusdialogue.com/interviews/susan-hefuna/ (accessed May 23, 2009).

Pécoil, Vincent. 2003. "Jens Haaning." In *Hello, My Name Is Jens Haaning*. Edited by Vincent Pécoil and Jens Haaning. Copenhagen: Le Consortium Dijon, in collaboration with Centre D'Art Mobile Besancon and Danish Contemporary Art Foundation. http://www.jenshaaning.com/HAANING_LO-RES.pdf.

Rancière, Jacques. 2003. *The Thinking of Dissensus: Politics and Aesthetics*. http://arditi.googlepages.com/Ranciere_Response.pdf (accessed May 30, 2009).

Tazi, Nadia. 2007. "The State of the Straits." *Afterall*. (winter): 91–106.

Van de Ven, Lidwien, and Vera Tollmann. 2007. *Interview*. Document 12. http://www.documenta.de/index.php?id=1175&L=1 (accessed May 30, 2009).

Kerry Oliver-Smith

Kerry Oliver-Smith is the curator of contemporary art at the Harn Museum of Art. She oversees an international collection of more than fifteen hundred works, in all media, from 1945 to the present. Oliver-Smith's research interests focus on the juncture of art and politics, with an emphasis on photographic and video practice.

She has organized twenty-eight exhibitions, along with the museum's *RISK* Cinema series. Select exhibitions include *Art, Media and Material Witness: Contemporary Art from the Harn Collection* (2009); *Momentum: Contemporary Art from the Harn Collection* (2008); *Vision/Revision: Contemporary Art from the Harn Collection* (2007); *Allan Sekula: TITANIC's Wake* (2004–5); *German Legacies: The Photography of Andrea Robbins and Max Becher, Sergio Vega* (2002); *Modernismo Tropical* (2002); and *Insistent Memory: The Architecture of Time in Video Installation* (2000). Exhibitions accompanied by catalogues include *Paradigms and the Unexpected: Modern and Contemporary Art from the Shey Collection* (2008); *Contemporary Cuban Art from the Farber Collection* (2007); and *The Swamp: On the Edge of Eden* (2000). She also contributed to *American Selections from the Samuel P. Harn Museum of Art* (2009).

Oliver-Smith has received several research grants from the University of Florida and has served on numerous panels and committees, including the National Endowment for the Arts and Art Museum Curators Association. Prior to her current appointment, she served as the Harn Museum curator of education. A founder and artistic codirector of Florida's Hippodrome State Theatre, she has worked extensively in film and theater, including projects in the United States, England, Scotland, and Spain. Oliver-Smith is a member of Phi Beta Kappa and holds a master's degree in film and media studies from the University of Florida, where she is currently pursuing her doctorate.

Marius Babias

Marius Babias studied literature and political science at the Free University of Berlin. Born in Romania, he currently lives and works in Berlin as a curator and arts theorist. Since 2008, he has been director of the Neuer Berliner Kunstverein (NBK). In 2005, he was commissioner of the Romanian Pavilion at the 51st Venice Biennale, and has curated the exhibitions *The New Europe*, at the Generali Foundation, Vienna, and *Formats for Action*, at NBK. In 2006, he cocurated the Periferic 7—International Biennial of Contemporary Art, in Iasi, Romania. From 2001 to 2003, he was the artistic codirector at the Kokerei Zollverein | Zeitgenössische Kunst und Kritik, in Essen.

Babias has worked as an art critic for *Kunstforum International*, *Kunst-Bulletin*, *Metropolis M*, and *IDEA arts+society*, among other publications. From 1997 to 2001, he was a visiting professor at the Städelschule Frankfurt/M., the University of Arts Linz, and the Center for Contemporary Art Kitakyushu, Japan. In 1997, he cocurated the exhibition *weitergehen*, at Kulturbehörde Hamburg. In 1996, he won the Carl Einstein Prize for art criticism. He edited *Im Zentrum der Peripherie* (1995) and coedited *Die Kunst des Öffentlichen* (1998), *Arbeit Essen Angst* (2001), *Campus* (2002), *Handbuch Antirassismus* (2002), *Critical Condition—Writings by Julie Ault, Martin Beck* (2003), and *The Balkans Trilogy* (2006). Babias is also the author of *Herbstnacht* (Berlin 1989), *Ich war dabei, als . . . Interviews 1990–2000* (Frankfurt am Main 2001), *Ware Subjektivität— Eine Theorie-Novelle* (Munich 2002), *Berlin, Die Spur der Revolte* (Cologne 2006), and *Kunst in der Arena der Politik* (Cologne 2008).

Boris Groys

Boris Groys is a philosopher, essayist, art critic, media theorist, and internationally acclaimed expert on late-Soviet postmodern art and literature and the Russian avant-garde. His writings engage the wildly disparate traditions of French poststructuralism and modern Russian philosophy.

Since 1994, Groys has been a professor of aesthetics, art history, and media theory at the Center for Art and Media Technology, in Karlsruhe, and has curated and organized numerous international art exhibitions and conferences. In 1981, he emigrated to West Germany, where he earned his doctorate in philosophy at the University of Müenster. From 1976 to 1981, he held a position as a research fellow in the department of structural and applied linguistics at Moscow State University. In the 1970s, Groys, who had studied philosophy and mathematics at Leningrad State University, immersed himself in the unofficial cultural scene in Russia's capitals, coining the term "Moscow conceptualism."

In the United States, he is best known as the author of *The Total Art of Stalin* (1992). This work is credited with introducing Western readers to Russian postmodernist writers. His philosophical writings include *A Philosopher's Diary* (1989), *On the New: A Study of Cultural Economics* (1992), and *The Invention of Russia* (1995), while his contributions to art theory and criticism can be found in *Vanishing Point Moscow* (1994) and *The Art of Installation* (1996). His most recent books are *Under Suspicion: A Phenomenology of the Media* (2000) and *Ilya Kabakov: The Man Who Flew into Space from His Apartment* (2006). Groys has also edited collections of articles in Russian and German and has written more than one hundred articles.

FRANCIS ALŸS

Francis Alÿs was born in Antwerp, Belgium, in 1959. He studied architecture at the Instituto Universitario di Architettura, in Venice, and the Institut d'Architecture de Tournai before moving to Mexico in 1990. His work has been seen in solo exhibitions at Tate Modern, London (2010); the National Portrait Gallery, London (2009); Los Angeles County Museum of Art (2008); and Portikus, Frankfurt (2006). It has also been included in group shows at the National Museum of Modern Art, Tokyo (2009); KW Institute for Contemporary Art, Berlin (2008); 16th Sydney Biennale (2008); and the 52nd Venice Biennale (2007). Alÿs currently lives and works in Mexico City.

FIKRET ATAY

Born in Batman, Turkey, in 1976, Fikret Atay received his degree of fine arts from Dicle University, in Diyarbakir, Turkey. His work has been featured in solo exhibitions at Bonner Kunstverein, Germany (2008); the Hammer Museum at the University of California, Los Angeles (2006); Kunstverein für die Rheinlande und Westfalen, Düsseldorf (2005); Museo de Arte Contemporáneo de Castilla y León, Spain (2005); and Büro Friedrich, Berlin (2004). His work also has been included in group exhibitions at the Lyon Biennial, France (2009); New Museum, New York (2008); Istanbul Biennial (2007); San Francisco Museum of Modern Art (2006); and Tate Modern, London (2006). Atay currently lives and works in Batman, Turkey.

KADER ATTIA

Kader Attia was born in Dugny (Seine Saint-Denis), France, in 1970. He graduated from the École Nationale Supérieure des Arts Décoratifs, in Paris. His work has been shown in solo exhibitions at the Centre de Création Contemporaine de Tours, France (2009); Centro Huarte de Arte Contemporáneo, Huarte, Spain (2008); Henry Art Gallery, Seattle (2008); Institute of Contemporary Art, Boston (2007); Haïfa Museum of Art, Israel (2007); and Musée d'Art Contemporain de Lyon, France (2006). His work also has been included in group exhibitions at the 10th Havana Biennale (2009); The Kitchen, New York (2009); Paris

Triennale, Grand Palais (2009); 10th International Cairo Biennale (2008); Artists Space, New York (2007); Centre d'Art de Neuchâtel, Switzerland (2007); Palais de Tokyo, Paris (2006) and the 50th Venice Biennale (2003). In 2010, he will take part in the Sydney Biennale. Attia currently lives and works in Berlin. He is one of the winners of the 2010 Abraaj Capital Art Prize.

MAJA BAJEVIC

Maja Bajevic was born in Sarajevo, Bosnia and Herzegovina, in 1967. She began her studies at the Academy of Fine Arts, Sarajevo, and completed them in Paris at the École Nationale Supérieure des Beaux-arts. She has had solo exhibitions at the Kunsthaus Glarus, Switzerland (2009); Fondazione Bevilacqua La Masa, Venice (2008); National Gallery of Bosnia and Herzegovina, Sarajevo (2006); Moderna Museet, Stockholm (2005); and P.S. 1, New York. Her work also has been included in group shows at the Centre Georges Pompidou, Paris (2009); Akademie der Künste, Berlin (2008); and Documenta 12, Kassel, Germany (2007). Bajevic currently lives and works in Berlin, Paris, and Sarajevo.

YTO BARRADA

Yto Barrada was born in Paris, in 1971. She was educated in Tangier, Morocco, and later studied history and political science at the Sorbonne, in Paris, and photography at the International Center of Photography, New York. Her work has been featured in solo exhibitions at the Göteborgs Konsthall, Gothenburg, Sweden (2009); Berkeley Art Museum and Pacific Film Archive, California (2007); and Jeu de Paume, Paris (2006). Her work also has been included in group shows at the San Francisco Museum of Modern Art (2008); Walker Art Center, Minneapolis (2007); The Arsenal, 52nd Venice Biennale (2007); 2nd International Biennial of Contemporary Art of Seville, Spain (2006); and Moderna Museet, Stockholm (2006). Barrada currently lives and works in Paris and Tangier.

TACITA DEAN

Born in Canterbury, England, in 1965, Tacita Dean studied at the Falmouth School of Art;

the Supreme School of Fine Arts, Athens; and the Slade School of Fine Art, London. Her work has been shown in solo exhibitions at the Australian Centre for Contemporary Art, Melbourne (2009); Fondazione Nicola Trussardi, Milan (2009); Dia: Beacon, New York (2008); and the Solomon R. Guggenheim Museum, New York (2007). It has also been included in group shows at Walker Art Center, Minneapolis (2009); Centre Georges Pompidou, Paris (2009); Hirshhorn Museum and Sculpture Garden, Washington, D.C. (2008); and Manchester International Festival, Opera House Manchester, United Kingdom (2007). Dean currently lives and works in London.

BEATE GÜTSCHOW

Beate Gütschow was born in Mainz, Germany, in 1970. She studied at the School of Fine Arts in Hamburg and the School of Fine Arts in Oslo. Her work has been featured in solo exhibitions at the Kunsthalle im Lipsiusbau, Dresden (2009); Kunsthalle Nürnberg und Haus am Waldsee, Berlin (2008); and the Museum of Contemporary Photography, Chicago (2007). Her work also has been included in group shows at the Nelson-Atkins Museum of Art, Kansas City (2008); Kunstverein Hannover and the Sprengel Museum, Hannover, Germany (2007); Martin-Gropius-Bau, Berlin (2007); Kunsthalle Hamburg, Germany (2007); and the National Museum of Modern Art, Tokyo (2005). Gütschow currently lives and works in Berlin.

JENS HAANING

Jens Haaning was born in Copenhagen, Denmark, in 1965. He studied at Det Kongelige Danske Kunstakademi, in Copenhagen, and the Akademie der Bildende Künste München. His work has been included in solo exhibitions at the Whitechapel Gallery, London (2008); San Francisco Art Institute (2008); Institut d'art contemporain, Villeurbanne, France (2007); and Wiener Secession, Vienna (2007). His work also has been in such group exhibitions as the Quadrennial for Contemporary Art, Kunsthal Charlottenborg, Copenhagen (2008); the 4th and 6th Gwangju Biennale, South Korea (2002, 2006); and the 9th Istanbul Biennial (2005). Haaning currently lives and works in Copenhagen.

SUSAN HEFUNA

Susan Hefuna was born in 1962. Her work has appeared in solo exhibitions at the Gallerie Volker Diehl, Berlin (2009); the Third Line, Dubai, UAE (2008); and Townhouse Gallery, Cairo (2007). It has also been included in group shows at Fare Mondi, Venice Biennale (2009); Martin-Gropius-Bau, Berlin (2009); Victoria and Albert Museum, London (2009); Seville Biennial Spain (2008); New Museum, New York (2008); Sharjah Biennale, UAE (2007); 2nd Riwaq Biennale, Palestine (2007); and the Louvre, Paris (2004–5). Hefuna has no fixed address, but works as she travels.

EVA LEITOLF

Eva Leitolf was born in Würzburg, Germany, in 1966. After studying at the Universitat GH-Essen, she earned her MFA from the California Institute of the Arts, in 1997. Her work has appeared in solo exhibitions at Pinakothek der Moderne, Munich (2008); Les Chiroux, Liège, Belgium (2007); Staatliches Museum für Völkerkunde, Munich (2005); and Rijksmuseum, Amsterdam (2000). It has also been included in group shows at Photo Phnom Penh, Cambodia (2009); Massey University, Wellington, New Zealand (2009); Gallery at University of Texas, Arlington (2007); and Mildred Lane Kemper Art Museum, St. Louis (2007). In 2008, she was nominated for the Deutsche Börse Photography Prize. Leitolf currently lives and works in the Bavarian Forest, Germany.

AERNOUT MIK

Aernout Mik was born in Groningen, Netherlands, in 1962. He studied at the Academie Minerva, in Groningen, and Ateliers '63, Haarlem. He has appeared in solo exhibitions at the Museum of Modern Art, New York (2009); Ludwig Forum, Aachen, Germany (2008); Dutch Pavilion, 52nd Venice Biennale (2007); and BAK, Utrecht, Netherlands (2006). He has also been in group exhibitions at the Contemporary Art Center of Palazzo Strozzi, Florence (2008); Stadelijk Museum, Amsterdam (2007); and Louisiana Museum of Modern Art, Copenhagen (2006). His work will be exhibited in a major solo exhibition in 2011 at the Jeu de Paume, Paris, and Folkwang Museum Essen, Germany, and at the Stedelijk Museum, Amsterdam, in 2012. Mik currently lives and works in Amsterdam.

MARCEL ODENBACH

Marcel Odenbach was born in Cologne, Germany, in 1953. In the 1970s, he studied at Technische Hochschule Aachen. His work has appeared in solo exhibitions at the Kunsthalle Bremen, Bremen, Germany (2008); 16th International Electronic Art Festival, SESC Videobrazil, São Paulo, Brazil (2007); and Hamburger Bahnhof Museum für Gegenwart, Berlin (2006). He has also been represented in group exhibitions at the Los Angeles County Museum of Art (2009); Museum of Modern Art, New York (2009); Martin-Gropius-Bau, Berlin (2008); Mildred Lane Kemper Art Museum, St. Louis (2007); and Witte de With, Rotterdam (2007). Odenbach lives and works in Cologne.

DAN PERJOVSCHI

Dan Perjovschi was born in Sibiu, Romania, in 1961. Since earning his MFA from George Enescu Conservatoire of Fine Arts in 1985, Perjovschi has worked as writer, cartoonist, and artist. His work has been shown in solo exhibitions at Castello di Rivoli, Turin (2009); Van Abbemuseum, Eindhoven, Netherlands (2009); Wiels Center for Contemporary Art, Brussels (2008); Museum of Modern Art, New York (2007); and Tate Modern, London (2006). His work also has been in group exhibitions at the 10th Lyon Biennial (2009); 16th Sydney Biennale (2008); 52nd Venice Biennale (2007); and the Centre Georges Pompidou, Paris (2006). Perjovschi currently lives and works in Bucharest, Romania.

MARJETICA POTRČ

Marjetica Potrč was born in Ljubljana, Slovenia, in 1953. Originally trained as an architect at the University of Ljubljana, Potrč went on to earn a second BA and MFA in fine arts. Her work has appeared in solo exhibitions at the Max Protetch Gallery, New York (2002, 2005, 2008); Nordenhake Gallery, Berlin (2003, 2007); The Curve, Barbican Art Galleries, London (2007); Portikus, Frankfurt (2006); MIT List Visual Arts Center, Cambridge, Massachusetts (2004); and Palm Beach Institute of Contemporary Art, Lake Worth, Florida (2003). Her work also has been included in group shows at the Venice Biennale (2003, 2009); Smart Museum of Art, University of Chicago (2009); Van Abbemuseum, Eindhoven, Netherlands (2008); São Paulo Biennale (2006); and Gwangju Biennale, South Korea (2004). Potrč has been the recipient of numerous awards, including grants from the Pollock-Krasner Foundation (1993, 1999), the Hugo Boss Prize, administered by the Guggenheim Museum (2000), and the Vera List Center for Arts and Politics Fellowship at the New School, New York (2007). Potrč currently lives and works in Ljubljana, Slovenia.

ANDREA ROBBINS AND MAX BECHER

Andrea Robbins was born in Boston, in 1963. Max Becher was born in Düsseldorf, in 1964. Robbins and Becher both graduated from the Cooper Union School of Art, in New York, in 1986. Their collaborative work has appeared in solo exhibitions at the Center for Art and Visual Culture, University of Maryland, Baltimore College (2008); SK Cultural Foundation, Cologne (2007); and the Sonnabend Gallery, New York (2006). Their work also has been included in group shows at the Museum of Contemporary Art, Barcelona (2008); Museum of Contemporary Art, Miami (2007); and the Museum of Contemporary Photography, Chicago (2006). Robbins and Becher currently live and work in Gainesville, Florida, and New York.

BRUNO SERRALONGUE

Bruno Serralongue was born in Chatellerault, France, in 1968. He earned a Maîtrise d'histoire de l'Art, in Paris, and a Diplôme at l'Ecole Nationale de la Photographie, in Arles. He has appeared in solo exhibitions at Wiels Center for Contemporary Art, Brussels (2009); Gallery Francesca Pia, Zurich (2008); Gallery Air de Paris, Paris (2007); and Centre de la Photographie, Geneva (2007). His work also has been in group exhibitions at Tate Modern, London (2008); Centre Georges Pompidou, Paris (2007); and Kunstmuseum Basel, Switzerland (2005). In July 2010, he will be featured in a major solo exhibition at Jeu de Paume, Paris, which will travel to La Virreina Centre de la Imatge, Barcelona. Serralongue currently lives and works in Paris.

SUPERFLEX

Jakob Fenger, Bjørnstjerne Reuter Christiansen, and Rasmus Nielsen joined together in 1993 to form Superflex. All three artists were educated at the Royal Academy, in Copenhagen. Their work has been featured in solo exhibitions at the South London Gallery, London (2009); De Vleeshal Middlesburg, Netherlands (2008); 1301 PE, Los Angeles (2007); and Gallery Vermelho, São Paulo (2006). They have also been included in group shows at the Museum of Contemporary Art, Miami (2009); Berlin Biennale (2008); Museu de Art Contemporáneo Castilla y León, Spain (2007); and the Gwangju Biennale, South Korea (2006). The artists currently live and work in Copenhagen.

LIDWIEN VAN DE VEN

Lidwien Van de Ven was born in Hulst, Netherlands, in 1963. She studied at St. Joost, in Breda, and the AKI I Enschede. Her work has been shown in solo exhibitions at the Museum of Contemporary Art, Antwerp; Museum Boijmans van Beuningen, Rotterdam; and Galerie Paul Andriesse, Amsterdam. Her work also has been included in group shows at the Van Abbemuseum, Eindhoven, Netherlands (2008); Documenta 12, Kassel, Germany (2007); and the Sydney Biennale (2006). Van de Ven is the recipient of numerous awards, including the 1989 Charlotte Köhler Prize for installations, the 1990 Raad voor de Kunst Amsterdam Award for installations, and the 2001 Maria Austria Award. Van de Ven currently lives and works in Berlin and Rotterdam.

LENDERS

Air de Paris Gallery, Paris

Francis Alÿs

Fikret Atay

Kader Attia

Maja Bajevic

Yto Barrada

Baker Botts L.L.P., Dallas, Texas

Carlier Gebauer Gallery

Collection Frac Île-de-France, Paris

Tacita Dean

Galleri Nicolai Wallner, Copenhagen, Denmark

Galerie Paul Andriesse, Amsterdam

Galerie Chantal Crousel, Paris

Galerie Peter Kilchmann, Zurich

Galerie Polaris, Paris

Beate Gütschow

Jens Haaning

Susan Hefuna

Rose Issa, London

Anton Kern Gallery, New York

Eva Leitolf

Lombard-Freid Gallery, New York

Aernout Mik

Museum Moderner Kunst Stiftung Ludwig Wien (MUMOK)

Christian Nagel Gallery, Berlin and Cologne

Marcel Odenbach

Dan Perjovschi

Marjetica Potrč

Private Collection, Zurich

Max Protetch Gallery, New York

Andrea Robbins and Max Becher

Bruno Serralongue

Sonnabend Gallery, New York

Nils Staerk Contemporary Gallery, Copenhagen

Superflex: Jakob Fenger, Bjørnstjerne Reuter Christiansen, and Rasmus Nielsen

The Third Line, Dubai

Lidwien Van de Ven

CROSSING OVER

RISK Cinema is presented this season as a counterpart to the Harn Museum exhibition *Project Europa: Imagining the (Im)Possible.* Focusing on both Europe and the United States, films in this series use found footage, and documentary and staged film in the exploration of art and politics. American filmmaker Amie Siegel looks at the legacy of the Stasi in East Germany while Belgian filmmaker Johan Grimonprez looks at America during the Cold War period. Deimantas Narkevičius, an artist from Lithuania, examines the juncture between history and personal experience. In a different vein, German filmmaker Helga Fanderl links documentary film to poetic and abstract work.

SCREENING AND ARTIST LECTURE
Amie Siegel, *DDR/DDR*, 2008, HD, 135 min.
February 9, 7 p.m.

Introduced by Barbara Mennel, Associate Professor, Department of English and Germanic and Slavic Studies

Amie Siegel's "ciné-constellation" *DDR/DDR,* 2008, combines vérité interviews with staged dialogue to unearth East German traumas associated with both the socialist state and reunification. Siegel's lens finds filmic lessons in her analysis of Stasi information operations and her inquiries into the suppression of psychoanalysis in the DDR. (artforum.com)

Born in Chicago, Illinois, in 1974, Siegel lives and works in Berlin, New York, and Cambridge. Exhibitions and screenings of her work include *The Russian Linesman,* The Hayward, London; 2008 Whitney Biennial, Whitney Museum of American Art; *Forum Expanded,* KW Institute for Contemporary Art, Berlin; and the Austrian Film Museum and Berlin International Film Festival. Siegel teaches in the department of visual and environmental studies at Harvard University. She has been a guest of the DAAD Berliner-Künstlerprogramm and is a recent recipient of a Guggenheim Fellowship.

This event was cosponsored by the Center for European Studies and the Center for the Humanities and the Public Sphere, with support from the Rothman Fund and the Harn Museum.

SCREENING AND ARTIST LECTURE
Helga Fanderl, Short Films
February 21, 7:30 p.m.

Introduced by Roger Beebe, Director of FLEX Films, Associate Professor, Department of English, University of Florida

Working exclusively in the small-gauge super-8mm film format and editing entirely in camera, Helga Fanderl has directed more than four hundred short films over the last several decades, ranging from observational documentary portraits to more abstract, poetic works. Born in Ingolstadt, Germany, in 1947, Fanderl turned to celluloid in 1990, after studying German and Romance languages and literature in Munich, Paris, and Frankfurt. She then attended art school in Frankfurt and Cooper Union, in New York. The recipient of numerous awards, Fanderl's work has been presented in major film museums and film festivals since 1990, including *Views from the Avant-Garde* at the New York Film Festival.

This event was cosponsored by FLEX Films, the Center for the Humanities and the Public Sphere, and the Harn Museum.

SCREENING AND ARTIST LECTURE
Johan Grimonprez, *Double Take*, 2009, 80 min., DVD
February 23, 7 p.m.

Introduced by Kerry Oliver-Smith, Curator of Contemporary Art

Grimonprez's second film essay, *Double Take,* questions how our view of reality is held hostage by mass media, advertising, and Hollywood. Written by award-winning British novelist Tom McCarthy, the film addresses the global rise of fear-as-commodity.

Grimonprez lives and works in Belgium and New York. His 1997 video *Dial H-I-S-T-O-R-Y* earned him the best director award at both the San Francisco Film Festival and Toronto's Images Festival. *Dial H-I-S-T-O-R-Y* premiered at the Centre Georges Pompidou, Paris, and was shown at Documenta X, Kassel. Since then, it has been seen worldwide. Grimonprez has exhibited his work at such institutions as Pinakothek der Moderne, Munich; the Santa Monica Museum of Art; Whitney Museum of American Art, New York; 24th São Paulo Biennale; and Tate Modern, London. He was the 2006 recipient of the Carnegie Art Award.

This event was cosponsored by FLEX Films and the Center for the Humanities and the Public Sphere.

SCREENING
Deimantas Narkevičius, Short Films
March 23, 7:30 p.m.

Introduced by Shepherd Steiner

Deimantas Narkevičius was born in 1964, in Lithuania and lives and works in Vilnius. His film and video work expresses a subjective and contemporary view of history; it is also a critical look at the medium, its ability to communicate, and its importance in a primarily visual culture. He connects the past with the present and history with personal experience, while pitting documentary truth against potential fiction. Narkevičius has gained recognition at the most exalted level of the international art scene; in 2001, he represented his country at the 49th Venice Biennale. His solid record of exhibitions worldwide is highlighted by solo shows in France, Belgium, Lithuania, and Germany.

Art and Democracy
April 9, 6 p.m., and April 10, 9 a.m.–5:30 p.m.

This event, organized by Kerry Oliver-Smith and Alex Alberro, was cosponsored by the School of Art + Art History Harn Eminent Scholar Chair in Art History, University of Florida School of Art and Art History, University of Florida Center for European Studies, University of Florida Center for the Humanities and the Public Sphere, University of Florida France-Florida Research Institute, and the University of Florida International Center. Symposium moderators are Barbara Mennel, Scott Nygren, and Maureen Turim.

KEYNOTE SPEAKER

François Cusset is a professor of American studies at the University of Paris and former director of the New York-based French Publishers' Agency, as well as an editor, translator, and regular contributor to major journals and magazines on both sides of the Atlantic. Cusset is an intellectual historian whose far-reaching body of work includes the critically acclaimed *French Theory: How Foucault, Derrida, Deleuze, & Co. Transformed the Intellectual Life of the United States* (University of Minnesota Press, 2008), the polemical *The Decade: The Great French Nightmare of the 1980s* (*La Découverte*, 2006), and the first French-language introduction to Queer Theory, *Queer Critics* (Presses Universitaires de France, 2002).

SPEAKERS

Alex Alberro is the Virginia Bloedel Wright Associate Professor of Art History at Barnard College of Columbia University. He is the author of *Conceptual Art and the Politics of Publicity* (MIT Press, 2003). He has also edited and coedited a number of titles, including *Museum Highlights* (MIT Press, 2005), *Recording Conceptual Art* (University of California Press, 2001), *Conceptual Art: A Critical Anthology* (MIT Press, 2000), and *Two-Way Mirror Power* (MIT Press, 1999).

Nora Alter is a professor of film and media studies in the department of English at the University of Florida. She has written *Vietnam Protest Theatre: The Television War on Stage* (1996), *Projecting History: Non-Fiction German Film* (2002), and *Chris Marker* (2006). She has contributed essays to *Camera Obscura*, *Cultural Critique*, *New German Critique*, *The Germanic Review*, and *Film Quarterly*. Alter has been awarded fellowships from the NEH, the Howard Foundation, and the Alexander von Humboldt Foundation. In 2005, she was awarded the DAAD Prize for Distinguished Scholarship in German and European studies.

Claire Bishop is an associate professor in the doctoral program in art history at CUNY Graduate Center, New York, and is a visiting professor at the Royal College of Art, London. Her publications include *Installation Art: A Critical History* (Tate, 2005) and *Participation* (Whitechapel/MIT Press, 2006). In 2008 she co-curated the touring exhibition *Double Agent* at the ICA, London, and edited the accompanying catalogue (2009). She is a regular contributor to *Artforum* and other magazines, and is currently working on a history and theory of socially-engaged art.

T. J. Demos is a lecturer in the department of history of art at University College London. He has written for such journals as *Grey Room*, *October*, *Artforum*, *Texte zur Kunst*, and *Art Press*. He is on the editorial board of *Art Journal*. His publications include *Vitamin Ph: New Perspectives in Photography* (Phaidon Press, 2006) and *The Exiles of Marcel Duchamp* (MIT Press, 2007). His current book project is provisionally titled *Migrations: Contemporary Art and Globalization*.

Tim Griffin has been editor of *Artforum* since 2003. During that time, he has written for the publication on Chantal Akerman, Paul Chan, Mary Heilmann, Philippe Parreno, Seth Price, Catherine Sullivan, and Kelley Walker, among others. He has devoted special issues of the magazine to art and politics, globalization, minimalism, the legacy of land art, and the rebuilding of New Orleans, as well as to such figures as choreographer Michael Clark, philosopher Jacques Rancière, and architect-designer Buckminster Fuller. Griffin is also the author of a book of essays, *Contamination* (2001). His essay on John Baldessari, "What do you do?," appears in the catalogue for the artist's retrospective that opened in February 2010 at Tate Gallery, in London.

Maria Hlavajova is the curator and artistic director of BAK (basis voor actuele kunst), in Utrecht, Netherlands, and the program director of Tranzit, an initiative in Bratislava, Slovakia; Budapest, Hungary; Prague, Czech Republic; and Vienna, Austria. She organized a three-part project, *Citizens and Subjects*, for the Dutch Pavilion at the 52nd Venice Biennale and numerous projects at BAK. She was the cocurator of Manifesta 3, Ljubljana (2000), and director of the Soros Center for Contemporary Arts, in Bratislava, from 1994 to 1999.

Shepherd Steiner is a visiting assistant professor in modern and contemporary art at the University of Florida. He recently published essays in *InTensions, Journal of Visual Culture*, *Becoming Dutch*, and *Formalist Literary Theory in America*. He coedited *Cork Caucus: on art, possibility, and democracy* (*Revolver*, Frankfurt, 2007), and is currently finishing a book of close readings in modernist painting, sculpture, and criticism in America in the 1950s and '60s.

LECTURE
Kader Attia, Artist in Residence
January 21, 6:30 p.m.

Kader Attia was an artist in residence for the Harn Museum exhibition *Project Europa: Imagining the (Im)Possible*. Attia spoke about the wall mural he created for the exhibition and his artistic process as a filmmaker, sculptor, installation artist, and painter. Focusing on the complex relations between the East and the West, his work reflects the tension that exists between an uprooted African culture and a seductive Western consumer culture in France. He also examines the effects of discrimination and segregation in the Muslim community.

ARTIST INSTALLATION
Dan Perjovschi, Artist in Residence
January 24–February 6
during museum hours

As an artist in residence, Dan Perjovschi used the entire space of the Harn Museum's rotunda to create an original work for *Project Europa*. Known as an artist, writer, and journalist, he has made drawing an object and a medium of performance and installation. Visitors were invited to watch as Perjovschi created his latest work.

GALLERY TALK
Dan Perjovschi, Artist in Residence
January 31, 3 p.m.

During this gallery talk, Dan Perjovschi explained *The Round Drawing*, commissioned and created for *Project Europa*. The artist's work satirizes the politics and culture of Europe as it draws parallels to the United States and, specifically, Gainesville and Florida. This gallery talk offered a great opportunity to gain insight into Perjovschi's artistic process as he explained the work in progress unfolding on the walls.

GALLERY TALK
Kerry Oliver-Smith, Harn Curator of
Contemporary Art
February 21 and April 18, 3 p.m.

Harn curator of contemporary art discussed and highlighted works in *Project Europa: Imagining the (Im)Possible*.

LECTURE
Dan Perjovschi, Artist in Residence
February 3, 6 p.m.

Perjovschi's caricatures for the Harn Museum use wordplay and slogans to blend criticism, irony, and humor. He combines everyday observations with reflections on such issues as terrorism, surveillance, militarization, Islam, capitalism, and climate change.

LECTURE
Michael Bernhard, Raymond and Miriam
Ehrlich Eminent Scholar Chair in Political
Science, University of Florida
February 16, 6 p.m.
"The Politics of Memory: Commemorating
the Fall of Communism in Poland Twenty
Years Later"

This engaging lecture illuminated events leading to the fall of communism in Poland in 1989. Bernhard examined public commemorations as events in which political actors attempted to transform political culture; he also demonstrated that such commemorations are not about history but the self-interested concerns of politicians to manipulate it.

Francis Alÿs (pp. 34–35, 43)
Belgian, b. 1959
The Nightwatch
2004
Video documentation of an action, National
Portrait Gallery, London
Color, no sound, 17 minutes 30 seconds
Dimensions variable
Courtesy of the artist and Galerie Peter
Kilchmann, Zurich

Fikret Atay (pp. 51, 56–57)
Turkish, b. 1976
Tinica
2004
Video projection
DVD, 7 minutes 32 seconds
Dimensions variable
Courtesy of the artist and Galerie Chantal
Crousel, Paris

Kader Attia (pp. 64, 72–73)
Algerian, b. 1970
Untitled
2010
Wall painting
Dimensions variable
Courtesy of the artist and Christian Nagel
Gallery, Berlin and Cologne

Maja Bajevic (pp. 88–91)
Bosnian, b. 1967
Double Bubble
2001
DVD projection, 3 minutes 36 seconds
Dimensions variable
Courtesy of the artist and Galerie Peter
Kilchmann, Zurich

Yto Barrada (pp. 10, 50)
French, b. 1971
Advertisement Lightbox, Tangier
A Life Full of Holes: The Strait Project
2003
C-print
23.62 x 23.62 in. (60 x 60 cm)
Courtesy of Galerie Polaris, Paris

Yto Barrada (pp. 48, 50)
French, b. 1971
Ceuta Border, Bab Sebta
A Life Full of Holes: The Strait Project
1999
C-print
31.5 x 31.5 in. (80 x 80 cm)
Courtesy of Galerie Polaris, Paris

Yto Barrada (pp. 49, 53)
French, b. 1971
The Strait of Gibraltar, Tangier
A Life Full of Holes: The Strait Project
2003
C-print
23.62 x 23.62 in. (60 x 60 cm)
Courtesy of Galerie Polaris, Paris

Yto Barrada (pp. 23, 49)
French, b. 1971
Wallpaper, Tangier
A Life Full of Holes: The Strait Project
2001
C-print
23.62 x 23.62 in. (60 x 60 cm)
Courtesy of Galerie Polaris, Paris

Tacita Dean (front cover, pp. 34, 38–41)
British, b. 1965
Palast
2004
Six color photogravures
19.63 x 27.5 in. (49.8 x 69.9 cm) each
Courtesy of Baker Botts L.L.P., Dallas, Texas

Beate Gütschow (pp. 96, 101)
German, b. 1970
S#1(M)
2004
Lightjet print, mounted on aluminum Dibond
55.9 x 48 in. (142 x 122 cm)
©2010 Artists Rights Society (ARS),
New York/VG Bild-Kunst, Bonn
Courtesy of Beate Gütschow; Sonnabend
Gallery, New York; VG Bild-Kunst, Bonn

Beate Gütschow (pp. 96, 99)
German, b. 1970
S#31
2009
Lightjet print, mounted on aluminum Dibond
55.9 x 48 in. (142 x 122 cm)
©2010 Artists Rights Society (ARS),
New York/VG Bild-Kunst, Bonn
Courtesy of Beate Gütschow; Sonnabend
Gallery, New York; VG Bild-Kunst, Bonn

Jens Haaning (pp. 76, 79)
Danish, b. 1965
Antonio
2000
Lightjet print on photographic paper
27 x 19 in. (48 x 68 cm)
Edition of 5
Courtesy of the artist and Galleri Nicolai
Wallner, Copenhagen, Denmark

Jens Haaning (pp. 76)
Danish, b. 1965
Aurangzeab
2000
Lightjet print on photographic paper
27 x 19 in. (48 x 68 cm)
Edition of 5
Courtesy of the artist and Galleri Nicolai
Wallner, Copenhagen, Denmark

Jens Haaning (pp. 76, 78)
Danish, b. 1965
Deniz
2000
Lightjet print on photographic paper
27 x 19 in. (48 x 68 cm)
Edition of 5
Courtesy of the artist and Galleri Nicolai
Wallner, Copenhagen, Denmark

Jens Haaning (pp. 76)
Danish, b. 1965
Dennis
2000
Lightjet print on photographic paper
27 x 19 in. (48 x 68 cm)
Edition of 5
Courtesy of the artist and Galleri Nicolai
Wallner, Copenhagen, Denmark

Jens Haaning (pp. 76, 78)
Danish, b. 1965
Ecevit
2000
Lightjet print on photographic paper
27 x 19 in. (48 x 68 cm)
Edition of 5
Courtesy of the artist and Galleri Nicolai
Wallner, Copenhagen, Denmark

Jens Haaning (pp. 76, 78)
Danish, b. 1965
Faysal
2000
Lightjet print on photographic paper
27 x 19 in. (48 x 68 cm)
Edition of 5
Courtesy of the artist and Galleri Nicolai
Wallner, Copenhagen, Denmark

Jens Haaning (pp. 76, 78)
Danish, b. 1965
Hakan
2000
Lightjet print on photographic paper
27 x 19 in. (48 x 68 cm)
Edition of 5
Courtesy of the artist and Galleri Nicolai
Wallner, Copenhagen, Denmark

Jens Haaning (pp. 76)
Danish, b. 1965
Murat
2000
Lightjet print on photographic paper
27 x 19 in. (48 x 68 cm)
Edition of 5
Courtesy of the artist and Galleri Nicolai
Wallner, Copenhagen, Denmark

Jens Haaning (pp. 76)
Danish, b. 1965
Ömer
2000
Lightjet print on photographic paper
27 x 19 in. (48 x 68 cm)
Edition of 5
Courtesy of the artist and Galleri Nicolai
Wallner, Copenhagen, Denmark

Jens Haaning (pp. 74, 76)
Danish, b. 1965
Radovan
2000
Lightjet print on photographic paper
27 x 19 in. (48 x 68 cm)
Edition of 5
Courtesy of the artist and Galleri Nicolai
Wallner, Copenhagen, Denmark

Susan Hefuna (pp. 6, 35)
Egyptian/German, b. 1962
ANA
2006
Handmade wood carving, ink
77.5 x 3.54 x 55.12 in. (197 x 9 x 140 cm)
Courtesy of the artist and The Third Line, Dubai

Susan Hefuna (pp. 35, 47)
Egyptian/German, b. 1962
Knowledge is Sweeter than Honey
2006
Handmade wood carving, ink
78.83 x 3.54 x 82.68 in. (185 x 9 x 210 cm)
Courtesy of a private collection, Zurich, and
Rose Issa, London

Susan Hefuna (pp. 35, 44)
Egyptian/German, b. 1962
SEE
2006
Handmade wood carving, ink
55.12 x 3.54 x 77.5 in. (140 x 9 x 200 cm)
Courtesy of the artist and The Third Line, Dubai

Eva Leitolf (pp. 62, 64, 67)
German, b. 1966
Althaldensleben ("Olln")
German Images—Looking for Evidence
2006
Color photograph
31.89 x 27.17 in. (81 x 69 cm)
Courtesy of the artist

Eva Leitolf (pp. 62, 64, 69)
German, b. 1966
*Disused Concrete Works (Ehemaliges
Betonwerk)*
German Image—Looking for Evidence
2006
Color photograph
31.89 x 27.17 in. (81 x 69 cm)
Courtesy of the artist

Eva Leitolf (pp. 15, 62, 64)
German, b. 1966
Hirschgarten, Munich (Hirschgarten, München)
German Images—Looking for Evidence
2007
Color photograph
31.89 x 27.17 in. (81 x 69 cm)
Courtesy of the artist

Eva Leitolf (pp. 62, 64, 71)
German, b. 1966
*Lake Schwerin, near Berlin (Schweriner See,
bei Berlin)*
German Images—Looking for Evidence
2006
Color photograph
31.89 x 27.17 in. (81 x 69 cm)
Courtesy of the artist

Eva Leitolf (pp. 32, 62, 64)
German, b. 1966
*Refugee Hostel, near Berlin (Asylbewerberheim,
bei Bahnsdorf)*
German Images—Looking for Evidence
2006
Color photograph
31.89 x 27.17 in. (81 x 69 cm)
Courtesy of the artist

Eva Leitolf (pp. 62, 64, 70)
German, b. 1966
Schöna, Sächsische Schweiz
German Images—Looking for Evidence
2006
Color photograph
31.89 x 27.17 in. (81 x 69 cm)
Courtesy of the artist

Eva Leitolf (pp. 62, 64, 68)
German, b. 1966
Tramstop, Potsdam (Haltestelle, Potsdam)
German Images—Looking for Evidence
2006
Color photograph
31.89 x 27.17 in. (81 x 69 cm)
Courtesy of the artist

Aernout Mik (pp. 24, 90, 92–95)
Dutch, b. 1962
Raw Footage
2006
2-screen video and sound installation (images
from found documentary material: Reuters &
ITN, ITN Source), digital video on DVD
Dimensions variable
Courtesy of carlier | gebauer, Berlin
Research: Danila Cahen
Mixage/Sound engineering: Hugo Dijkstal
Online: Joke Treffers
Courtesy carlier | gebauer, Berlin
Raw Footage has been produced by the artist
and BAK. It is realized in partnership with
Treaty of Utrecht. Additional support has been
generously provided by The Netherlands Foun-
dation for Visual Arts, Design and Architecture;
Mondriaan Foundation; Galleria Civica di Arte
Contemporanea, Trento; ThuisKopie Fonds
and Fentener van Vlissingen Fonds.

Marcel Odenbach (pp. 33, 36–37)
German, b. 1953
*Niemand ist mehr dort, wo er hinwollte (No one
is where they intended to go)*
1989–90
Video installation, DVD player, monitor,
glasses, pedestal
Dimensions variable
Courtesy of the artist and Anton Kern Gallery,
New York

Dan Perjovschi (pp. 51–52, 58–59)
Romanian, b. 1961
The Round Drawing
Wall drawing, mixed media
2010
16-ft. wall and rotunda walls
Courtesy of the artist and Lombard-Freid
Gallery, New York

Marjetica Potrč (pp. 97, 102–105)
Slovenian, b. 1953
The Future is Now
2003
Installation
Wall drawing, acrylic paint, dimensions variable
10 drawings, ink on paper
each 8.27 x 11.69 in. (21 x 29.7 cm)
Courtesy of the artist, Max Protetch Gallery,
New York, and Collection of Gary L. Wasserman,
Naples

Andrea Robbins and Max Becher
(pp. 75–76, 83)
American, b. 1963, and German, b. 1964
*BUT, America in France: Strip Malls of
Toulouse*
2003
Chromogenic print
30 x 34.75 in. (76.2 x 88.3 cm)
Courtesy of Sonnabend Gallery and the artists

Andrea Robbins and Max Becher
(pp. 75–76, 84)
American, b. 1963, and German, b. 1964
*Griff Plus, America in France: Strip Malls of
Toulouse*
2003
Chromogenic print
30 x 34.75 in. (76.2 x 88.3 cm)
Courtesy of Sonnabend Gallery and the artists

Andrea Robbins and Max Becher
(pp. 75–76, 85)
American, b. 1963, and German, b. 1964
*Jardiland, America in France: Strip Malls of
Toulouse*
2003
Chromogenic print
30 x 34.75 in. (76.2 x 88.3 cm)
Courtesy of Sonnabend Gallery and the artists

Andrea Robbins and Max Becher
(pp. 75–76, 82)
American, b. 1963, and German, b. 1964
*Salon Center, America in France: Strip Malls
of Toulouse*
2003
Chromogenic print
30 x 34.75 in. (76.2 x 88.3 cm)
Courtesy of Sonnabend Gallery
and the artists

Andrea Robbins and Max Becher
(pp. 75–76, 80–81)
American, b. 1963, and German, b. 1964
*Toys 'Я' Us, America in France: Strip Malls
of Toulouse*
2003
Chromogenic print
30 x 34.75 in. (76.2 x 88.3 cm)
Courtesy of Sonnabend Gallery and the
artists

Bruno Serralongue (pp. 50, 55)
French, b. 1968
Abri #6, Calais, avril 2007
2007
(from the series *Calais*, 2006-)
Ilfochrome mounted on aluminum with
Plexiglas box
50 x 62.5 in. (127 x 158 cm)
Courtesy of the artist and Air de Paris Gallery,
Paris, Collection Frac Île-de-France, Paris

Bruno Serralongue (pp. 50, 54)
French, b. 1968
*Passer en Angleterre. Accès terminal
transmanche, Calais, juillet 2007*
2007
(from the series *Calais*, 2006–)
Ilfochrome mounted on aluminum with
Plexiglas box
50 x 62.5 in. (127 x 158 cm)
Courtesy of the artist and Air de Paris Gallery,
Paris

Superflex (pp. 16, 76, 86–87)
Jakob Fenger, Bjørnstjerne Reuter Christiansen,
and Rasmus Nielsen
Danish
Burning Car
2008
Blu-ray projection, 11 minutes
Produced by Propeller Group (Ho Chi Minh
City) and co-produced by the Vleeshal,
Middelburg, Netherlands
Dimensions variable
Courtesy of the artists and Nils Staerk,
Copenhagen

Lidwien Van de Ven (pp. 60, 62)
Dutch, b. 1963
*London, 04/09/2004 (International Hijab
Solidarity Day)*
2007
Inkjet print on photo rag paper mounted on
Dibond
59 x 88.5 in. (150 x 225 cm)
Courtesy of the artist and Galerie Paul
Andriesse, Amsterdam

Lidwien Van de Ven (pp. 61, 63)
Dutch, b. 1963
Paris, 11/02/2006 (demo Danish cartoons)
2007
Inkjet print on photo rag paper mounted on
Dibond
47 x 71 in. (120 x 180 cm)
Courtesy of the artist and Galerie Paul
Andriesse, Amsterdam

Lidwien Van de Ven (pp. 61, 65)
Dutch, b. 1963
Reichstag, Berlin
2001
Offset print on paper
9 ft. 10 in. x 14 ft. (300 x 425 cm)
Courtesy of the artist and Galerie Paul
Andriesse, Amsterdam